Copyright

Copyright © 2014 by Matthew Bennett

All rights reserved. This book or any portion thereof may not be reproduced or used in any manner whatsoever without the express written permission of the publisher except for the use of brief quotations in a book review or scholarly journal.

First Printing: 2014

ISBN 978-1-326-15025-9

MBIT Training Ltd, 2014

Worcester, UK.

www.MBITtrainingLtd.com

sales@mbittrainingltd.com

Introduction - Welcome to Network+ v6 (N10-006)

Welcome to Matthew Bennett's training series covering the CompTIA Network+ certification. The Network+ certification is an internationally recognised course aimed at Network administrators, engineers and other IT practitioners interested in Enterprise-level network administration. This book is focussed on the v6 edition of the course which goes live at the end of 2014 and will be valid for 3 years.

The Network+ course is accredited by ANSI and is compliant to ISO 17024. It is part of the Continuing Education programme whereby IT exams are renewable every three years and by so doing the course content is updated to reflect the latest in hardware, skills, techniques and procedures. By completing the course and passing the exam, not only are you displaying competence as an IT professional but are also showing your dedication to your chosen career path and convincing others of your currency as a 'relevant, recent and professional' to your workforce.

Why listen to me? Well, I've been training for 14 years now. I'm a key member and partner of the UK Malvern Cyber Security Network and endorser of the National Cyber Security Centre. I have been an IT teacher at school, college and university level. I'm a bit of an academic, but realise that this is a theory exam as much as you also need hands-on experience of a network.

If you're a parent, then you may understand what I'm about to say here. Your network is analogous to a baby. It needs attention, support, care and security. If it is threatened in any way, you will feel its pain. For a corporate network, data is invaluable and vital to the livelihood of the company and also for its staff. You will soon realise that if your goal is just to pass an exam, you will be helpful to the It industry as your head will hold a lot of information, but your heart – your diligence and care for your network will keep the bad people away from your prize.

Upon completion of the course you are encouraged to affirm your skills by taking the Network+ exam. The exam will allow you to demonstrate that you have a good level of skills and knowledge to be able to configure, to troubleshoot and to manage network devices. You will consider the fundamentals of network design, process and operations and also of the latest in industry standards and practices.

In order to undertake this training it is expected that you already have some experience of IT networking and have at least worked as part of a corporate domain. Ideally you will be able to consider how domains are joined and be aware of the concept of an Enterprise network. A typical exposure of 9 to 12 months work experience in IT networking is advised and a basic understanding of IT operations, IT hardware, customer support and IT troubleshooting as offered be the A+ certification would be ideal.

At the time of writing Network+ forms part of the US government Department of Defence directive 8570 requirement and meets IAT level 1 along with A+ CE. Network+ is further complimented by the Security+ qualification which meets IAT level 2. A large number of public sector and government organisations across the world use the IAT model as a benchmark for their own determinations so although CompTIA courses are not mandatory outside of this DoD directive, they are considered to be the benchmark of a good IT technician and there is an expectation on the individual to be able to attain the certification in order to perform their normal duties. It is for this reason that it is common to see Network+ along with other CompTIA certifications on Job Descriptions.

Domains

The following table lists all of the domain areas covered in the course and the weighting for each within the examination:

Domain	% of Examination
1.0 Network architecture	22%
2.0 Network operations	20%
3.0 Network security	18%
4.0 Troubleshooting	24%
5.0 Industry standards, practices, and network theory	16%
Total	100%

About the Author

Matthew Bennett is an IT educator and has been supporting networks since 1987. His early experience of computing was as a coder using 8-bit Machine Code, adapting and creating his own homebrew 8-bit games in the 1980s although he worked as a Network professional in the 1990s and later on supported Network transitions from IBM systems to Microsoft NT and later migrations to Domain networks.

Matthew became a teacher in 2000 and has been supporting Network classes as well as consultancy for 14 years. He has been teaching A+, Network and Security+ over the past 5 years for FE, apprenticeship and the corporate market.

Domain 1

Network architecture

"What is a Network?"

A network is a collection of devices able to share data and services between them. A network can exist in one of two logical forms:

A workgroup (peer-to-peer). Here, each computer is set up independently and each machine manages its own services and own connections to other network resources.

A domain (client-server). Here, common shared services are maintained by one device (centralised) and so wastage or duplication can be avoided. We will talk about a 'centralised' network to refer to one specially designed PC which can perform additional services for other PCs on the network, even newly joined ones. This 'dedicated PC' is referred to as the 'server'. It is often made of more robust hardware, or has been 'scaled up' to enable it to perform these additional duties.

Services which might be included on your network are:

File services – the server can be used to store documents which need to be accessed by several people on different PCs.

Print services – the server can render print jobs, manage who can access printers across the network and act as manager to ensure that documents are printed out in a timely manner. If a manager urgently needs a document to be printed on the same printing device that somebody else is using, if the manager has priority over the printer, the job will be moved higher in the queue and will be printed faster on the print device.

Active Directory – the main role of a server on a domain network is to authenticate both connecting computers, devices and users. When a user attempts to log on to the network, their credentials are actually stored on a central database. Likewise, when your client computer was switched on, it also connected to Active Directory and had to be authenticated. Through authentication your account exists as part of a logical grouping of similar people (e.g.' IT Managers' group) which has been given access to certain areas of the network, also certain rules (called 'Group Policy Objects') have been applied. Therefore, when you log in on any computer in the network, you will be able to access your team resources, but also certain restrictions may apply to your account due to the level of access you have been granted.

IIS / Web services – whether you are using an Apache server, or Microsoft's Internet Information Services, you can host a secure website for public or for internal use (internet site v intranet site).

SQL database – it is common to house a variety of big data stores which need to be accessed regularly, repeatedly from different team members and on different PCs across the network. These 'high availability' services require most often the use of a dedicated server.

Network services – there are a collection of services offering network administration functionality so that other PCs and access network resources easily. These include DHCP, DNS, Routing, Firewall and other key functions discussed within this domain which enable a computer new to the network to be able to learn how to navigate the network and to discover the resources and services available to it.

BYOD v CYOD. A key challenge for Network managers pertinent at the present time is the concept of 'Bring your own device'. This is the process of allowing your employees to connect devices (irrespective of the make or model) to install a certificate file you have provided for them to use which effectively joins the device to the network. This provides the user with functionality of network resources but raises issues around device and network security, also data security. For this reason manufacturers are now making it very easy to allow the user to casually join and disjoin a domain at the press of a button. This is good for the user as when the device is joined it has to ascribe to any policies listed by relevant GPOs already set up. Until the device is disjoined, these policies will apply, even when away from the physical corporate network which may limit the normal functions of the device (e.g. a smartphone).

To meet this problem some companies are instead opting with 'Choose your own device' – the company will pay for a business smartphone, which is to be used for business use only, therefore negating the need to concern themselves with mixing business and personal data, or the use of a private smartphone on a corporate network.

Collision Domain is an area on the network which is defined physically. It is an area where data packets may collide across the network cables when two network devices transmit along the same cable. A subnet comprising of one hub connected to 10 PCs would be a prime example of a collision domain as the other PCs may also transmit at the same time.

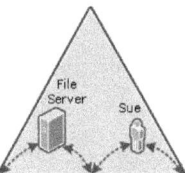

Broadcast Domain is different to a Collision Domain. It is instead logically defined. It is the area which defines the boundaries of the domain itself. It is usually the collection of PCs and switches which makes up the subnet. The domain is usually ended at a router because routers are set to block broadcast packets. A broadcast domain might consist of several PCs in several buildings spanning different countries and is not defined by physical location.

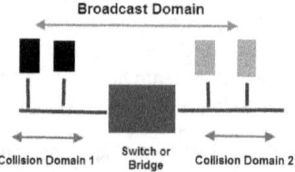

Child domains (such as a remote or branch office) would form part of the domain, but one boundary would be the junction point between the child domain and the larger head office. Within Active Directory users and devices will be grouped by site to determine the domain boundaries. This way you might wish a person in the branch office to access the local DNS server in order to reduce network traffic.

1.1

1.1 Explain the functions and applications of various network devices

- Router
- Switch
- Multilayer switch
- Firewall
- HIDS
- IDS/IPS
- Access point (wireless/wired)
- Content filter
- Load balancer
- Hub
- Analog modem
- Packet shaper
- VPN concentrator

Network Devices:

A network device is a physical, dedicated piece of hardware which performs a specific defined task. Its task can be considered in relation to the OSI model as we consider what form the data is in as it travels through the device.

Router – A router is a device designed to act as a 'doorway' allowing data traffic out of the local subnet. Devices are connected together logically by using a numeric grouping system called 'IP addressing'. Each device is informed of another IP address within the same internal subnet which is the gateway point through which it can direct traffic onto the larger network.

As with a physical door, it has two handles (or IP addresses), one on each side (the internal network and the external network).

Routers operate at layer 3 of the Open Source Interconnect (OSI) model and by so doing manage access to other networks by using the IP address and subnet mask of each data packet being sent. The IP address is split into two portions – the network portion and the host portion and so the subnet the data is being sent on to is determined.

Routers are relatively 'chatty' themselves. Routers have their own common language (the Routing Protocols) and several of these are covered later on in this course. As with switches, a router contains a small computer which stores a table containing the IP address of the connecting computer and the physical port it is connected through. Unlike a switch which stores the physical 'MAC' address of the Network Interface Card (NIC) this time IP addresses are used and one cable may carry traffic from an entire group of computers (the subnet).

Routers use their own routing protocols to talk with other routers to determine which other subnets are serviced and by so doing can determine the best route to get to a particular part of the network. Different routing protocols work in different ways but it is interesting to note that this is an automatic process and allows a router to be 'aware' of other connections beyond its own physical confines.

Routers are also designed to block traffic not intended for a specific device. 'Broadcasts', namely a packet intended for everyone on the network to hear would cause congestion on the wider network and so Request for Comments paper RFC 1542 details the need for Routers to effectively block broadcasts. Without this the internet, or the local network would become congested as PCs try to discover network services. This is particularly true for two network functions:

- Imaging and Deployment – as part of the imaging process, the image and the preliminary Preinstallation Environment are streamed across the network to the waiting PC which initially has no data on the hard drive. The PC 'boots up' from data received across the NIC. The protocol which is involved in this process is the BOOTP protocol, so if a router is in the way of the data stream it will effectively block the process and stop the image data from reaching the waiting PC.
- DHCP – the DHCP service allows client PCs to request and obtain a leased IP address for a length of time. Part of the process involves the sending of Broadcast packets. If a Router was in the way of the data flow, the server may not be contacted and the DHCP process may not even begin.

Routers are also capable of adapting traffic so that device designed for another network can be adapted and the reply data also adapted. The process, referred to as Network Address Translation enables the router to remember the IP address of a sending PC on its routing table and it is very common to see this process in use on the external-facing router as this service negates the need to but individual public IP addresses for each PC in the organisation. Instead, we can use one public IP and share this amongst every PC on the network. It works as follows:

- The PC wishing to send data to the Internet (the public network)'s IP address is recorded on the router.
- The router removes the sending PC's IP address from the return data and replaces it with its own IP address.

- The augmented packet is sent across the public Internet.
- The returning data is addressed to the router's external IP address, but the router realises that the packet needs to be sent on, so the incoming packet is augmented and the external IP is replaced by the original PC's IP address.
- The augmented packet is sent across the internal network

Finally, it is important to remember that we are concerned with data security starting by protecting our own internal data. The router is a bastion of protection for our local network so it is helpful to think that the router is a line of defence rather than a means to connect beyond the network. We therefore talk about blocking data coming into the network rather than extending capabilities of the internal network.

Switch

As opposed to a 'hub' a switch is a device which allows data to be sent within the local subnet. It is a physical device acting as a central wiring point where each local PC is connected to the rest of the network. Where a Hub would copy the electrical signal and replay this on every other port, a switch is able to determine which port the data is required and a virtual connection is created between the two ports allowing other virtual connections through other unused ports. A switch is therefore extremely efficient as there may be many different data streams being sent through the switch at the same time. The switch is able to deal with each data request without loss of data, or data collision.

A switch is a device operating at layer 2 of the OSI model. There are typically two types of switches we will encounter here:

Unmanaged switch – this is a dedicated device capable of transferring data from one port to another with a very fast turnaround time. The switch keeps a basic table of port and MAC address of the NIC connected to that port and this table is updated regularly. Once the MAC address is learned the switch can use this data to determine which port I needs to send the data on to.

Managed switch – a managed switch, also called a 'multi-layered' switch because it has a web-based management portal to configure the device can provide additional functionality. One common control would be to set the direction of traffic as one-way or two-way, also if it is one way which actual direction the data should be sent ('uplink' or 'downlink'), also to set the speed (baud rate) of the connection on a specific port. As the device has an IP address in order for the administrator to effect changes to the device, the device is said to operate at both layers 2 and 3 of the OSI model.

One common advantage of using a switch is the fact that, as with Routers, a switch can communicate with another switch to determine the best route through the network. Whilst it is common to see switches within one building it is only usual to see a router be used to connect the subnet to another subnet, or to another part of the network, or even to the internet.

Switches can be grouped together to form a 'cluster' and by so doing large subnet sizes can be created by connecting several switches to operate in tandem. Switches operate at layer 2 of the OSI model by using MAC information to determine pathways through the network. A Switch is also capable of sectioning some of the physical ports available to work along with another switch it is clustered with (i.e. ports 1-4 on Switch 1 and ports 15-18 on switch 2) to form a segmented network across the wired network referred to as a VLAN. This is helpful for the creation of a Sandbox or test network where devices are in different locations, building or even cities across the physical network.

Firewall – this term tends to mean different things to different people. Whilst it is true that there is a software firewall (in fact with Microsoft systems there are two firewall screens available to you) built into the PC, there is a hardware firewall – an expensive but dedicated device designed to limit data from accessing your network. Each data stream is allocated a number which determines the type of data being sent through the network. These are controlled by two different transport protocols:

Transport Communication Protocol – TCP is used to ensure that data sent is received correctly and is said therefore to be a 'reliable protocol'. With TCP the two PCs will first attempt to 'handshake', that is to establish communication before any data is sent. If a packet receipt is not received in good time, then the packet is resent. Therefore the receiving PC can maintain and check the packets as they are received until the file is re-structured. There is also a degree of error-checking taking place which ensures the validity of the data received. TCP is therefore a very reliable protocol making it good for file transfers.

User Datagram Protocol – UDP is not a connection-oriented protocol. Here, a stream of data is sent. There may be errors in the data stream and there is no consideration as to if the data is being received or not. As there is no error-checking mechanism built into the packet, the packet can contain slightly more data, making receipt a little faster, but the data stream will be prone to errors. This however makes it a good protocol to use for video conferencing, online video streaming and webcam streams where the end user will not be too concerned if there is a slight glitch, or where the user may want to opt in or out of a video conference.

There are 1024 system ports (from 0 to 1023) which are known as the 'commonly known ports'. Above this 1024 to 49151 are the registered ports. They are registered with the Internet Assigned Numbers Authority (IANA).

The number range from 49152–65535 are 'ephemeral ports' used for temporary access. These are not used by IANA but are used internally within the network. For example, to transfer a file from PC to PC using FTP you could assign a rule to use Dynamic FTP. Here, port 21 would be used to establish the connection but for security reasons rather than use port 20 to transfer the data another dynamically assigned port is used by both PCs.

A port is simply a 'doorway'. Traffic can flow in or out of the port and the port can be set to allow one or two-way traffic. There are 0-65535 ports for TCP and another 0-65535 set of ports for UDP.

It is possible to use any port number, but the port being used must be open at the firewall and known to be used for that specific purpose by both PCs involved. As we are often dealing with public networks there has to be a common standard so that everyone uses the same port for the same purpose. There are only a few port numbers that it would be useful to remember:

Port	Purpose
20	FTP -- Data
21	FTP -- Control
22	SSH Remote Login Protocol
23	Telnet
25	Simple Mail Transfer Protocol (SMTP)
53	Domain Name System (DNS)
67	DHCP (server use)
68	DHCP (client use)
69	Trivial File Transfer Protocol (TFTP)
80	HTTP
110	POP3
123	Network Time Protocol
143	Interim Mail Access Protocol (IMAP)

As well as port numbers a software firewall can trigger the opening of a port based on an application requesting it. This will be on a temporary basis and when the job is done the port is re-closed. Dynamics ports are opened through application rules and this service would usually feature on either a software firewall 'with advanced security' or on a Host-based intrusion detection system / internet management software.

Intrusion Detection and Prevention.

These devices are often dedicated hardware resources which accompany the firewall offering logging and prevention services. The Intrusion Prevention system uses heuristics (common patterns in data) to determine if there data is a threat to the network (e.g. a virus signature). The Intrusion detection system however does not stop the traffic from entering the network, but does log traffic as it travels through the device.

When IDS and IPS systems are placed on the network infrastructure they are designed to bulk-process a lot of data entering the domain. These are referred to as 'Network based' systems (NIPS and NIDS).

Where the IDS or IPS is software-based and located on the client PC, these are referred to as Host-based (HIPS and HIDS). These programs tend to be resource-heavy in that every file in use is scanned for any known signatures which may look like a data string located on the virus database Norton Internet Security would be an example of a HIPS.

As you can imagine, if the corporate hardware scoping allows for no margin of production beyond the original scope the PCs will struggle to run IDS software. This is why it is common to see problems with domestic end-user computers as they did not allocate for the additional demand on the system an IDS system will bring.

Offsite and cloud

One positive argument for a move to cloud storage and processing is the fact that hardware is no longer a concern to the end user. Such systems provide legal protection to the end user to safeguard their data. Centres are often also SO/IEC 27001:2005 or BSI: IS 577753 data security compliant and promise 100% uptime.

Demilitarised Zones

It is possible, in fact quite popular to see a reserved, controlled area accessible from the public, but leaving the internal network protected. This 'Demilitarised Zone' is a logical area housed between two firewalls in which specific public-facing services can be placed. It is possible to place the public website's web server, but also a file server should the company wish to share any documents with the public. One common trap for the unwary would be to place a logging IDS onto the file server and to leave attractive-seeming files to download. Any potential hackers may attempt to download the files and their details will be caught in the process. This is known as a Honeypot, or Honeytrap. A collection of such machines across the corporate network are referred to as a 'Honeynet'. (2.4)

Access Point – this is a device other than a NIC which enables network-ready devices such as a laptop or a smartphone to be able to connect into the wider network. This is typically a Wireless access point – a device which can re-transmit wireless data as wired packets across the wired network. Loosely speaking, an access point on an ad-hoc network is another laptop's wireless NIC.

Content filter – this is usually an application installed on a web proxy server. The job of the proxy server is to act on behalf of the client. The webpage request is checked against an acceptable use list of known websites. This can be set up in one of two ways – either specific websites are blocked, or only sites on the list are permitted. Proxy server can also scan website content for key words in either the META head tags or on the page itself and refuse to load a site if a certain word, phrase or topic is found.

A common UNIX system used as a dedicated proxy server and content filter is 'Smoothwall'.

http://www.smoothwall.org

One the client-site client browsers contain a 'SmartScreen' filter which also will scan for unacceptable content, although this is more designed to safeguard against malware, adware or impersonation.

Load Balancer – this is not necessarily a device in itself but a means of providing resilience by adding multiple servers and devices configured to complement each other and by so doing reduce traffic on the network. For example the introduction of local DNS servers will negate the need for all client PCs to communicate with one 'master' DNS server which otherwise may congest the network. Equally a cluster of file servers could take multiple requests for file transfers and ensure that all of the requests were met, assuming that the network was capable of also transferring the data load. Switches also can be 'clustered' to ensure that data requests are serviced and congestion is minimised.

Hub – simply put: "Hubs are stupid". A hub is a simple electronic device which replicates the electrical signal sent on one port and sends this signal out on every other port. The receiving devices have to check the header information on the frame to determine if the data frame is meant for them. If not, the data frame is discarded, but this clearly stops the NIC from being able to send out data frames of its own at the same time as the 'line' is busy. Hubs are therefore only used when connecting a small network, such as a **Small Office Home Office (SOHO)** network or might be used for a connection point on a network where there is no concern over when devices might access. For example if we have 2 PCs wired into the network and a hub provides the interlink, with only one user and only one PC is likely to be used at any one time, then there will be no congestion and the use of a Hub can be justified.

The important takeaway is that unlike a switch a hub does not store any information concerning ports and therefore is not 'aware' of the rest of the network other than the completion of an electrical circuit through the connection of a network cable to a live device. There is no 'on-board computer' storing a MAC or IP table and so no means to manage the flow of data. Hubs are however very inexpensive and are a simple solution. They should never be used as part of a more complex network, or as a central connecting device.

Analogue Modem – this device performs two roles – to convert from a digital electronic signal (as with a NIC) to an audible generated tone which represents an analogue number. This tone can be transmitted along the traditional voice phone network (as engineers in the United States would refer to it, the '**Plain Old Telephone System**' POTS). The term 'Modem' refers to the two roles: Modulator (to generate a noise) and 'Demodulator' to read the audio signal and recode as digital binary data. A modem would typically connect to a PCI or ISA (or CMR) slot on the mainboard and would connect to the phone line. A telephone can also be added to the Modem in order to make standard telephone calls when the modem was not in use. More advanced modems would also support the sending of a fax, which is why it became a popular tool for early networking.

Analogue modem speeds were very slow by today's standards at approx. 56kb per second, so a typical web page with only 3 small GIF images and approx. 200 words of text might take up to 8 – 30 seconds to load. A modem is therefore not an effective tool for today's networking.

Packet shaper – this device is used for bandwidth management across large domains, typically across multi-site locations. Traffic is analysed based on the type of data being sent. Data is classified and certain data is prioritised based on pre-defined rules. This device is placed on the very edge of the network and is used to prioritise traffic being sent to other sites, or across the internet.

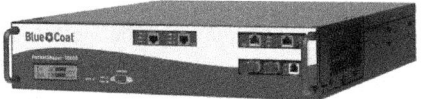

VPN concentrator – it is usual in an enterprise network to receive a large number of staff 'dialling in' to the network from across the internet, particularly as more of us work from home. To assist in servicing this facility a VPN concentrator is a dedicated hardware device which will take the different encrypted data packets (referred to as 'host to site tunnels' and enable the router to manage each of these data streams in turn. Conversely (and easier to imagine) the returning data streams can be combined to sent across the same internet channel (the process of combining data signals and sending the combination across the network is referred to as 'multiplexing').

1.2

1.2 Compare and contrast the use of networking services and applications

- VPN
    - Site to site/host to site/host to host
    - Protocols
        - IPsec
        - GRE
        - SSL VPN
        - PTP/PPTP
- TACACS/RADIUS
- RAS
- Web services
- Unified voice services
- Network controllers

1.2 Networking services and applications

A **VPN** or 'Virtual Private Network' is a means of extending your network by the use of the internet as a medium. This may sound unsecure, even unsafe and yes you are correct in this assumption. In order to ensure that our corporate data is kept secure the connection between the two end points (e.g. branch office and main office sending data via the internet) has to be mutually authenticated (at both ends) and also encrypted. We consider two different aspects to the data flow:

Communication – a theoretical 'tunnel' is created to signify a secure connection. If someone on the internet were to attempt to copy a data packet and interrogate it, the data they would be looking at would be heavily encrypted to the point where we consider it to be difficult, or even impossible to 'break' (to decrypt). This process is referred to as 'packet sniffing' as the observer is attempting to analyse and make sense of data packets.

Data – the actual data stream itself (payload) is also heavily encrypted, so even if the outer communication is decrypted, the actual file you are attempting to send from site-to-site (for example) is also encrypted at various levels.

VPNs can operate at layer 3 of the OSI model, or layer 2. Point to Point Tunnelling Protocol (PPTP) operates at layer 3 and each Router is responsible for forwarding the data on, whereas Layer 2 Tunnelling Protocol (L2TP) provides security to the very end device. PPTP is also often referred to as a '**site to site** tunnel' although in truth every router on the internet involved in sending the data to the other site will also inspect the packet before re-sending it. With L2TP operating at switch level, Routers are not involved in inspecting the packet and so the tunnel is more secure.

A **Host-to-site** tunnel is more common to see where a staff member 'dials in' to the network, authenticates with a RADIUS server with their Active Directory credentials and continues to work as if they were physically located and logged in to an office PC. There are however drawbacks of this system, for example if you were working on a train and were using your phone to dial in, the session is live on your laptop. If the train goes through a tunnel, or the signal is too weak, the session is lost and any work you had open is also lost. To overcome this is a new feature, DirectAccess available on Microsoft Server 2012 where the client session is actually run on a server on the internal network, so the client is effectively 'Remote Desktop' connecting to their session. If the signal is lost, the user can re-join and reconnect to the existing session.

A **host-to-host** is an ad-hoc connection which is typical of Personal Area Networks. An example of this would be to temporarily connect to your friend's phone and to send them a file. Here, the file would be encrypted as would the data packet being sent, but it is unlikely that a tunnel itself will be formed. An example of this type of sharing is a Bluetooth connection in which a connection Personal Identifiable Number (PIN) is needed to be able to connect both devices to each other. Connection would be within a very limited physical range (of up to 10 metres).

Protocols:

IPSec – this is a suite of protocols providing security at the Internet layer of the TCP/IP protocol. With IPSec, the IP packet itself is both authenticated and encrypted.

The following services are therefore available with IPSec:

Authentication of the remote connector

Encryption of the enclosed data

Hashing code is used to ensure that the code is genuine and has not been changed en-route.

Anti-replay – a sequence of number s are used to ensure that an attacker cannot simply re-send the same packet multiple times to obtain entry.

Encapsulation – the packet contains additional header information with security information needed to direct the packet along its route.

IPSec allows us to create a connection between two PCs using the following protocols:

Internet Security Association and Key Management Protocol (ISAKMP) – as there are several different security protocols available to create the connection, both devices have to agree protocols which are installed and available for both PCs. A similar analogy would be to negotiate a common language in which two people who have different native languages would speak, or in WiFi terms contention between 802.11b or g, with WEP or WEP2. However here, these procols are Internet protocols responsible for creating the connection.

Internet Key Exchange (IKE) – security keys are created and used at both ends of the network. These keys have to be securely sent to the opposite PC and also secured from being copied by attackers on the internet. The IKE protocol is able to secure the key mid-transit from typical Internet related threats.

Diffie-Hellman (DH) – this is an algorithm used in the exchange of keys to ensure that the encrypted data sent cannot be re-constituted back into its original form. Some key algorithms run the risk of being determined as large keys may have repetition of encrypted data sections which may serve as a clue to the attacker. Diffie-Hellman is famous for being an encryption method which is hard to break.

IPSec can operate in two modes – transport mode and tunnel mode.

Transport mode – complete, end-to-end protection for the length of the entire tunnel.

Tunnel mode – a site-to site tunnel from the endpoint gateways. Internal data transmission is outside of the tunnel, therefore insecure, but can be presumed to be 'safe' as is within your physical site and therefore under your control.

Both IPSec elements can operate in either mode.

Authentication Header – this is used to prove that the data packet has come from the sending PC and verified its authenticity, but provides no encryption on its own. The protocol number and packet length are changed and this second header is added before the IP data packet payload.

AH also uses the Integrity Check Value (ICV) – a hash created using all of the fields within the packet except for those which may change as part of the transmission itself. The hashing algorithm used is either Message Digest 5 (MD5) or SHA-1.

A Hashing Message Authentication Code (HMAC) is used. This includes in the hash the secret keys known by both PCs. This acts as a form of digital signature to ensure that other traffic is legitimate. This 'signature' attests that data matching its data has not been altered.

Encapsulating Security Payload (ESP) – Here, both encryption and authentication of parts of the packet are provided. ESP is harder to crack and is also contains more elements to ensure that both authentication and encryption are provided.

Here, the original data is preceded with an ESP header containing the security parameters and sequence number. The original IP header is adapted to reflect the longer length of the packet and the protocol number of changed to 50, which is the number specifically used for ESP.

Additional padding is added to the original IP data payload to make it difficult to determine the endpoint of the payload within the packet. After the padding is a 'next header' block which identifies the payload by the protocol number. These sections are then encrypted, typically using AES, but the encryption algorithm used can be changed, but must be agreed by both PCs. Finally an authentication block is added to the end of the packet which contains data calculated from the shared security key and the earlier fields.

The padding, padding length, payload and next header sections are all encrypted.

It is important to realise that the IP addresses used to send and receive the packet are not changed, so routers can still pass on the packet.

It is possible to use a combination of both ESP and AH should you wish to do so, but the AH data is applied first.

GRE – Generic Routing Encapsulation is a tunnelling protocol created by Cisco systems which allows you to encapsulate and use other protocols whilst tunnelling across an internet network. Cisco routers can therefore send on encrypted traffic which used non-Cisco recognisable protocols.

SSL VPN – often used as the last option for creating a secure connection for DirectAccess is the option to use **Secure Sockets Layer, Virtual Private Networking**. This communication method relies on the server's digital certificate, sending encrypted traffic using port 443, as with secure websites.

PTP – An advancement from the Network Time Protocol, Precision Time Protocol is used to synchronize clocks throughout the network. This systems is extremely accurate (to the sub-microsecond), allowing for far greater accuracy and synchronisation than NTP alone.

This could be a useful way of overcoming the 'Domain Controller problem'. It is good practice never to virtualise the Domain Controller in a network, because if this server was not available the network would be unable to authenticate and so nobody would be able to log on and to service the network other than with local accounts. When a computer falls out of synchronisation with the domain controller for more than 5 minutes time difference, Active Directory will refuse to respond to the affected PC. Virtualised computers do not work in 'real time' in that as processing demands rise and fall the amount of processing power the virtual PC will use will cause a 'speed up' or 'slow down' effect when compared to the relative time of the host PC. With generation 2 virtual machines this is even more prevalent as there is no host PC to control the virtual machine. The elastic concept of time therefore makes it highly likely that the virtual PC will de-synch from the rest of the network.

Point-to-Point – When we consider networking topologies 'Point-to-point' (PTP) refers to a direct connection between 2 PCs such as can be found in a Fully Connected ('Mesh'), or Bus network.

The Point-to-Point Protocol (PPP) is a data link protocol used to establish a direct connection between two nodes. It can provide connection authentication, transmission encryption (using ECP, RFC 1968), and compression. It is typically used when making a telephone modem connection and describes how the communication, authentication and encryption of the data stream is handled.

PPPoE – one modern variant of PPP is the Point-to-Point-Protocol over Ethernet. This is typically used to manage the transmission of broadband traffic enabling the client connect from their DSL modem, or combined router to their Internet Service Provider (ISP).

PPTP- The Point-to-Point Tunnelling Protocol (PPTP) is a method for creating and operating virtual private networks. It uses a control channel over TCP port 1723 and a GRE tunnel is created which encapsulates PPP packets. PPTP is synonymous with VPN networking. On Microsoft systems the tunnel is authenticated with MS CHAP v2 although v1 can still be used as can CHAP or PAP but these are less common. PPTP was first introduced for dial-up connections but was limited.

Partly due to its age and extensibility there are a number of security problems and vulnerabilities with PPTP. The preferred tunnelling system now in place is L2TP with IPSec.

TACACS & RADIUS – The concept of a RADIUS (Remote Access, Dial In User Service) server is now quite common in large corporate networks where you will encounter VPNs and remote workers. The RADIUS server acts as a proxy – a gateway where incoming VPN users can authenticate with the network. The RADIUS server checks with the Domain Controller to ensure that the user's authentication details are valid without compromising the DC through a direct connection into the heart of the network. RADIUS is therefore an 'edge' server ensuring that the internal network is protected. TACACS (Terminal Access Controller Access-Control System) is protocol developed in 1984 for use with Unix systems which managed authentication and access control on the Unix environment. It was replaced by TACACS+, developed by Cisco as the advancement to TACACS. TACACS+ is not backwards compatible. It uses the TCP protocol (whereas RADIUS uses UDP).

DUN/RAS – Registration, Admission and Status (RAS) is a suite of commands which manage the process of authenticating and managing the data stream. This is often found within telephony to control a modem connection (Dial-Up Networking).

Web Services – a web service is any network function which can be accessible from a website. Most end-user applications on modern systems are designed using C# or HTML5 due to its platform independence, making it the ideal means to produce corporate applications which will work great on any system, at any resolution. These applications may also need to connect to data held on a central location (e.g. a SQL database Server, or for files a SharePoint Server).

To enable web services to be accessible, we host web pages for internal (Intranet), external for remote workers (extranet) or public (Internet) use. These are held on an Internet Information Services server (IIS), or for Linux systems an Apache server.

It is also common to be able to service some network-enabled devices, such as printers by using the printer's landing page. Managed switches and Routers also have administration pages which are accessible by a known IP address. These IP addresses are typically not added to the corporate DNS records but are known only to maintenance Network Administrative staff.

Unified Voice Services - UC is not necessarily a single product, but a suite which provide a consistent unified user-interface and user-experience across multiple devices and media-types. For Microsoft users the corporate communications platform is Lync, which integrates with Exchange Server and for the client Outlook. Lync Client offers chat and IM capabilities, also video conferencing and desktop sharing allowing teams to collaborate regardless of their physical location. There are a variety of different service providers but the key to UC is that these services are integrated with Voice over IP, so that all communications elements are offered within the suite.

A **Network Interface Controller** (NIC) is an expansion card which is capable of transmitting binary data frames as electrical signals across a medium. This is typically for transmission across Ethernet CAT 5 or CAT 6 cable, although earlier NICs also supported Coaxial cable as a medium. It is also possible to obtain optical NICs capable of transmitting the data stream as a sequence of light pulses along fibre optical cable.

The NIC will also be able to perform the reverse operation of converting received impulses into a data stream for use internally by the PC.

NICs have again become quite popular with processes such as NIC teaming and virtual switches for virtualised servers in which an array of NICs can be used to create a large bandwidth 'trunk' connection where a larger bandwidth is possible.

It is now also not a requirement to have a hosted operating system – a Storage Area Network consists of an array of hard drives connected to a fibre NIC allowing iSCSI access and data transfer across the network.

1.3

1.3 Install and configure the following networking services/applications
- DHCP
    - Static vs dynamic IP addressing
    - Reservations
    - Scopes
    - Leases
    - Options (DNS servers, suffixes)
    - IP helper/DHCP relay
- DNS
    - DNS servers
    - DNS records (A, MX, AAAA, CNAME, PTR)
    - Dynamic DNS
- Proxy/reverse proxy
- NAT
    - PAT
    - SNAT
    - DNAT
- Port forwarding

The **Dynamic Host Configuration Protocol** (DHCP) is an important server service offered across the network. As a concept it is fundamental to the Network+ course.

A DHCP server will listen for any broadcast packets from no registered PCs. A DHCP server is designed to lease out IP addresses to devices as they need it. Typically a device keeps the IP address for 8 days after which time the request for another 8 days is made.

There are four stages to the DHCP lease:

Discover – a broadcast packet is sent from the new requesting PC across the network. The DHCP hears this packet and the DHCP process starts.

Offer – the DHCP server checks its cache of available IP addresses. If there are sufficient IP addresses available within the range (the scope), then an IP address is offered.

Request – the PC requests to use the IP address it has been offered.

Acknowledge – an acknowledgement packet is sent to the PC which then starts to use the IP address. It is at this point that the lease starts.

An image which may help you to remember the mnemonic is the children's TV series, "Dora the Explorer".

When the IP address is issued to the PC, other information can also be provided, in fact DHCP will act as a gateway to other important services and network locations:

- The router default gateway IP address
- Location of the DNS server
- Location of the IIS web server
- Local printer IP addresses for this subnet.

It is up to you as a Network designer to determine if you want to issue information to your clients through DNS, or through DHCP. Usually it is common to signpost services (e.g. IIS and printers) through DNS but to place the location of the DNS server as a DHCP signpost, without which the new PC will be unable to locate network resources.

When setting up a DHCP scope it is important to remember that the scope is a logical set if IP addresses, but physically it is likely that the devices will be local to each other, within the same building, floor or even room. They exist as part of the same subnet and will likely be connected to each other via a switch. They will access the rest of the network outside of their subnet via a router. This poses a problem – by default, Routers block broadcast traffic, as is detailed in RFC 1542. Effectively Routers 'block broadcasts'. As the initial stage of the DHCP process involves the DHCP server hearing a broadcast on the subnet the DHCP server would be unable to service requests on the same subnet if a router was stopping broadcast traffic. It is quite sensible for Routers to block broadcasts – without this a network 'storm' would be created as your new PC attempts to ask the entire internet for the location of a helpful DHCP server.

The DHCP service is significant on the network, so it is the role of the Network Architect, or Manager to approve any new scopes added to the network. Your network might have several DHCP servers, or one for every subnet on the network, or possibly one at each branch of your organisation. To avoid conflicts the scopes have to be checked, the scope activated and the DHCP server authorised before DHCP will start to issue new IP addresses.

DHCP Relay - Where one DHCP server serves two subnets linked by an internal Router, the Router must either allow broadcasts (it is possible to disable the BOOTP block) or a DHCP Relay Agent service can be installed on the local subnet which does not contain the DHCP server. Here, the broadcast is encapsulated by the listening DHCP relay agent which then sends the request as a Unicast packet directly to the DHCP server (the DHCP server is already known to the Relay Agent). The DHCP server sends the DHCP Offer via the Relay Agent which then is able to forward the offer to the requesting PC.

Across the life of the lease, the leased PC will contact the DHCP server at 50% and then again at approx. 75% of the lease in order to remind the server that the lease is active. Where there are limited IP addresses available within the lease range (the 'scope'), this would allow the DHCP server to be aware that leases are due for renewal and to accommodate accordingly.

The problem occurs when a PC is not in use for a length of time. Imagine the scenario where a worker has gone on holiday for a fortnight and there are limited IPs within the scope. Here, the PC may now have been used for the interim period and another new PC might have taken the last IP address. When the worker returns from holiday the PC attempts to request an IP. As the old IP number has been issued to someone else a different IP address will be given if there are sufficient IPs left in the scope. If there are any applications which specifically rely on an IP address (this is considered to be poor programming) then the application may fail.

Alternatively, if the DHCP lease request has not started yet the old PC will still be using its old IP address. As two PCs will be trying to use the same IP on the same subnet this will cause a conflict. The old PC will have to relinquish its IP address and the TCP/IP protocol will revert the IP address to 0.0.0.0 (network 0, Host ID 0), meaning that the network is currently unreachable. By using the IPCONFIG /RENEW (IFCONFIG on Linux systems) the DORA process is started and a new IP is requested. In this example, this is only possible where the IP address has been automatically assigned by DHCP – if the IP address was manually assigned (a 'static IP') there will be no change to the old PC and the DHCP-controlled new PC will instead be affected.

Another common issue is the 'Network 0 problem'. From Windows 2000 onwards an auto-configurable IP protocol was in place, called APIPA (the Automatic Private IP Addressing protocol). This IP address is a randomly assigned address starting 169.254.x.x and was originally used as a means to communicate on an internal network without the need for a DHCP server. When a DHCP server is not broadcasting its heartbeat on the network (e.g. the service has stopped or the DHCP server is switched off), the IP address will automatically change from the DHCP-assigned IP address to an auto-generated APIPA address. This will enable devices within the subnet to continue to have network connectivity until the problem is resolved. It is however worth mentioning that APIPA addresses are non-routable and therefore internet connectivity will be lost although local services will still be available.

Static vs dynamic IP addressing – a manually configured address or 'static' address is assigned by the network administrator manually at the PC. This IP address will not change over time. The information required for a device to access the network and supplied at the time of entering a static address is:

- The devices' static IP address
- Subnet mask
- Default gateway (local router which allows traffic out of the subnet. This is the internal IP address as the router is known by the subnet, not the external-facing IP address of the router).
- DNS Server – You can add several DNS servers and it is usual to do so. If the device is located in a corporate location such as a branch office, the local DNS server should be the closest DNS server logically to it, therefore a DNS server based at the branch. This may have been configured to store local information pertaining to the branch and will reduce traffic to other DNS servers such as the Head Office DNS server.

Alternate location – as laptops are portable there may be a situation where the device is used away from the office, such as at home. As the second network will have different configuration to the corporate network it is highly likely that you will need a second, different IP configuration for the laptop when it is used at home. The 'Alternate configuration' tab therefore provides an opportunity to place a second 'static IP', or even to look for a different DHCP server whilst you are connecting to the home network.

One common problem is when the 'alternate configuration' setting is not used and IP is supplied by DHCP at both locations. Here, the home DHCP will be providing a heartbeat signal, so the office DHCP-supplied IP address will be used on a different network at home. As the IP will not match the home subnet, the device will not communicate with other devices on the home network subnet. To overcome this it may be necessary to change the IP address. This can be done by using the IPCONFIG /RENEW command mentioned earlier. A new IP address is provided for this new location, however you will have the same problem when you return to the office.

Reservations – A DHCP reservation is an IP address within a defined scope which will always be used for a particular device. For example a legacy, network-enabled print device may only work if you use the IP address of 192.168.1.5 hard-coded at the factory and it may not be possible to change this. In this situation you still wish to issue an IP address by using DHCP, but can instruct DHCP to reserve this specific number for a particular device. The device reservation also requires the Network Administrator to inform DHCP of the MAC address for the device you wish to reserve.

An advantage of DHCP Reservation over Static IPs is that you can still provide the additional signpost information to the device.

Exclusions – It is possible to exclude an IP address from a given scope. This is also useful in the situation where you have a hard-coded device where the IP address is already assigned and cannot be changed by DHCP (e.g. early laser printers required the operator to set the IP address on the firmware of the printer itself). The print device's IP may be within the range and part of the same subnet but you need to ensure that this IP is not re-issued to any other devices therefore causing a conflict. Therefore, if the device already has an IP address statically assigned then the exclusion will ensure that the IP is not mistakenly re-used.

A typical IP to exclude is 192.168.0.1 as this is the IP used for Internet Connection Sharing and is a default IP for early routers and ADSL modems.

Scoping strategy – Both Microsoft and Cisco have advice on how to scope your network. As a rule of thumb, IP addresses at the lower end of the list (e.g. 1-9) are reserved for servers and local devices such as printers, although you may wish to create a scope dedicated to managing printers. From 10-250 you would assign your client devices and from 254 downwards we tend to have the management IP addresses for our routers and managed switches. Remember that any IP address ending in 0 cannot refer to a device itself, but is referring to the network. Also, any IP address ending 255 (the maximum number in an 8-bit octet) is in fact a 'broadcast' to all devices on the subnet.

Leases – although this can be changed, DHCP wired connections are typically leased for 8 days and wireless connections are only leased for one hour. This duration is set on the creation of the scope, so you will need to consider this first before building your network.

IP options – as discussed, the DHCP services provides more than the devices' own IP address. There are a range of options each with their own identifying number to offer information to the new PC such as the IP of the local DNS server, gateway, IIS servers and so on.

Domain Name System (DNS) – this service is usually dedicated on a server which is capable of serving requests across a portion of the network. The DNS server regularly receives information from devices, acting as a kind of 'phonebook' to the devices, offering 'lookups' or resolutions and helping the PC to find where a network resource is located. DNS is at the topmost level of the directory services model:

- DNS – a lookup service which translates name requests to resources or other devices to their IP address.
- DHCP – the service which issues an IP address to a MAC address.
- ARP / RARP (Address Resolution Protocol) – a local table or cache, stored on each PC which describes which IP address is used by known local MAC addresses.

DNS is a database of known resources. Referred to as a 'Zone'. Different domains can each be services within one DNS server.

A request can be of one of two types:

Forward lookup – this is a resolution from name to IP. This is the most common form of lookup used across a network to find where resources are located.

Reverse lookup – these are not common and on an internal network there is no need to set up a reverse lookup zone. These are typically used for web servers, where the IP address is known and we want to determine on which web server (from many in a cluster) a particular website is located.

Within the zone there are a number of different record types:

SOA – the Start Of Authority. It may be highly possible that you have many DNS servers located within your network. Which one should a newly joined PC start with? The SOA denotes the starting point for any new device – this is the 'primary' DNS server within the network.

SRV – The Service record denotes key services within the network, usually these tend to be DNS servers. Other information stored within the record would be the protocol type and port used to communicate with this service.

A – an IPv4 address of a device on the network. The name and IP address are stored.

AAAA – an IPv6 address of a device on the network. The name and IP address are stored.

MX – the location of the Mail Exchange server

CNAME – canonical name. By setting a CNAME another alias can be used to refer to known device on the network. This can make it easier for network administrators to refer to resources and devices by using non-technical names or 'nicknames' to access a particular server. Where a CNAME is known by the client PC it will then continue to use the CNAME rather than the actual name for the device it is trying to communicate with.

LOC – a location record is used to specify the geographical location record for a device. This is useful if you have different branches located in different cities and want a way of geographically grouping resources.

PTR – used on reverse lookups, the PTR or 'pointer' refers back to the name. Resolution is the opposite of a forward lookup, this time the IP address is resolved to the device's known name.

Dynamic DNS is a service which addresses the problem of changing IPs on the public 'internet' network. Most Internet Service Providers give residential customers a public IP which is assigned by their own DHCP service. This IP address will regularly change. Because of the changing nature of these addresses, a residential customer will have difficulty in connecting to their network from an external source, or to access services contained within the network, such as web hosting. To get around this problem the IP address used is assigned to a Dynamic DNS database operated by a third party. This enables the resource, accessed by name (a Uniform Resource Locator, or URL) to still link to the correct IP address every time the IP address changes.

A **web proxy server** is a network service offered to the client where the proxy acts on behalf of the client to obtain the requested resource. The website is loaded onto the proxy only if the requesting URL complies to corporate acceptable web addresses. The page is first loaded onto the proxy server and then the content is forwarded to the client's PC. By doing this, if the website is popular and contains a large number of static areas, information is cached on the proxy therefore reducing load time for other users on the network.

Proxy can be enforced as a hidden process, so the end user is not always aware that a proxy is in use. Usually the web proxy IP address has to be added to the browser configuration, but this process can be implemented by Group Policy, or by the proxy server itself (as is the case with Smoothwall systems).

A **reverse proxy** acts as a vanguard to protect the real server from access by other users. For example, requests to access a web server may lead the web server vulnerable to attack. Therefore, requests are handled through an intermediary server called the 'reverse proxy' which is more secure and can handle such attacks.

Network Address Translation – NAT is the process offered by a router where the packet sent from a local subnet is adapted by the router and the public IP address (or external facing IP address for internal routers) is replaced so that traffic can be sent on from the subnet to other subnets, or the wider, external network. The return packet is also checked and augmented with the internal IP address of the client PC replacing the IP address of the router. This way internal traffic can be sent out to the wider network.

NAT is a vital service. Without this, each PC would need to have an IANA assigned public IP address. As it is a router can adapt internal traffic and allow it to be sent on the wider, or the external network with this feature.

Port Address Translation extends the capabilities of NAT. Where NAT is the adaptation of the IP address, we can 'overload' the IP address by also specifying the Port we are going to use to communicate through. PAT is the facility for different services to travel through the same IP address (e.g. HTTP and HTTPS traffic both entering the router through the router's external ports 80 and 443). This provides additional security to the monitored IP address to ensure that traffic entering from the external network is for defined services only.

Static NAT – Routers can have their IP addresses assigned to their table manually, or automatically. Where the Network Administrator has added manual entries we refer to this as Static NAT (SNAT). This is typically used for resources on the network which do not reconfigure and the IP address is permanent.

Dynamic NAT – Modern routers also communicate with each other to determine other routers, optimal paths and also some information about key IP addresses known to the neighbouring router. When using NAT for the internal network, the internal IP addresses are dynamically assigned and are not accessible directly from an external source. The Dynamic portion of NAT in this case refers to the fact that the routing table is self-configurable and that as IP addresses for end client devices change this is updated within the internal network.

Port forwarding – the firewall usually allows only a few main ports open for common services. There are however 65535 x 2 ports which could be used. Some of these may allow inbound only, outbound only or 2-way traffic. With Port Forwarding we are adapting the IP address and port number (the socket) to a new destination, allowing the socket through the firewall and then forwarding the packet onto its destination based by information about the IP address stored in the Routers' routing table.

It is also possible to manage a dynamic port system where the firewall has ports closed by default. One packet sent through a common port may 'trigger' the opening of another port (the dynamic port) allowing further data through. It is quite common with File Transfer Protocol to use a dynamic port. Here, port 21 establishes the connection at which point the firewall opens another dynamic port rather than the more typical port 20. When the connection is closed, the port is re-closed.

1.4
1.4 Explain the characteristics and benefits of various WAN technologies
- Fiber
  - SONET
  - DWDM
  - CWDM
- Frame relay
- Satellite
- Broadband cable
- DSL/ADSL
- ISDN
- ATM
- PPP/Multilink PPP
- MPLS
- GSM/CDMA
  - LTE/4G
  - HSPA+
  - 3G
  - Edge
- Dialup
- WiMAX
- Metro-Ethernet
- Leased lines
  - T-1
  - T-3
  - E-1
  - E-3
  - OC3
  - OC12
- Circuit switch vs packet switch

Fibre – a fibre optical cable is used typically to send a large amount of data, extremely quickly. An LED light beam is used to signal from a sending laser transmitter. The light bounces within the cable strand and is eventually received by a receiver which re-converts the signal back into a binary stream. Two cables are used – one for each direction of travel and at each interface there are both a transmitter and receiving sensor. The cost of fibre has been quite prohibitive for it to not be the main medium of choice for end users, but reductions in costs and durability of the cable have led to increasing use.

One of the great advantages of fibre is that it is not susceptible to electro-magnetic interference which makes it the ideal solution in an environment with high EMF, such as a factory floor where unsuppressed motors and high-power equipment may cause interference.

The single-mode fibre is the best solution for long-distance connections and where speed is required. This single fibre strand is often made of high-quality glass, although cannot be bent over 30° without damaging the fibre.

Multimode fibre is more commonly used to connect the vertical backbone of a network within an office building, or to connect two neighbouring buildings together. Speeds are slower and the quality of the fibre strands is not as good as with single-mode, therefore this is a better, cheaper solution for local connectivity.

Our interest now extends to ISPs and Telecoms providers as they now offer fibre to residential customers. 'Fibre to Home' (also known as 'Fibre to Premises') is still not prevalent, although is starting to become established in the larger cities. This reduces the single point of data reduction (or 'bottleneck') completely from the provider to the end user's home where the demarcation point is placed (the master socket in the home would act as the end of service for the telecoms provider. If the end-user's laptop has a slow NIC, this would be the end-user's responsibility.) Fibre to Premises can deliver at present download speeds of 300Mbit/s for residential customers.

'Fibre to Cabinet' (FTC) is more common. Here, the telecoms provider has laid fibre cable from their operations area to the local street exchange in each district. At this point media conversion takes place within the cabinet and the data is bridged to the existing copper network already laid within the street. Here it is possible that there may be a bottleneck and reduction in service as the copper cables cannot transmit at the speeds Fibre is capable of. With FTC download speeds of 80Mbit/s are reasonable.

Synchronous optical networking (SONET) is the ANSI standard for sending data over optical media. This ensures that the data transmission can be understood by all parties irrespective of the country the traffic is being sent over. The standards support transmission at up to 9.9 gigabits per second, although some lines will support higher, even 20 gigabits per second. As with the earlier ISDN technology, SONET defines a base rate of 51.84 Mbps and then different channels 'trunk' together to provide the overall bandwidth at these larger speeds.

Dense Wavelength Division Multiplexing (DWDM) is a technology where data from different sources together on an optical fibre, with each signal carried at the same time on its own separate light wavelength. This combination of light is then filtered and segmented when it is received as the multiplexed light signal is re-constituted into different data streams.

Coarse Wavelength Division Multiplexing (CWDM) is a similar technology which can support up to 16 channels of data with each operating at 2.5, 4 or 10 Gbit/s, but the technology has only a small reach at 100 kilometres. It is the system used by Cable TV providers in their faster broadband technologies and allows different information to be streamed along the same physical medium.

Both multiplexing systems support SONET which has therefore become the 'backbone' for metropolitan data transfer.

Frame Relay is a protocol designed to work at levels 1 and 2 of the OSI model, designed originally for ISDN. Data is placed into a data block called a 'frame' and error correction is managed at the end points, not at every point of the transmission. Bandwidths of 128Kbps are possible, and this system is often used amongst telecommunications carriers.

Frame Relay is based on the X.25 standard, but is typically used for digital transmission. Frame Relay is often found at the local area network endpoints, where they would link to a corporate backbone, or within the telecommunication provider network and is seen typically across T1 lines.

Satellite communication is the ideal solution where the user is located in a remote, or rural area, with no means to connect to the Internet backbone. Satellite requires the transmission of a signal to an orbiting satellite managed by the telecommunications provider.

Satellite can produce a good, high-speed data transmission but there is a problem – because of the distance of the dish and the satellite there is a time delay before the data stream is received (this is referred to as high latency).

Broadband cable (commonly just referred to as 'cable') is another method of using existing cabling to enable access in urban areas. Here, existing cable originally laid for cable TV streaming can be also used to take a data signal. Coaxial cable is the dominant medium, but is often a mixture of fibre and coaxial within the district, but would be coaxial to the end-user's home where the signal is split and used separately by the broadband modem and TV. Speeds are often similar to ADSL broadband.

Digital Subscriber Lines are a term for what is commonly described as 'Broadband'. The most common form is Asynchronous DSL, where download speed makes up approximately 80% of the download bandwidth and the remaining 20% is reserved for uploading.

DSL relies on the fact that digital data transmission can be sent at higher frequencies than the human voice, therefore within the conversion of the telephone network to digital, we are now able to send two channels of data along the same medium – lower audio for telephone calls and the higher frequency for data transmission. With ADSL speeds of up to 16Mb are typical with advancements caused by upgrading the backbone to use Fibre rather than coaxial, therefore effectively increasing transmission speeds and bandwidth possible.

Two forms of DSL are available on the market – ADSL is the most common, whereas Synchronous DSL is used by web development teams as they would have a need to upload more data than standard end users.

Integrated Services for Digital Network is by today's standards a limited, costly solution but was the precursor to ADSL. ISDN lines were commonly used by business in the 1990s to provide a dedicated private line between two buildings, provided by the telecoms provider. ISDN is a circuit-switched solution provided by telecoms providers. The line requires a dedicated ISDN modem.

ISDN is in itself a data stream where the data sent is broken into discrete 'channels' transmitting at 64 kbps. The initial ISDN model is the Basic Rate Interface (BRI) which offers 144 kb/s payload as 128 kb/s for data and then a 16 kb/s signalling channel. This is referred to therefore as 2B+D, meaning 2 'bearer' channels and one data channel.

The Primary Rate Interface (PRI) is carried over an E1 line and is common for corporate use. Here, we are using 30 B channels and 1 D channel to provide a maximum throughput of 2048kb/s.

Asynchronous Transfer Mode (ATM), unlike Frame Relay transfers data packets of a fixed size. Each data packet is relatively small. Unlike TCP/IP, a fixed channel is created from endpoint to endpoint and a set route to send the data is defined across the network.

There are four types of ATM:

constant bit rate (CBR): As with a leased line, a constant stream of data cells is sent as a regulated stream.

variable bit rate (VBR): Here, data can be condensed and the channel can favour sending more or less data cells at a point in time. This makes it useful for situations where there may be a need for a burst of data, such as the case in video-conferencing as call demands increase the data throughput required.

available bit rate (ABR): With ABR it is possible to 'burst' data as with VBR, but there is a guaranteed minimum data bandwidth available at all times.

unspecified bit rate (UBR): Here, there is no guaranteed throughput, so there may be a delay whilst the data is sent. UBR is useful for systems which can cope with delays such as when transferring a file.

The **Point to Point Protocol (PPP)** as described earlier is used to ensure error checking and correction take place whilst the packet is sent. PPP operates in the data link layer by first transmitting the packet to an Internet-enabled server (such as your local ISP server) that will in turn send the traffic onto the Internet.

Multilink PPP (or MP) allows several physical connections to one server (e.g. a server with many NICs) to share these connections as one logical connection, thereby increasing the available bandwidth. MP allows for bonding whilst the need for further expansion is present. Channels link for the needed duration and unlink dynamically. This is different to channel bonding which is a manual process.

Multiprotocol Label Switching (MPLS) is designed to simplify IP packet information exchange. Layer 2 information about the network route used is added to the layer 3 data. This enables telecoms network systems to manage around network issues. A disconnected route, a bottleneck or other transport problems can be overcome by known information contained within the packet, so other routes can be used to navigate around problems on the network.

We tend to consider an MPLS enabled network as part of the existing network. Labelling 'Edge Routers' give the packet an identifier which contains destination and source information, the socket used and so forth. The packet is classified and a Label ID is added. The routes through the MPLS network region are defined by Labelled Switch Paths and the paths which will be taken are used by the Label Switched Routers. Network operators can diver the route the packet will take therefore based on the data type and traffic on the network, but also by information about the customer (e.g. corporate customers paying for an 'always available' service may get priority and overcome congestion on the MPLS network).

The **Global System for Mobile Communications** (GSM originally stood for **Groupe Spécial Mobile**) is a standard developed by the European Telecommunications Standards Institute to describe the protocols used for 2G cellular phone data transmission.

The original 1G system relied on circuit-switched telecommunications, whereas started out life as a circuit-switched system, but then extensions were added to make GSM a packet-switch oriented system. Initially GSM was extended by the addition of the General Packet Radio Service (GPRS) and later with the Enhanced Data Rates for GSM Evolution (EDGE), which are still widely used as 'fallback' systems for our 3G and 4G cell systems today.

GSM is a cellular network, so an array of aerial transmitters (cell transmitters) are needed across a city to provide coverage.

Code division multiple access (CDMA) is a channel accessing method used within radio communications. Several transmitters can send information at the same time on the same channel. Each transmitter is assigned a code to maintain uniqueness within the multiplexed radio stream. This system extends the capabilities of mobile phone data transmission by allowing many different data streams to be sent from the same transmitter, on the same channel.

Long-Term Evolution (LTE) is a packet-switching standard based on GSM and EDGE for use in high-data transfer and focusses on network improvements made to deliver better transmission speeds, using digital signal processing technologies. It is considered to be a global cellular standard based on GSM. It has downlink peak rates of 300 Mbit/s, also uplink peak rates of 75 Mbit/s and is considered to have low latency, therefore extremely responsive.

4G – the Fourth Generation mobile telecommunications standard is now prominent as the main standard and by so doing can provide high-speed IP telephony, High-Definition TV and other services where a high transfer of data is required. 4G is a cellular service and is packaged as one of two main systems: Mobile WiMAX, or LTE.

Current 4G transfer rates are 300 Mb/s (used when the individual is in transit) and 1 gigabit per second (Gb/s) (when the user is not in transit).

HSPA+ Evolved High-Speed Packet Access is a wireless standard used on 3G networks, but is compatible with LTE. Here, downlink speeds of 168 Mb/s and uplinks of 22Mb/s are possible and are generated by using the MIMO ('multiple input, multiple output') wireless aerials. By using Dual-Cell HSDPA (two parallel transmission channels) and 4-way MIMO can allow for speeds of up to 168Mb/s downlink.

3G the Third Generation of mobile networks are the current standard for mobile communications with capable speeds typically (on its own) of 200 Kb/s.

Enhanced Data Rates for GSM Evolution (EDGE) is also known as Enhanced GPRS. It is a backwards compatible standard which will operate with GSM and allows for higher bit rates per channel than GSM alone. With EDGE it is possible to determine peak rates of 1Mb/s a typical rate of 400Kb/s. The extension, 'Evolved EDGE' is a further improvement still - transmission times have also been reduced to half and bitrates have been increased to 1Mb/s.

Dialup refers to the process of transmitting data as an audio analogue stream. This was the earliest form of internet connectivity and allowed the user to authenticate with their ISP, establish a connection and transmit data. Transmission was extremely slow with a MODEM (Modulator-Demodulator) attached to either a mobile phone, or landline telephone would send the analogue signal as audio 'noise' which would be decoded as a data stream by the receiving modem. It did not take advantage of the nature of the digital network and relied on the circuit-switched network which often would have interference which would weaken and garble the signal, leading to a loss of connection. Dialup speeds were typically 54Kb/s on a 64Kb/s connection, at best.

Worldwide Interoperability for Microwave Access (WiMAX) is wireless system making use of Microwaves to transmit data. It can provide data transfer speeds of 40 Mb/s and 1Gb/s for a WiMAX station. WiMAX is recognised by IEEE as the 802.16 standard (called 'Fixed WiMAX'). It is analogous to Wi-Fi, but can send data over larger distances and at a faster speed. It would however be an ideal 'wireless' solution for end users, enabling Internet-based TV, VoIP, smart metering of power, gas and water devices as well as internet access without the need of a Satellite dish or cable to premises.

Mobile WiMAX has been used to support the existing 3G/4G cell network allowing for greater speeds and the reduction of congestion by carrying 'trunk' data.

WiMAX can therefore provide long distance data transfer, or fast speeds enabling it to operate as a trunk carrier, supporting the existing network. The main difference with Wi-Fi is that WiMAX is designed to be a long-distance solution, such as to take information from district to district, or city to city.

Metro Ethernet is an Ethernet-based Metropolitan Area Network enabling companies to connect local offices to each other across the wider Ethernet network. This eliminates the previous need of a dedicated leased line. As we are here discussing the internet 'backbone' within a city, speeds tend to be measured in the 10Gb/s up to 1Tb/s.

Leased Lines – a leased line is a dedicated cable supplied by the telephone company. In the case of a 'circuit switched' leased line such as with ISDN, the line was completely dedicated from endpoint to endpoint. A specific connection was created, identified with a number (as with a telephone connection) which was unique to the user.

Leased lines are measured in terms of their speed of data transmission:

T-1 is a digital transmission system developed by Bell Labs, originated in 1962. T1 trunks were used to connect together telephone exchanges using copper wire. T1 is capable of carrying 1.544 Mb/s (DS1) (24 user channels at 64kb/s) The T1 typically now also supports Fibre as the medium of choice and can transmit 60 times more data than a standard ADSL modem.

T-3 is a wider implementation with speeds of 43.232 megabits per second achieved by bonding 28 x T-1 (1.544 Mb/s each) connections together, however transmission distance was limited at 180m. T-3 is therefore not a viable long-distance solution, but more a 'bonding' solution within neighbouring buildings.

E-1 is the European standard for data communication. Whereas the T-1 transmits at 1.544 Mb/s the E-1 transmits using 32 user channels, therefore 2.048 Mbit/s created from 32 time slots of 8 bits.

E-3 is also a European standard multiplexing solution capable of transfer speeds of 34.368 Mb/s – that's 512 User Channels.

OC3 (Optical Carrier 3) is a standard developed for bulk transmission over fibre. It is capable of 155 Mb/s (84 T1s).

OC12 (Optical Carrier 12) is a standard developed for bulk transmission over fibre and is used by ISPs and also the creation of Wide Area Networks to bulk transfer 'trunk' data. OC-12 transmits at 622.08 Mb/s and is therefore equivalent to 4 OC3 connections.

Circuit switching is a system of creating a channel by establishing a dedicated communications circuit through the network before the 'line' is used for communication. The circuit works as though the endpoints are connected as by an electrical circuit. The line is 'opened' and 'closed' at the end of the call at which point the circuits are reset and can be used for other calls. Here an electrical state is created whereby a communications line through the network is created.

Packet switching is the system of creating a logical link between the two endpoints by addressing the data packet as it travels across the network. Routes are determined based on known congestion and routers will share routing information to determine that the data packet being sent is using the best available connection to be able to send the packet across the myriad of routers which make up the network. No electrical circuit is made up but instead routing protocols dictate the route taken to send the packet. Based on the congestion and availability of routes different routes are chosen, also multiple packets can be sent at the same time along different routes to reach the same endpoint.

Circuit v packet switching – With a circuit-switched line, the line is open throughout the call. All data is sent across the dedicated circuit and is sent in sequence. Typically a circuit-switched approach is ideal for a phone call whereas a packet switched approach is ideal for the transmission of data. Data transfer is managed by the TCP/IP protocol in which data packets may arrive at the endpoint node out of sequence. Any incorrect packets are resent and the file is re-pieced. Packet switching involves the identification of an IP packet on the subnet and for the router to determine the best route along the network without the need for creating dedicated lines but instead basing the route on available connections between routers, the connection speed and metrics of the connection to ascertain the best route. The route is therefore considered dynamic.

1.5

1.5 Install and properly terminate various cable types and connectors using appropriate tools

- Copper connectors
    - RJ-11
    - RJ-45
    - RJ-48C
    - DB-9/RS-232
    - DB-25

- UTP coupler
- BNC coupler
- BNC
- F-connector
- 110 block
- 66 block
- Copper cables
  - Shielded vs unshielded
  - CAT3, CAT5, CAT5e, CAT6, CAT6a
  - PVC vs plenum
  - RG-59
  - RG-6
  - Straight-through vs crossover vs rollover
- Fiber connectors
  - ST
  - SC
  - LC
  - MTRJ
  - FC
  - Fiber coupler
- Fiber cables
  - Single mode
  - Multimode
  - APC vs UPC
- Media converters
  - Single mode fiber to Ethernet
  - Multimode fiber to Ethernet
  - Fiber to coaxial
  - Single mode to multimode fiber
- Tools
  - Cable crimpers
  - Punch down tool
  - Wire strippers
  - Snips
  - OTDR
  - Cable certifier

Copper connectors – here a variety of connectors are used across network components to attach to network devices. We will consider each of the connectors currently in use:

RJ-11 – the Registered Jack type 11 is a small, clear plastic plug with 6 gold/copper pins on one side and a locking clasp on the other. Of these only 2 are typically used for standard analogue phone networks although all 6 are usually wired. For the UK, it is common to only see 4 wires in use. The RJ11 is used to attach a serial connection to a device such as a managed router, but is more commonly used for connecting to a Modem to allow connectivity between the PC and the telephone line. A second RJ11 line is used to plug in the telephone as a 'monitor' device and also to enable the telephone to operate normally when the modem is not in use.

In the UK, British Telecommunications (BT) have held the monopoly of the telephone network throughout the 1980s and 1990s. BT developed their own equivalent phone connector plug based on RJ11 but has a wider connection. Typical ADSL filters till have a BT jack and BT female input, but will use an RJ11 input for the digital DSL signal.

RJ-45 – Registered Jack type 45 is the most common network port. This is the standard Ethernet connection port as found on NICs, Hubs, Switches and Routers. The RJ-45 is the common connectivity standard for connecting any network device. It consists of 4 pairs of twisted-pair wires arranged in the configuration 568A or 568B at both ends. This would create a straight-through or 'patch cable' capable of adding the device to the existing network.

By mixing 568A at one end of the cable and 568B at the other end of the cable the swapping of wires 1 (end A) and 3 (end B) and 2 (end A) and 6 (end B) creates a 'crossover cable'. This is used to connect together devices of a similar type where a data loop is required to create a circuit between the two nodes. This is typical if you were to connect two routers together, or two PCs directly to each other.

RJ-48C – this connector is a differently wired RJ-45 seeming cable used for T1 lines. The modular connector is identical to that of the RJ-45, so it is the wiring which denotes the difference to RJ-45. There are two different configurations used to create a T1 connection. First, we use pins 1, 2, 4, and 5. The alternative is to use pins 1, 2, 7, and 8. Also you will notice that the cable used is Shielded Twisted Pair with a T1 cable.

DB-9 / RS-232 – The serial connection is used to monitor data sent to one port, but can also be used to send data via a serial communication line. On Routers and Managed Switches it is also possible to connect to the management instrumentation software via an RS-232 connection however this connection needs to plug into the administrator's laptop so that they can manage the device. Here, the administrator would connect via the modem plug and visit a specific management IP address, or create a TELNET session in order to administer the device. The DB-9 is a D-shaped female connector which plugs into the only male socket on the PC. The socket is configured with pins on 2 rows – 5 and 4.

DB-25 as with the DB-9 the standard connector is of a D-shape configuration with 2 rows of pins – this time 13 and 12. The communication is again serial but is typically female on the device, whereas DB-9 is male. They can be used for direct serial connection including status updates from a UPS box, or direct connection to another PC. It is also sometimes used within professional recording studios and can also be used as a connection out to a printer (the DB-25 to Centronics cable is a standard connection type for line and early laser printers. This communication method however is parallel, not serial so the presence of a DB-25 on its own does not signify that the communication is always serial.)

A **UTP coupler** is a small plastic device containing two directly-joined RJ45 sockets. This enables the cable run to be extended on the network.

A **BNC coupler** is a small metal cylinder with bayonet connection pins. It enables the BNC connection to allow for a longer cable run by connecting a new cable at this point. The coupler is a small, cheap, inexpensive means to extend the network for Coaxial cable networks.

The **Bayonet Neill–Concelman (BNC)** or 'Bayonet' connector is a standard connection type used with coaxial cable. The main copper wire makes connection with the metal tube to which the signal is sent. One the outside of the BNC is a ¼ turn screw with a track cut into the outer collar to form a lock. This locks against two pins on the 'female' end. The connector is also commonly known as the 'British Naval Connector'.

It is common to find a BNC connector not only in use for networking but also due to its versatility the 50 Ohm BNC is commonly used in the Broadcasting industry for TV, editing and also for radio production.

The **F-connector** is a similar sturdy connection allowing the middle copper wire to be locked into position. Here, the F itself is a hexagonal threaded ring which locks the cable into place. It is commonly found on the rear of satellite and cable TV set-top boxes.

A **110 block** can be found within the switch room at the back of a patch panel. It is used to connect the Cat 5 cables running to the connection points in each room on the floor through to the patch panel, where each socket can then be wired into the switch. The 110 block is a series of metal v-shaped blocks stored which capture and cut into the plastic surround of the wire, therefore making connection whilst also holding the wire in place. Each Cat-5 cable connects to a series of blocks which in turn are connected to the patch panel. In order to attach the wire to the block, a punchdown tool is used to force the wire into the slit, making the process of attaching the cable relatively easy.

110 blocks are preferred over the older 66 blocks as they produce less crosstalk.

A **66 block** is also a punchdown block, but is used for the telephony system, not for networking. It consists of a variety of 'punched' wires – one block is from the telephone provider and one block is from the internal telephone network. These two arrays are 'bridged'. The 66-block is considered to be a 'demarcation point' – the final point in the sequence under the management of the telephony service.

The family of copper cables used within networking are often the more significant medium – they are found within almost all networks and can produce excellent local speeds. Copper is also the medium of choice for cost reasons as the cable is relatively inexpensive in comparison to other network media. The two main cables we will consider as the twisted pair and the coaxial cable.

A **shielded cable** is one which contains further plating, or shielding to protect the data signal being sent along the wire from interference (random notice from other equipment, or electromagnetic interference) or from 'crosstalk' (signal bleed from other local data wires).

The **unshielded cable** contains no additional shielding – crosstalk is removed from the wire only be protecting it from opposing data – the wire is twisted with its opposite – the data stream is sent on one wire and the opposing binary signal is sent on the other wire twisted with it. This way, any crosstalk would in fact negate the original signal rather than adding additional data to it and from the deduction of the inverse signal from the original, the original data stream is still received. The process is known as 'balancing' and is also used widely in the Broadcast media, specifically audio engineering industry. Here, an 'unbalanced' cable such as a phono cable can only run for approx. 1 metre before the cable has also picked up sufficient interference to interfere with the signal, generating audio 'hiss'. This is because a wire run across a room would act as an aerial as well as transmitting its own signal. The signals it would pick up would interfere with the data signal we are trying to send which will garble the original signal.

'Balancing' is the process of using the binary opposite signal. In audio, a microphone is attached to a sound desk by the use of an XLR (Cannon) plug – the cable is rubber sheathed and has three wires – LR wires carry the stereo and inverse stereo signal, but the 'X' is used to earth the two opposite devices together, ensuring that both have the same Earth Potential Difference, therefore eliminating excess 'hum' generated by the other device.

Unshielded cable therefore typically would provide a run of 100 metres without significant loss of signal (attenuation).

A shielded cable comes in one of two forms:

i) Each wire is shielded (or each twist is shielded)
ii) The complete set of wires are shielded before the cable is sheathed in plastic.

Either way, the intention is to eliminate interference and to minimise crosstalk if possible. (The first option will also help to reduce crosstalk, but the second will combat outside interference only).

CAT3 is a common cable designed for short, internal use, for the transmission of telephone signals (Voice-Grade). It can be used for networking and will transmit up to 10Mb/s. However, CAT3 would not be sufficient for modern data networks.

CAT5 is the more common networking cable for internal use. It can transmit 100Mb/s over 100 metres. Due to high demand, costs are considerably low, so this is the most ubiquitous of cables available on the market. Of the 4 pairs of copper wire, only 2 pairs are actually used to send the signal.

CAT5e is a development on the existing CAT5 cable where all 4 pairs of wires are used to transmit the signals. Here, speeds of 1000Mb/s are possible using the existing physical infrastructure. Cat5e ('e' referring to 'enhanced'). The cable is also backwards compatible with CAT5 and CAT3.

CAT6 is the standardised cable for Gigabit Ethernet, allowing typical speeds of 10Gb/s. The cable twist appears to be much tighter than in CAT5 and subsequently there is greater reduction of crosstalk allowing for faster transmission speeds. CAT6 is not widely used within the UK due to cost, but is the standard cabling type in the US. The pairs are not themselves coiled around each other but are straight along the run of the cable, forming a body of wiring around a small, flimsy centre plastic core. There is a slight barley twist in the centre core, but not to the extent of CAT6e.

CAT6a is a more robust cable. The cable jacket is quite sturdy and its diameter is equivalent to a 25-pair CAT3 type cable, so almost double the diameter in comparison to standard CAT6 UTP cable. Every pair is twisted and coiled around the centre plastic core which itself is barley-twisted to ensure a distance between each pair. The CAT6e jacket is quite sturdy, made from thick plastic. The jacket also has sections which again separate the four pairs from each other, reducing crosstalk within the cable. The cable is much heavier and is typically used for internal use when cabling an office to its switch room.

Polyvinyl Chloride is a common plastic jacket found in most 'patch' cables. In the event of a fire the concern is that PVC will melt and itself be used by the fire as a fuel, but will exude toxic gasses which may be harmful to any persons attempting to leave the building. Flame retardant chemicals can be added to the manufacture of the PVC to impede the flames from spreading but the toxicity of PVC is a concern.

Plenum cable on the other hand is made from a different form of plastic which will not produce toxic fumes when it burns. This also would be manufactured with flame retardant chemicals to impede the fire from spreading. It is called 'plenum' because of where the cable is used. The ducting space, or 'void' space above a false ceiling and the real ceiling is used to lay power cables, lighting and air-conditioning pipes as well as air-conditioning units. It is also a perfect space to lay networking cable. Plenum cable is therefore typically the cable connecting each network point (wall socket) in the room to the switch room's patch panel. The cable would typically be 25-pair plenum-rated cable although sometimes individual 'plenum' 8-wire cables are bundled and the bundle is run across the ceiling space within trunking, or on metal cable trays. The cables terminate onto a 110 block at the back of the patch panel.

RG-59 is a coaxial cable used for low-power video signals, such as for CCTV. It consists, as with other coaxial cable of a solid copper core (75 Ohms) surrounded by a plastic insulator, a copper braided wire mesh which shields the inner wire from external interference and finally an outer plastic jacket. RG-59 is commonly used with broadcast video equipment, but for short range only, such as to connect a satellite dish to the set-top box. This is comparable to RG-58 which is used for radio and was in use within the early 1990s as 'Thinnet' (10BASE2). RG-59 is not commonly used for networking but is used where broadcast video may need to be transmitted, such as from a security camera to a receiving station before media conversion onto the TCP/IP network.

RG-59 also carries 2 wires which can be used to supply power to your external device (e.g. your security camera) although it is also possible to use these wires to provide audio.

RG-6 is a low-quality alternative used for short-range connections such as to connect a video recorder to a TV. RG-6 is also 75 ohms but lacks the power wires.

The main deciding factors here are install time (do you want to run additional power cables to your external device) and impedance (if the equipment is designed to run above 50 MHz then you will want to consider RG-59.

Straight-through cable (patch cable). Earlier I introduced the concept of a 'patch' cable, which is a cable where the wires are in the same pinout sequence at either end of the cable. Here, the cable extends the device's reach and allows for direct connection to another device. In relation to the OSI model, a PC would be connected to another device via direct physical connection into a switch. The process of connecting data from one port on a patch panel into a switch is referred to as 'patching' (creating an electronic circuit to a specific port).

A **Crossover cable** differs to a straight-through (patch) cable in that it can remove the need of an intermediary device such as a switch if all that is required is to create a direct connection with another PC. A data loop needs to be created and for this two wire positions are adjusted at end B. Most modern switches are now able to sense the type of cable connected to it, so if the wrong type of cable is used the circuitry will automatically compensate for this, for each port separately.

Crossover cables are typically used for devices at layer 3 of the OSI model or above to connect directly to other devices operating at layer 3 or above (e.g. Router connecting to another router, or Server connecting to Router, or PC directly connecting to another PC).

A **rollover cable** is a null-modem cable used to monitor switches and routers and to access the management console. They are also known as Cisco console cables, or a Yost cable. The pinout at one end of the cable is the opposite of the other. (e.g. pin 8 goes to pin 1 at the other end.)

Fibre optical cable consists of a strand of glass of platic material which will carry a light beam. The process of sending light across time produces a signal which can be re-coded as a binary data stream. By sending light of slightly different frequencies it is possible to send several light signals across the same medium at the same time. This process is known as multiplexing. Each light signal is decoded and re-coded as a digital binary electronic stream.

Fibre cable actually consists of two strands, even though we refer to 'single mode'. This is because one cable strand will send the light stream one way whilst the other can send returning data in the opposite direction. The fibre cable attaches to two ports, one consisted of a laser or LED emitter and the other is a light sensor capable of receiving and decoding the various signals.

There are two main types of cable:

Single mode – here, a high quality strand of glass or plastic is used to transmit signals over a long distance (up to 40km). Single mode is high speed and long-distance, but is usually only found within metropolitan networks, or within the telecoms infrastructure to carry trunk (bulk) data. The core glass fibre is cladded by a plastic sheath which traps the light inside, ensuring that the light emission is not lost in transit (total internal reflection).

Multimode is more commonly found within one building, or between neighbouring buildings. Speeds are slower and the data distance is also shorter. The cable is made up of several strands of plastic or glass each of which capable of carrying a signal over a short distance. The light rays bounce off the walls of the core strands allowing for several rays to be sent at the same time, as a multiplexed signal, however is only effective at short distances.

Fibre connectors are used with specific types of cable and are remembered as much by how they are operated as common names have now developed for these connectors:

ST – Straight Tip (common name: 'Shove-Twist'). The ST connector encloses the cable in a rubber sheath terminating with a bayonet cap to lock the cable in place. It is commonly used with Multimode cable but can be used with either type.

SC – Standard / Subscriber connector (common name: 'Shove-Click' or 'Square Connector'). The SC connector ends with a grey plastic coupling and this 'dual plug' attaches the cable pair into the receiver/transmitter unit (a dual SC), although it is common to also buy SC plugs which are for each individual cable. SC can be used with either cable mode type.

LC – the **Lucient connector** is ideally suited for single mode fibre, although both versions are again possible. It sends in a dual grey plug with ceramic ferrules at the tip of the fibre on each cable. LC is half of the size of an SC connector. It is again square shaped and has a locking clip on the top of the plug. The ferrule is half of the diameter of an SC connector. Given the size difference it is possible to increase the density of fibre connections within your switch room. LC is used typically for single mode cable only.

MTRJ – the **Mechanical Transfer** (common name: 'media termination') **Registered Jack** is a multimode connector has rectangular rather than round ferrules. It is extremely small, so is popular due to the space saved. The MTRJ endpoint port is analogous to an RJ45 port and allows end devices to communicate directly using fibre.

FC – **Ferrule connectors** (common name 'Fibre Channel' or 'Fibre Connector') are used in environments where there may be high vibration, so it is important that the cable does not jolt loose. They are now less common due to the propensity of SC connectors. The end of the plug is threaded so that the plug can be screwed into place. Although it can be used on both types it is typically used on single fibre cables.

Fibre coupler – this is a junction box-style device capable of extending the run of a cable. They are typically used in underwater repair where the cables have to be joined together, but are essentially 'dark boxes' where the two fibre cable ends can be joined and the signal repeated. Advanced couplers can read and re-transmit the data stream, acting as a repeater to extend the length ('the run') of a data stream over several miles.

APC v UPC – when the fibre terminates there is normally an air gap which can impede the light signal and interfere with how the light is received. By adjusting the end of the fibre from a direct, straight Physical Contact to an Angular Physical contact. Ultra Physical Contact is an improvement on the standard connection in that the cable end has been polished so any back reflection has been slightly reduced. With Angular Physical Contact the endpoint is angled by 8 degrees reducing any back reflection still further.

Media converters – a media converter is a device capable of reading the data delivered in the first medium and retransmit it using a different media. Converters typically would have to transmit the data stream at different speeds, and because of this there is a degree of data caching required.

A switch is the most common type of media converter in that data input into one port can be transmitted out on another port which happens to transmit the data using a different medium. Switches can house a mixture of ports which are coaxial, Ethernet or fibre. It is common to use a multimode fibre cable as an uplink connection to connect the switch to the remainder of the network.

The advantage of a media converter is that you can still make use of the existing network infrastructure. **Single-mode fibre to Ethernet** tend to be used on entry points to the existing Ethernet network on edge-facing switches, or an edge router. **Multimode fibre to Ethernet** converters, or switch adapters are also available and are commonly found in rack-mounted switches to connect floors, or buildings together.

It is less common to see Fibre to Coaxial other than in a customisable switch as the data transfer speeds are quite different. Multimode to RG-59 is possible and is used more commonly by broadcast TV companies to separate a multiplexed ('muxed') signal to several, sometimes even thousands of homes. Cable TV providers would plan their TV network with the 'head' end and the neighbourhood hub site where the signal is broken down into component streams and sent across the various coaxial cables to each customer.

This section draws greatly on the differences of 'Fibre to Cabinet' and 'Fibre to home' to impress the fact that the existing coaxial infrastructure is used as much as it possible without significant reduction of signal quality or speed, negating the actual need of laying fibre to each home.

Single mode to Multimode fibre – as with the above 'head' and 'feed' sections are considered where a multiplexed signal can be broken into its component parts for transmission at lower speeds. Typically single mode fibre is used for long-distance, high-speed travel and multimode for shorter, close distance travel.

Network tools:

Cable crimpers are a multi-purpose device used to strip, align and cut the cable and internal wires, but also to attach the RJ45 pinouts to their respective wires. A Crimper blade is first is used to cut the cable to length, the jacket is then carefully cut revealing a length of wire, which is untwisted, straightened and put into the correct positioning. The wires themselves are then 'dressed' (placed against each other) and the wire tops are again cut to ensure equal length. The wires are then passed into the RJ45 plug and pushed to the very end where they lie behind the copper pins, within their respective 8 wire channels. The crimper is then used to apply pressure onto the copper pins which bite into the wire ends, making contact with the copper below the plastic sheathing. At the same time a 'bridge' component is pushed down onto the cable jacket at the base of the plug, tightening a grip over the wires and cable, holding the array into place.

A **punchdown tool** is a pen-like device with a v-shaped metallic end. It is designed to apply pressure onto a wire, forcing it in the v-slit of the 110-block. The same tool is also used on telephony headers such as are at the reverse of RJ45 network points, or ISDN sockets, although screw-held equivalents are also still possible to buy.

As the force is applied to the wire, the punchdown tool allows downward force to push the wire into the slit. As the slit narrows the plastic jacket is cut and the wire is exposed, making tight contact to the V-slit, also holding the wire into position.

Wire strippers are a nutcracker-like device screwed at the very end with a series of pre-cut holes where it is possible to apply pressure to and cut into the plastic sheathing around a wire and therefore allow the external plastic sheathing to be severed so that it can be manually pulled away from the wire and removed by the operator. Different size diameter holes are present to enable the operator to strip different types of wire, from power-rated wires to small telecoms 'thinnet' or telephone cabling.

Snips are the technical term for wire scissors used to remove stray strands from braided wire, or to cut the ends of a wire to the same length. They look similar to pliers but end in a flat blade, allowing for greater force to be applied to cut into the wire than can be done with conventional scissors which would not be able to cut into the wire as effectively.

A **Time Domain Reflectometer** is an electronic device used where there is a break in a cable. It measures, against time the point at which the resistance in the wire changed and by so doing can calculate the distance a cable break is away from you. An **Optical TDR** is an advanced variant of the same device capable of determining the point at which light was no longer reflected along its path.

A **Cable Certifier** is an advancement on a cable tester which sends a pulse along one end of a cable (each wire in turn) and provides a visual readout for both ends of the cable to prove that there is connectivity. A Certifier is used for custom-made cables to ensure that not only is the resistivity of the cable acceptable at both ends, for each wire but that the overall cable design and cable endpoints are secure and meeting regulations. A Certifier will either upload this result to a database, or print off a confirmation slip which can be used for insurance purposes to prove that the cable is fit for purpose.

1.6

1.6 Differentiate between common network topologies
- Mesh
    - Partial
    - Full
- Bus
- Ring
- Star
- Hybrid
- Point-to-point
- Point-to-multipoint
- Client-server
- Peer-to-peer

Until now we have considered the physical layout of the network. This section will consider the logical, or rather the flow of data from device (node) to device (a 'hop').

The simplest form of network would share a common cable (or 'fat pipe') which would allow one packet to travel along it from any node on the network to any other. The use of one common cable reduces cost although transmission speed is reliant on the effectiveness of the common cable. Theoretically, it would be possible to transmit a packet from one end node across the network to another node in only one hop, however network protocol might cause other nodes to check to determine if the packet is intended for them, or not and if not to send on the packet. The disadvantage of a **Bus** network, as we are describing here is that a break in the cable would not cause the network to break into two, but would fail the overall cable and render the network inoperable. For this to work, the common cable has to be terminated at either end. This system is of course also seen within a SCSI chain (for RAID arrays using one data cable to attach to several SCSI hard disks).

A further adaptation of the bus network would be a line, or rather fully a '**ring**' network where each device is connected to each of its neighbours by the use of two NICs within each node. Here, the packet is transferred along the ring in a 'pass the parcel' fashion until the eventual recipient is found. A break in a cable in this scenario would actually leave the network still working as no repeater is needed. A break in the cable would simply cause the packet to be sent along in the other direction until the recipient is reached.

The above example is theoretical, but impractical. Each node would require two IP addresses (one per NIC) and this would involve some creative network management to make it work. The fact that there are several 'hops' would render the network to be considered slow. If one PC was switched off this would render as a 'break' in the cable. Two breaks at different ends of the ring would split the network in two.

There was however a practical example of 'ring' which is now discontinued, but useful in a historical context. A Token Ring network was in face wired as a 'star' network where the Media Access Unit (MAU) acted as the central device to which all nodes were attached, but the packet was sent to each node in sequence from the MAU until the correct node was found.

The **star** network is the most common type of network. It is cheap, easy to set up and requires only one IP address per NIC, making it easy to manage. The broadcast domain is the extent of the switch to the Router as the exit point out to the remainder of the network. As switches are capable of reading the data frame (at level 2 of the OSI model) by using the ARP address, the data can react its destination in two 'hops' (device to switch, switch to end device).

A **hybrid** is a combination of the above designs. This is quite common when you will create a connection between two subnets using a 'backbone' or 'uplink' such as two star networks linked by a fibre backbone. A typical office building design would be of a star network for each floor with a vertical 'trunk backbone' made from fibre uplinks.

A **mesh** network (or 'fully connected') is a theoretical design used for research purposes only due to its complexity and constraints. A Mesh network would contain a series of nodes which are connected to each other. Every node would be connected to each other via only one hop. This would be possible through a series of crossover cables. In practical application it would be costly, each node would contain several NICs each with their own IP address (so one node might have many IP addresses) and each would need to be carefully managed to ensure that the one-hop solution, if available is taken rather then bypassing the packet through a neighbouring NIC.

The formula to calculate the number of connections in a full mesh is $n(n-1)/2$ where n are the number of nodes in the network.

Thus, with 4 nodes:

$4(4-1)/2 = 4(3)/2 = 2(3) = 6$ connections (cables) used.

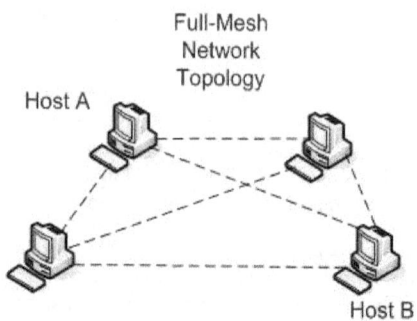

Full-Mesh Network Topology

Host A

Host B

With a **partially connected mesh** it is possible to ensure that all nodes have redundancy without the need for full connections on every PC.

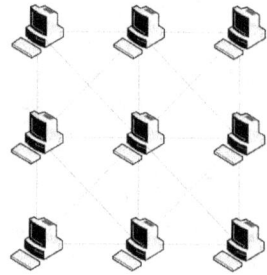

Point-to-point refers to a dedicated channel with one node at either end of the cable (the channel). This is the typical operation of sending a unicast data packet into a switch and out though one other port.

Point-to-multipoint refers to a point at which a single connection can branch into several other possible connections. Usually the connection is transient in order to send the data packet and is closed at the end of the connection. A connection device such as a switch would class as a multipoint device in that the client PC has a dedicated line which can send data to the switch, but the switch may broadcast the data to all nodes (if the data packet was a broadcast the switch would have to do this.)

In a lower tech example, the use of a hub does just this – the input data packet is duplicated and sent out on all ports.

The **Peer-to-Peer** model is a logical design of a network where each PC is independent and runs its own services. A user would have separate accounts on each PC, so in a scenario of 10 users and 10 PCs would potentially mean 100 different separate accounts each with their own shared folders and documents. This can create backup and network management problems which can be overcome by centralising the services and documents, stored in a single location. In Microsoft terminology, this is referred to as a 'Workgroup', or more recently with systems from Vista onwards a 'Homegroup' which enables common network security and sharing by using a public folder.

The **client-server** model a better answer to the network problem and is used where there is a large number of users or PCs. Here, servers take on network management roles and by centralising these services reduces the network requirements of the individual workstations. The client-server model requires several common services to be used on the network:

A domain controller holds the Active Directory database and is a central point where network enabled users and PCs can authenticate and be authorised. Login attempts are logged forming accountability. Granular control of users and computers can be established and security rules (known as Group Policy Objects) can be applied to both the user and the PC based on location, type of PC and role within the company (the group to which the user, or PC is a member of).

DNS service acts as a global phonebook allowing known network names of devices or shared folders to be found and resolved to the IP address of the device your PC needs to make contact with.

DHCP service is used to issue IP addresses on a lease basis to network devices, but also to signpost other useful IP addresses such as the location of the DNS server, the router (default gateway) and other network resources.

File server – a central repository of files. This could be the actual location of the user's profile – there is no need to store the profile on the local machine and by so doing a user can now log onto any permitted PC on the network.

In Microsoft terminology we refer to a connected centralised 'client-server' network as a Domain. The DNS principle extends on the original concept of naming first established with Windows NT where NetBIOS names defined the uniqueness of the PC and also its function on the network to a more hierarchical system with the concept of the Fully Qualified Domain Name which can be used to determine the setting of the PC, or share within the wider context of a domain. (e.g. west.comptia.org may refer to PCs stored at the western region of the company domain).

1.7

1.7 Differentiate between network infrastructure implementations
- WAN
- MAN
- LAN
- WLAN
  - Hotspot
- PAN
  - Bluetooth
  - IR
  - NFC
- SCADA/ICS
  - ICS server
  - DCS/closed network
  - Remote terminal unit
  - Programmable logic controller
- Medianets
  - VTC
    - ISDN
    - IP/SIP

The Network+ course infers some prior knowledge of Network infrastructure – you will need to focus on the newer concepts than the fundamentals which have been in existence for over a decade now.

Wide Area Network (WAN) – this concept is the extension of the Local Area Network in that a variety of network resources (usually a department, PCs or specific users) who need to work away from the main office location. The connection of a branch via a secure Virtual Private Network (either a dedicated leased line or a secure IPSEC 'tunnel' through the Internet network) will extend the capability of the network to other users based away from the head office. The remote user will have exactly the same experience as if they were logging on at the head office.

WANs come in various types but is a general rule the term WAN refers to any remoting user attaching to a main network located within one central building (the LAN).

Metropolitan Area Network (MAN) – Where there are two or three defined areas within one city, we refer to this as a MAN. Usually the MAN sites are connected by a leased line or secure tunnel making use of the existing internet infrastructure within a city. WiMAX and Metro Ethernet are ideal systems to support the creation of a MAN and negates the costly need of a leased line to send 'trunk' data between sites.

A **Local Area Network (LAN)** is a network confined within the local building, or local site (a cluster of neighbouring buildings defined as one site). The network is contained within one logical site. All accessing users are local to the site.

A **Wireless LAN (WLAN)** is the extension of the LAN to support users who may be roaming, but within the connectivity via a wireless router, or access point. A wireless LAN is more dynamic in that the user may roam across the site, connecting to different access points which serve the physical site but address themselves on the network by MAC address, not by switch port.

A **hotspot** is an area where the user can connect to a wireless access point (the area where the device may connect and the user authenticate to the network is considered 'hot').

A **Personal Area Network (PAN)** is a small, discrete network, usually ad-hoc in nature which enables the user to create a connection with neighbouring devices in order to transmit data. A PAN is typically Bluetooth, or Wi-Fi and would be a direct link between two devices. Or example a smartphone can connect via **Near Field Communication (NFC)** to transmit a file to a wireless printer in order to print a copy of a document. Also, two smartphones may connect via Bluetooth and send an image.

As a connection system **Bluetooth** is a reliable and easy-to-use, ubiquitous facility now present in most modern smartphones and laptops. Bluetooth enables point-to-point connections with one other device, such as a Bluetooth keyboard connecting to a smartphone, and works by sending radio signals to the connected device. Bluetooth operates on the 2.4GHz band and typically would send 1Mb/s over 10 metres, although recent versions of Bluetooth are being developed which increase the speed and range at reduced power. Bluetooth is the connection system of choice for local gadgets, or personal accessories (e.g. a Bluetooth headset, earpiece, hands-free kit).

Infra-red is an unreliable network system. It is now not often used because it requires a direct line of sight from the emitter to the sensor and has a slow connection over a limited range – usually 1 metre but in more advanced IR systems is limited to 5 metres:

- IrDA-SIR (slow speed) infrared supporting data rates up to 115 Kb/s
- IrDA-MIR (medium speed) infrared supporting data rates up to 1.15 Mb/s
- IrDA-FIR (fast speed) infrared supporting data rates up to 4 Mbps

Supervisory Control And Data Acquisition (SCADA) – this is a coding system used widely for remote control devices, issuing information and status about the remote device. A SCADA system can be used to automatically program machinery in the response to telemetry data. Taking the analogy further an **Industrial Control System Server (ICS)** can use telemetry to manage operations within an industry (within a plant). For example, it would be possible to switch on water pumps and redirect the flow to areas in a system where the water would be needed. SCADA systems are often used within electricity plants and wider on the National Grid to ensure that electricity generated is stored and redirected to where it is needed. SCADA is an example of an Industrial Control System.

An ICS Server should not be confused with **ICS – Internet Connection Sharing**, which is now a depreciated element. Internet Connection Sharing is the ability of a client PC to act as a sharing point to allow other PCs of the same subnet to make use of the ADSL modem connected to the ICS computer, enabling internet access to all PCs on the subnet.

A **Distributed Control System (DCS)** is a dynamic system where production is computer controlled. A hierarchical control system is used to control production from initial scheduling of work to controlling (coordinating computer) which govern each plant's supervising computer. These in turn manage the control of automated plant machinery.

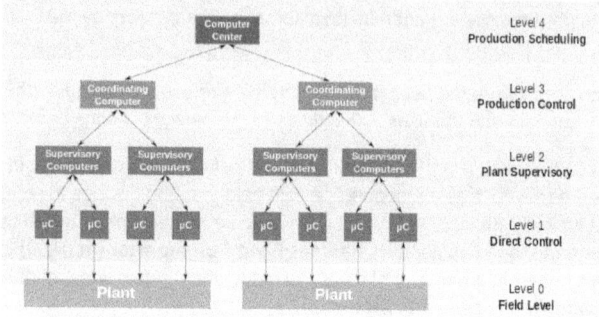

The DCS network is a 'closed system' meaning that it is isolated from the internet, or from other external factors which may impact on production. Machinery which comprises the DCS is dedicated to its function.

Within SCADA, the **Remote Terminal Unit** is a processor-controlled device which enables interaction with the physical world. An example would be a Lego Technic processor attached to a motor, which is designed to open a window in an automated greenhouse. The RTU may also have a thermometer which will sense when the temperature of the greenhouse rises beyond a defined tolerance. The RTU will pass sensor input into the processor for calculation within the computer program, but also will use instructions from the processor to operate the motor (the output).

The **Programmable Logic Controller** is the device which holds the computer program. This receives sensor data from the RTU which is then used by the program. Its output responses are also sent to the RTU.

A typical example of an integrated RTU/PLC system would be the automatic car. Here, radar and sensor data would pass into the PLC which would make safety decisions, turning and speed decisions in order to control the car.

Medianet refers to a network architecture deliberately constructed for media applications. It is used specifically for voice, telephone (VoIP) and video conferencing and refers to the network components which carry, process and manage this data. Typically the VoIP network was separate to the data 'Intranet' network but it is now commonplace to see telephony network solutions integrated with the standard network as providers offer Medianet capabilities.

VTC refers to Video Teleconferencing – the use of voice over IP (VoIP) telecommunication networking to transmit a video feed. Within the corporate sector providers such as Cisco and Microsoft have specific solutions which can offer teleconferencing facilities (e.g. Lync). For the public sector, lower quality, lower bandwidth solutions across the public internet are available (e.g. Skype).

ISDN – We have looked at the data makeup of ISDN earlier in this module. With a PRI solution bandwidth would allow high-quality voice and video transfers across a dedicated channel. An example of use here would be the BBC who have dedicated ISDN lines to connect each radio station and post-production edit facility to enable voice-overs and news reports, also interviews to be conducted remotely at another office. ISDN can be daisy-chained to enable support from news reporters or actors located a long distance away.

IP/SIP as with ISDN, SIP allows for secure session connections over closed networks. It relies on the PSTN network to be able to make a telephone call through which we can send the data packet. It is however a legacy technology and can be unreliable. It is therefore a circuit-switched technology.

H.323 – this is the new protocol for multimedia transmission over IP networks which although it is not specifically referred to in the course, is becoming the more common transfer method. It is a packet-switched technology and true multimedia over IP.

1.8

1.8 Given a scenario, implement and configure the appropriate addressing schema
- IPv6
  - Auto-configuration
    - EUI 64
  - DHCP6
  - Link local
  - Address structure
  - Address compression
  - Tunneling 6to4, 4to6
    - Teredo, miredo
- IPv4
  - Address structure
  - Subnetting
  - APIPA
  - Classful A, B, C, D
  - Classless
- Private vs public
- NAT/PAT
- MAC addressing
- Multicast
- Unicast
- Broadcast
- Broadcast domains vs collision domains

In this section we will focus on how the data is addressed and sent across the network.

IPv6 is a relatively new format but in truth was introduced publicly by the Internet Engineering Task Force in 1998 although it was not until the wider migration to Windows

Vista which used IPv6 as the default IP addressing scheme that IPv6 became the standard addressing system.

IPv6 is a larger data packet with a 128-bit addressing system in comparison to IPv4's 32-bit. (There was no public release of IPv5, rather further development led to the eventual release as IPv6).

The main problem we have faced with IPv4 is that we would soon run out of IP addresses. This has now happened. Internet routers tend to support IPv4 as the main common system, although there is an initiative to upgrade the internet to IPv6-capable routers. CompTIA refer to the IPv6 Internet but in truth IPv4 are widely used.

IPv4 is still used internally for private addressing as Network Designers may wish to create subnets of specific sizes and can use now older methods such as CIDR, Subnetting or Supernetting to do this. The sheer large number of IP addresses available with IPv6 negate the need to produce a complex subsystem.

IPv6 provide for use a large address space, advanced protocol headers for the data packet enabling us to control more advanced packet forwarding. IPv6 nodes can determine their own IP address, simplifying IP configuration. We now use large packets called 'jumbograms' capable of carrying bulk data transfer between ISP provider systems, or across different networks. The packet can be both authenticated and encrypted. The packet can also support QoS labels to identify which data packets are to be prioritised.

IPv6 no longer supports broadcast packets. Instead we use **Multicast** (specific PCs) or Anycast (whoever is able to join the data stream).

IPv6's capabilities are further extensible making it an ideal future technology. On Windows 8.1, IPv6 support is the default addressing system and is enabled by default, but was optional with Vista and 7. Other technologies such as IPSec tunnelling and DirectAccess both make use of IPv6. Windows 8.1 secure file sharing and Remote Access Service also now use IPv6.

IPv6 is also capable of Neighbour Discovery. By sending the host MAC address it can register received solicited MAC addresses from other devices, or IPv6 routers.

Address structure:

For a General Unicast address, the 128-bit IPv6 packet is broken into three parts: a 48-bit routing prefix, a 16-bit subnet id and a 64-bit host identifier.

A **Link-Local** address consists of a 10-bit prefix and 54-bits as zero-padding, with the 64-bit host identifier.

A General **multicast** would have an 8-bit prefix, a 4-bit flag, a 4-bit scope and then 112 bits as the group ID.

Address compression - an example IPv6 address is:

2001:0bc2:25d2:0000:0000:8bbd:0261:6231

Therefore we can see eight groups of four hexadecimal digits. Each group is separated by a colon.

Where the group starts with a 0 these zeroes can be omitted, e.g. *0bc2* can be written as *bc2*

Where there are groups of zeroes, the entire section can be removed and replaced by double colon. This can however be done once, thus:

2001:0bc2:25d2:0000:0000:8bbd:0261:6231

Can be written as

2001:bc2:25d2::8bbd:261:6231

IPv6 addresses are recognisable by looking at the first group:

- A 'network zero' IP address with all 128 zero bits refers to an unspecified address (e.g. 0000:......)
- ::/0 refers to the default route.
- ::1/128 refers to the loopback address for NIC 1 on the current host.
- fe80::/10 refers to a local address on the same subnet ('link-local'). This is the equivalent of a private IPv4 local address, (or even APIPA)
- fc00::/7 refers to a unique local address between sites which are set to support unique local.
- ::ffff:0:0/96 refers to a '4 to 6' IP address where an Ipv4 packet is used on the Ipv6 address space.
- 2002::/16 as above, this is used for 6to4 translation.
- 2001::/32 is used for Teredo tunneling.

DHCP6 - IPv6 will **auto-configure** without the need for any network administrator intervention. A DHCPv6 server can supply the details of neighbouring nodes and the groups set up for the node to then decide which number it should use as next in the sequence. It is also possible for the node to auto-configure by using nearest neighbour identification.

EUI-64 - a host can automatically assign itself with a unique IPv6 IP address by using the existing 48-bits of the MAC address and adding the additional code "FFFE" as padding.

Tunneling – the process of encapsulating data within outer data used by other equipment to forward data is considered 'tunneling'. Imagine a tunnel and a hacker trying to look at the outer wall of the tunnel, from the outside. They will see a brick/concrete wall and are obfuscated from the data being transmitted inside. Imagine the data packets as being similar to carriages on a train, travelling through this tunnel. Each carriage could have dark glass windows, locked doors and no recognisable livery to identify what it contains. This is akin to encrypted packets sent through the tunnel.

6to4: This is a system allowing IPv4 packets to be transmitted across the IPv6 network it assigns address information of the IPv6 network to any IPv4 host. Next, the IPv6 packet is encapsulated into an IPv4 so that the packet can be transmitted over the IPv4 network.

4to6: This is a system allowing IPv6 packets to be transmitted across the IPv4 network by attaching IPv4 header information to the top of the packet.

Teredo tunneling – This is a system whereby IPv6 packets are encapsulated within IPv4 packets. The problem with 6to4 is that there is a need for public IPv4 addresses to be used. As there is a shortage of IPv4 addresses available the other option is to use Teredo-enabled routers. The Teredo-injected packet is a 6to4 packet sent as a User Datagram Protocol (UDP) packet which is able to be sent by standard IPv4 routers.

Teredo was designed to be a transitional system until IPv6 has matured. There are plans to deprecate Teredo in 2014.

The Teredo prefix is 2001:0::/32

Miredo is the open-source Teredo IPv6 tunneling software, for Linux.

IPv4 is a 32-bit addressing system using 4 bytes (8-bits) to determine the number system used. IPv4 is split into two key items of information – the Network address and the Host address. The four sections are referred to as w, x, y and z. These are denary numbers within each section (an Octet).

The IP addresses fall into two categories – the majority of addresses available are in fact purchased from the Internet Assigned Numbers Authority (IANA). These are referred to as 'public' addresses and make up the majority of addresses available. There are however reserved sections of the address space for each class where 'private' addresses can be used for internal purposes. These private addresses are not transmitted across the internet but are used within the local site.

An IPv4 address is therefore a 32-bit binary stream which can provide two key pieces of information:

- The Network subnet ID
- The Host ID on that subnet.

This is done by the use of an additional piece of information: The Subnet Mask. A Subnet Mask is another 32-bit binary stream which is used to separate the IP address into the two pieces of information. After splitting, the remaining information 'gaps' are padded with zeroes. Therefore:

192.168.0.1 can be written as: 1100000 . 10101000 . 00000000 . 00000001

This is used in conjunction a subnet mask of
255.255.255.0 this can be written as: 11111111 . 11111111 . 11111111 . 00000000

The process of combining this information uses a logic AND gate where each column provides the A and B input.

An AND gate is a logic gate (an electrical switch) which uses the following rule:

"The output is only live (1) when both inputs are also live (1)".

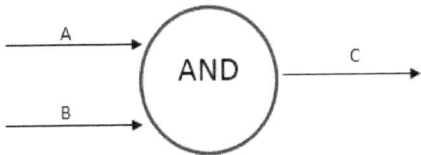

INPUT	INPUT	OUTPUT
A	B	C
0	0	0
0	1	0
1	0	0
1	1	1

In our example we will and each bit column:

A	192							168							0							1							
B	1	1	0	0	0	0	0	0	1	0	1	0	1	0	0	0	0	0	0	0	0	0	0	0	0	0	0	0	0	1
C		255							255							255							0							
D	1	1	1	1	1	1	1	1	1	1	1	1	1	1	1	1	1	1	1	1	1	1	0	0	0	0	0	0	0	0
E	1	1	0	0	0	0	0	0	1	0	1	0	1	0	0	0	0	0	0	0	0	0	0	0	0	0	0	0	0	0
F	0	0	0	0	0	0	0	0	0	0	0	0	0	0	0	0	0	0	0	0	0	0	0	0	0	0	0	0	0	1

Legend:

A = IP address (dotted decimal)

B = IP address (binary)

C = Subnet mask (dotted decimal)

D = Subnet mask (binary)

E = Network ID. This is the AND result.

F = Host ID. This the IP address with the NID subtracted.

To assist with identifying the classes of an address base on its IP, use the following power table:

2^7	2^6	2^5	2^4	2^3	2^2	2^1	2^0
128	64	32	16	8	4	2	1

Simply add the binary into the columns below one bit at a time and add the numeric values where the column is flagged as 1 together. Thus, 10101000 would be: 128 + 32 + 8 = 168.

To convert from denary to binary, start with the high most number and subtract it from your denary number. If the subtracting number is higher than the number you are trying to convert, then the binary is '0' and you start on the next column across to the right until you are able to find a subtracting number which is lower than the starting number. Subtract the number from your starting number and any remainder is carried over to be worked on by the next column until zero is reached. This way you are distributing the number across all columns.

For example, 30 would be distributed as : no 128, no 64, no 32, one 16, one 8, one 4, one 2, no 0.

So 3 is 00011110

Also, where there is a row of 1's there is no need to add all of these together to determine your denary equivalent. Simply imagine what the next leftmost column would look like (e.g. in the above column 9 would be 256) and deduct 1.

So: 11111111 would be 256-1 = 255

Classful addresses are an addressing scheme where the initial octets of the IP address determine the class of the IP address. By 'class' we are referring to how many networks we can create and subsequently how many hosts can be supported in each network. IANA records each of these, although there are a series of 'private' IP addresses which remain unsold, for internal network use. These are to be issued within your organisation by DHCP server, or for manual IP configurations.

The table below lists the table and approximate information to recall private IPs for the first 3 classes:

A	10.0.0.0 - 10.255.255.255
B	172.16.0.0 - 172.31.255.255
C	192.168.0.0 - 192.168.255.255

Although there are private address regions for all classes defined by IANA, only the above are commonly used.

Class D addresses are specifically used for **multicasting**, e.g. video conferencing. Class E and F are used by research, government and military establishments and their use is out of the scope of this course.

Addresses ending with .0 infer no host on this subnet and therefore are simply describing the subnet.

.255 are **Broadcast** addresses – a 'shout-out' to all nodes within the same network. The DHCP process is an example of where Broadcasts are used. Also, internal routers would need to be able to route broadcasts (referred to as BOOTP requests) for the process of imaging and deployment as the initial stage of imaging a 'blank' PC is to boot across the network from the PXE-enabled Network card (NIC).

Automatic Private IP Address translation (commonly referred to as **APIPA**), also referred to as 'Zero Configuration Networking' was designed originally to circumvent the need for manual IP configuration on a corporate subnet ('link-local'). The Operating System (in this case Windows 2000 and above) will auto-assign an address in the range 169.254.x.x where x is a randomly generated number between 0 and 255 (not inclusive as these are reserved) in the hope that other local clients on the same subnet will do the same, allowing the PCs to connect.

APIPA link-local addresses are non-routable and as most corporate network rely heavily on the DHCP service, it now infers a wider problem with the DHCP server, or that the router connecting the subnet to its DHCP server is now not broadcasting DHCP heartbeats. Assuming that network connection is good to the DHCP server, also that the DHCP server is authorised and active, the process of 'IPCONFIG / RENEW' will release the APIPA address and the service re-established. This is usually an automatic process – there is no need to manually force a renewal, also the DHCP server will have broadcasted to the subnet typically within 10 minutes, so if several PCs are affected patience is all that will be required.

Classless Internet Domain Routing (CIDR) is a technique used to explicitly define and describe a more tightly managed subnet and by so doing you can reduce the number of IP addresses defined within the subnet. A CIDR address is usually written with a suffix which denotes the number of bits used to describe the network portion of the IP address. On a standard classful system we use blocks of 8 bits to define the standard classes, A, B and C thus:

- *10.0.0.1 / 8 defines 255.0.0.0 as the subnet mask*
- *172.16.10.1 /16 defines 255.255.0.0 as the subnet mask*
- *192.168.1.10 /24 defines 255.255.255.0 as the subnet mask*

With a CIDR notation, the number of bits used does not fall into this common pattern. We have 'borrowed' a bit to be able to double the effective number of PCs within the subnet, but by doing so we have halved the amount of subnet networks available.

It is also important to note that on a CIDR system the starting IP address numbers used give us our starting position. Usually therefore a '192' address started out life as a class C, so if the suffix is /22 this infers that 2 bits have been borrowed. However, there is no real correlation between the numbers used and the suffix.

When we are describing a subnet mask by its bit length we use the term **'Variable Length Subnet Mask' (VLSM)**. Each section can be 'carved up' into areas of differing lengths until the space available is used up.

In the example 192.168.1.10 /22 we are 'borrowing' 2 bits from the network portion and will quadruple the number of available PCs within our network.

The formula to calculate the number of hosts is: $2^{(32-n)} - 2$

Here, 'n' is the number of bits as defined by the suffix. In the above case, n = 10.

Therefore $2^{(10)} - 2 = 1022$ hosts within each subnet.

In this example the number of subnets which can be created with a /22 CIDR mask is 4194304 subnets. This is using the equation 2^n

The first block IP range would be: 192.168.0.1 - 192.168.3.254

As discussed earlier IANA defined a series of reserved IP addresses which could not be purchased. These are referred to as **Private** addresses and are reserved for internal corporate use. **Public** addresses however define the addresses which can be purchased by IANA and are used to identify a router on the internet. Some of these addresses are defined dynamically so that a group or area within the telecommunications provider can service several thousands of customers within one area through only a small handful of IPs, originally the **Public** address was purchased by a company to provide access from the edge router to the internet.

Network Address Translation is the service provided by a Router whereby any traffic intended for the internet can be sent onto the internet without the need of a public IP address for every host. This would otherwise have been a very costly procedure where each PC would have to have needed its own dedicated public IP address. The router augments the IP header data by remembering which internal PC was sending the packet. The packet IP is changed to instead place the router's public IP address as the sender, rather than the internal IP packet of the PC. When the traffic is sent on across the network, the returning packet will be sent to the router. The router remembers the originator and the oncoming packet is augmented so that the packet can be sent to the recipient to the internal network.

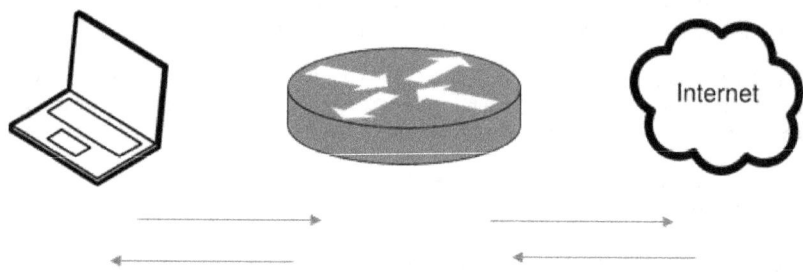

So:

1. Original packet is sent internally from the PC to the router
2. The router augments the packet and records the internal originator's IP address
3. The returning packet is sent from the internet provider
4. The packet is augmented by the router and sent internally.

Where NAT is the service, **Port Address Translation** refers commonly to the process of allowing external internet access to the internal PCs. The router makes a note of the port number to which the internal host is connected. This port number is recorded in the routing table to enable multiple internal hosts to connect.

Be careful not to confuse PAT with firewall ports. Although firewall ports designate the type of data accessing the network and a 'socket' defines the IP and data type, PAT does not pertain to firewall ports.

The **MAC address**, also referred to as the Physical address is an ID system recorded on the very NIC chip itself. This is a hexadecimal number (e.g. 00-16-D4-E2-5F-7E) where the first part is specifically describing the NIC provider and NIC model. The final sequence of numbers are a unique identifier for the network card and has to be unique on the network.

We tend to think of MAC addresses are quite random, but unique and set at the factory, however it is possible to alter the MAC of a NIC quite simply (in fact, it can be done in Device Manager). MAC spoofing is the process of changing the existing MAC address for a known one already pre-programmed and used on the network. Sometimes this is a process a hacker will do to obtain access to the network, but more commonly a Network Administrator may decide to replace a failing NIC and will find it easier to change the MAC address used by the new NIC to that of the old one rather than have to adjust MAC filtering already in place on the network.

The local PC stores a table referred to as the Address Resolution Protocol (ARP) cache. This is a table of known MAC addresses and the IP address associated to each.

To recap, a **Multicast** is a stream of data sent to a group of individual IPs on the network. This is usually performed when videoconferencing, or sharing a group session such as a collaborative Lync meeting, with application sharing.

A **Unicast** refers to a single IP transmission to a specific PC. The IP address is single – there is only one recipient. This is the most common form of network transmission.

An **Anycast** transmission refers to an IPv6 multicast used in video conferencing where anyone who can hear the data stream can join it.

A **Broadcast** refers to a transmission to all nodes on the subnet. Broadcasts are non-routable. In IPv6 broadcasts no longer exist.

A **broadcast domain** is the extent to which a broadcast can be sent. Limits are usually the edge of the subnet as defined by a router. At its lowest denominator, data traffic is defined by the MAC addresses used, but all traffic within the subnet is considered to be within the domain. For example, a Virtual LAN (vLAN) can be used to separate the connected physical hosts into several different groups, or networks. The MAC address is used by the switch to determine which group the data frame is part of (which group the data is intended for).

IP addresses are also useful for the network administrator as we can define a range of IP addresses which describe our subnet. The Router defines the extent of the subnet and connects our subnet to another.

A broadcast domain is considered to be a logical grouping structure.

A **collision domain** is the physical cabling of the subnet. Packets may interact with each other causing a conflict (a 'collision') at which point the nodes will have to re-transmit their packets across the shared network cable. Collisions are common where multiple hosts share a common cable (e.g. a bus network).

A collision domain is defined by the physical cabling used to create the network. Here, we are considering where a 'collision' might occur within the hardware. It is a physical grouping structure.

1.9

1.9 Explain the basics of routing concepts and protocols
- Loopback interface
- Routing loops
- Routing tables
- Static vs dynamic routes
- Default route
- Distance vector routing protocols
    - RIP v2
- Hybrid routing protocols
    - BGP
- Link state routing protocols
    - OSPF
    - IS-IS
- Interior vs exterior gateway routing protocols
- Autonomous system numbers
- Route redistribution
- High availability
    - VRRP
    - Virtual IP
    - HSRP
- Route aggregation
- Routing metrics
    - Hop counts
    - MTU, bandwidth
    - Costs
    - Latency
    - Administrative distance
    - SPB

The loopback interface is a means of testing the connectivity of a NIC port. Within TCP/IP, Loopback also refers to a pre-set reserved IP address used for testing purposes.

The Loopback plug is an RJ45 plug which has two wires to complete the circuit at pins 1 to 3 and 2 to 6. By connecting the plug to the NIC the status light should register the presence of a cable.

The Loopback instruction in the TCP/IP protocol suite explains the sending of a test packet to the NIC circuitry itself. This tests the ability of the Operating system to communicate with the NIC. For IPv4, the test range 127.0.0.x defines the network card to be tested, so if the first registered NIC in the PC is 1, then 127.0.0.1 is used.

For IPv6, loopback is ::1 (the shorthand for 127 zeroes followed by a 1, meaning no network, first NIC card).

For routers, the Loopback Interface is a common record in the table. It is an IP address used to test that the router is on. It does not define the router or any one node on the network, but is used for testing purposes. The OSPF (Open Shortest Path First) routing protocol uses a loopback interface as part of its initial setup.

A Routing loop is a problem which occurs on larger networks containing many connected routers where the data packet is being sent in a loop (A to B, B to C, C back to A). For this to happen there will need to be physical connections from A to B, B to C and C to A, but more importantly the route is established by taking the quickest path, or one based on a metric. The problem may well be because there are many different ways to get to router D, but the routers are deciding that the quickest way to send the packet is to send it on (e.g. router A is connected to router D directly, but it's a slow link, so its sent through another router).

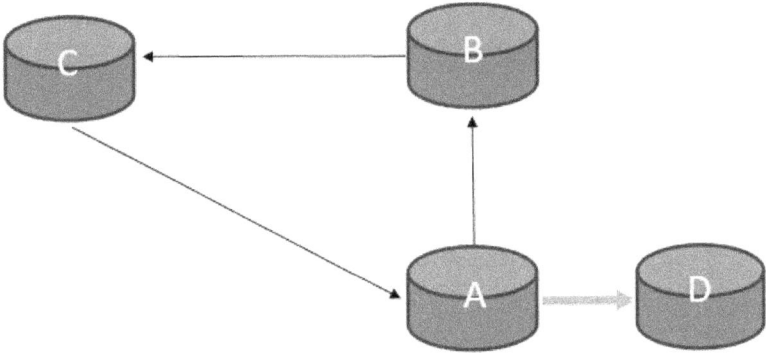

Router protocols either work by determining the shortest distance based on a metric (hop count, for example, or quickest 'hop' (shortest path). Switches however can combat this problem with the Spanning Tree Protocol which is able to determine when loops occur and close down the last link (e.g. if the above diagram were switches, A would know to temporarily close down incoming traffic from C).

A router contains a rudimentary computer capable of storing information about the port and IP address associates on that port (the **Routing Table**). The speed at which data can be sent to the device on that port can be set as can also a preference if data flow is up or down. A metric can also be assigned used to determine the better route to an endpoint.

Routing protocols are able to update the table on a regular basis. In fact, some such as the older distance vector protocol RIP is quite chatty, making it unpopular for use in larger networks (the new or changed information in the routing table is broadcast to its neighbours every 30 seconds.)

For the Network+ exam please be aware that you will be presented a series of questions in which you will have to read firewall logs and routing tables to determine which device is misconfigured, or failing on the network.

You would expect to find a number of entries on a routing table which do not conform to normal unicast logic. The first is the entry 0.0.0.0 on a network with a gateway x.x.x.x which implies that the router is part of the x.x.x network (e.g. a gateway of 192.168.1.254 imples that this router serves the 192.168.1.x network). The router will use an interface address – this is its internal IP address as it is known by other PCs within the subnet. The router will have two entries to list its own internal and external IP addresses within the table. Finally, the table will contain other known PCs which have been manually configured and added to the table (e.g. specialist servers) but also other neighbouring routers.

Address	Mask	Gateway	interface	metric
0.0.0.0	0.0.0.0	185.75.129.1	185.75.142.16	20
127.0.0.0	255.0.0.0	127.0.0.1	127.0.0.1	1
185.75.128.0	255.255.224.0	185.75.142.16	185.75.142.16	20

Table 1: An extract from a routing table

Static routes are manually defined by the network administrator by logging onto the router and programming a route. They are normally connecting to 'always on' links, or devices which are key to the integrity of the network. Static route metrics are not changed but settings remain permanent.

A **Dynamic route** is a route to another device which may re-configure based on other known variables. For example, if there are two cables connecting device A to a router via another router and changes were made to the interim router to adjust the speed on cable 1 (or the cable is replaced by a faster cable, e.g. cat 5 to cat 6) then this change is reflected as a change to the metric, giving preference to this newer route. Other neighbouring routers (such as the edge router in this example) will be updated to know that there is now a faster route and their respective (copied) settings from the internal router will update automatically.

Dynamic routing is extremely useful to retain a steady state on the system without the need for reprogramming lots of routers. As information is shared between routers, if a cable is removed, we would want the network to automatically adjust to the change. Static programming would require further work as neighbouring routers would also need to be updated as well. With dynamics routing the newer changes are rolled out across the network quickly and then the network returns to a steady state (this is referred to as 'contention'.)

Default route – quite simply, where two different paths exist on a router to reach the same endpoint, it is possible to indicate a preference. This route is referred to as the default route.

Distance vector protocols:

As discussed earlier in this section, there are two categories of routing protocol – link state and distance vector. Distance Vector determines the shortest distance and direction (path) the data would take to determine the shortest route, whereas link state is able to determine if the link is down first before making its decision, also deciding which of the active links is the fastest.

The most common DV protocol in use today is RIP v2. More advanced than its predecessor uses multicast addressing to advertise itself to its neighbouring routers. This is a more efficient use of bandwidth. RIP uses a 'hop count' (the number of nodes traversed through to reach the endpoint). RIP v2 can be configured as either classful or classless (meaning that it can be set to, or to not broadcast the subnet mask).

As some of the speeds vary on a wire, RIP v2 would need to regularly and dynamically change. If the hop count was large (16 is considered 'infinite' or 'unreachable'), if you have a variety of routers within your network it is possible that a hop count may not be the best determinant.

Two key Link-State protocols in use are OSPF and IS-IS. Open the Shortest Path First is the most widely used protocol. It is based on the Shortest Path algorithm developed by Dijkstra. OSPF is scalable and works well on enterprise networks, so is the protocol of choice.

Intermediate System to Intermediate System (IS-IS) was developed by the Digital Equipment Corporation (DEC) as a solution for large service providers such as communications companies to forward traffic. It also uses the Dijkstra algorithm separating the traffic into various levels to shape data flow. The IS-IS protocol is associated with IPv6 as a modern solution.

Hybrid protocols are ones which combine the qualities of Link State and Distance Vector together. **Enhanced Interior Gateway Routing Protocol (EIGRP)** is a Cisco-specific protocol which does combine the two protocol types and is widely used amongst Cisco routers on an enterprise network. The EIGRP metric is more advanced than RIP – it uses both the delay and the bandwidth of the connection to determine the fastest and most effective path.

Border Gateway Protocol (BGP) is also a hybrid protocol used by telecommunications companies to move bulk data from one domain to another. For example, Virgin Media may move traffic onto the BT network and vice versa irrespective of the physical location of the routers passing the data.

This therefore has identified the different **Interior and exterior gateway protocols**. In the above list, BGP only is used for exterior connections whereas the other protocols are interior (within one domain).

Autonomous system numbers – to this point we have described how data is transferred within the domain. The internet however connects multiple domains together and each domain is configured and managed separately to each other (e.g. www.comptia.org network and www.microsoft.com) for a higher level view each of these domains is assigned a number, referred to as the Autonomous System Number. This is used by the Border Gateway Protocol to route traffic across the Internet from domain to domain. Each domain is therefore a node on the wider Internetwork. By passing data in the node order 1,2,5,6 we can establish a path through the internet to the end domain.

Route redistribution – usually we agree on one common standard for all routers within the domain. However, there may be times where we want traffic to travel onto a route managed by a router configured to use a different protocol. By default routing information is only shared if the routing protocol is the same on the sending and receiving routers. With Route redistribution enabled however we can share data with other routers using other protocols.

High availability is the concept that a route is always available. This is usually achieved by adding redundancy to the network to ensure that data is always accessible. This is one of the key characteristics of the 'cloud' in that the user buys into legal protection in the form of a contract ensuring 'uptime' because data may be stored on many storage devices at different locations and the recipient will connect to any one available to them. This way, if a router on the internetwork were to fail, other routes are available and the traffic will still reach its destination. Other storage facilities are also available, so if the main file server is unavailable other SAN / NAS devices can serve as secondary supports. The data is synchronised across the network to ensure that all servicing devices share the same data. Uptime is defined as the 'up time' divided by the total time (this is represented as a percentage) and is considered good the closer it can be to 100%. No system is however completely fault tolerant and always available so 100% is a difficult goal to reach.

VRRP – In order to attempt to achieve High Availability, **Virtual Router Redundancy** is a protocol used to assign virtual routers to hosts as they are needed, bringing on more to ensure that there is no single point of failure. These serving routers act as a cluster, providing a backup route to the master (physical) router. VRRP provides the health of the router to the cluster so that others can support in the case of an offline router ('failover').

Virtual IP addressing – it is possible, in fact often desirable to provide more than one IP address to a physical NIC, thereby allowing access from different services to the same physical device. Conversely one host PC (e.g. a server) can host a variety of Hypervised Virtual PCs each of which is carrying out a different service on the network. Each virtual host will have its own virtual Network card with its own virtual IP address. In reality however the virtual IPs can all link to the main physical NIC and share the physical IP address. On Hypervisor software such as Oracle Virtualbox it is possible to set a private network so that the virtual PCs can talk to each other without affecting the physical machine, or connecting to the physical network. This is often used for 'sandbox' environments where a test network should not interact with the physical network, yet the physical PC still needs to connect to the physical network.

Virtual IP addressing can cause problems when a virtual server running DHCP is active on a local subnet – some renewing physical PCs will see the virtual server and connect to it through a DORA lease rather than connecting to the physical DHCP server. This problem can also be encountered through PXE-booting during a deployment as the blank PC needs to boot across the network and obtain an IP address from a DHCP server within the subnet. If it connects to the virtual server rather than the deployment server running DHCP the deployment will fail.

HSRP – the **Hot Standby Router Protocol** is a Cisco product which will establish a fault-tolerant default gateway. If the primary router acting as the subnet default gateway were to fail PCs will be able to use a replacement router to access data in the wider network. HSRP is however not a routing protocol in that it does not broadcast its known information, rather checks the health and status of the primary router acting as the gateway and can take over for any interfaces on the primary router which may have gone offline (e.g. through a poorly connected cable).

Route aggregation is the process simplifying the routing information stored on the various routers within the domain. Multiple routes are consolidated into one single route advertisement sent out, rather than broadcasting each separately. Route aggregation is also referred to as 'route summarisation'. In order to aggregate we use a CIDR network strategy and to create a 'route topology'.

Routing metrics – in order to determine the performance of a route we can use a variety of metrics supplied by the differing protocols:

Hop count – this is a measure of the number of intrermediate devices used within the path to reach the final destination. It does not include the starting or ending devices, only the ones in-between. A high hop count (e.g. 16) is considered to be 'infinity' therefore the packet at this stage is often discarded. The hop count is also associated with the 'time to live' as it is possible on some systems to set the maximum hop as the TTL metric.

The **Maximum Transmission Unit (MTU)** is the largest allowable size of an IP packet sent across the network. The larger the packet, the fewer the number of packets a file needs to be broken into, therefore this can reduce the time taken to send the file. For Ethernet this is typically 1500 bytes.

Bandwidth – this is the amount of data which can be transmitted across a medium. EIGRP uses this along with the delay to produce a metric to determine the effectiveness of a line. By increasing the bandwidth (e.g. clustering / trunking connections to another router) it is possible to shorten the time taken to send the data between two key nodes.

Cost – when using a numerical metric to determine one link in comparison to another we discuss its 'cost', namely a numeric system used to rank routes. We can make the 'cost' calculation quite complex involving services needed and dedicated lines but in its most simplest form it is the time taken to transfer the data on the bandwidth available along the selected line.

Latency – this refers to the delay before data is fully received and is usable. An example here would be satellite as the signal is sent from the transmitting station, bounced off a satellite and is sent on to a receiving station thousands of miles away. Even though the data is sent at incredibly fast speeds, the time taken to get the data to the endpoint and also to receive a reply is considerable (often quite a few seconds).

Administrative distance – this is an arbitrary value assigned by the routing protocol to weight one connection over another where two or more pathways exist to the same endpoint:

Meaning / protocol	Administrative Distance
Directly connected	0
Static route	1
Static route, next hop	1
EIGRP summary route	5
External BGP	20
Internal EIGRP	90
IGRP	100
OSPF	110
IS-IS	115
RIP	120
EGP	140
DHCP learned	254
Route unknown	255

Shortest Path Bridging (SPB) is a routing system used to provide multipath routing and is designed to replace Spanning Tree Protocol as the new and easier system for creating a variety of multipath routes. SPB is based on IS-IS but is backwards compatible with Spanning Tree. Each path to the endpoint is evaluated and its metric is used to favour the commonest path.

1.10

1.10 Identify the basics elements of unified communication technologies
- VoIP
- Video
- Real time services
    - Presence
    - Multicast vs unicast
- QoS
    - DSCP
    - COS
- Devices
    - UC servers
    - UC devices
    - UC gateways

Unified communications is the combining of a number of communications services to operate over the same system. Until recently the telecoms network within an office was completely separate to that used for data traffic. Now we can see that a device such as a PC is capable of seamlessly integrating presentations, calls, conferencing, speech recognition, email and a variety of other communications types with common networking activities using the same hardware irrespective of the type of hardware. I can therefore make an internal call from my Skype account on my work laptop to a colleague who will take the call on their Cisco VoIP phone. The hardware is designed to seamlessly integrate as VoIP UC technologies share common protocols and can manage the data in a 'platform independent' yet 'platform integrated' fashion.

Voice over IP (VoIP) is a system which allows the company to transmit voice and audio telephony data across the standard IP network. VoIP systems manage the ability to create and to close a call, using common audio codecs and standards across the network to ensure that the call can be made effectively. VoIP allows users to have a telephone number and often VoIP systems have the ability to transfer calls onto the wider POTS or PSTN network, allowing the user to send and receive calls to existing clients outside of the company domain. As these numbers are stored within existing contact management software such as Exchange and Outlook, a hyperlink will now simply start the call session and Lync, Skype or equivalent software will manage the call itself.

Video – as with VoIP, video conferencing was offered as a separate service. It used to be high-cost and relied on a dedicated ISDN line to provide connectivity between conference parties. Now with UC it is possible to stream video data creating a session using the existing hardware. As video is bandwidth intensive even after heavy compression by video codecs, Quality of Service (QoS) packet scheduling is used to bandwidth shape and prefer video traffic across the bandwidth when sent alongside other traffic.

Realtime services are used to transmit realtime information across the network. For example Dynamics AX would store transaction data and need to dynamically update this with other systems across the network. Realtime services manage the flow of data ensuring that all devices using and accessing data are able to access the same data at the same time. This is currently a problem for users wishing to access databases online and is why servers hosting databases (e.g. Oracle, or SQL Server) require a high specification of hardware to allow users to access data without reducing performance, or delay for other users.

Within UC, the most common realtime service would be Instant Messaging, or an online 'virtual classroom' where several users are sharing the same session and seeing the exact same information at the same time, also each can collaborate with the session.

One of the factors we consider when discussing realtime services is **presence** – if a user is active and online the software will stream all video, audio and other information to the machine. However there is a limit on the number of users who can be connected to the session at any one time. By not streaming the session but instead recording it offline users can access the material at a later date.

Another significant factor is how the data is streamed – video and UC sessions use class D **multicast** addressing, meaning that the exact same data is streamed to a group of IP addresses at the same time. This is considerably more efficient than copying the same data packet to multiple users and attempting to send x copies of the same packet at the same time (unicast).

Quality of Service is used to bias video traffic over normal data, ensuring that bandwidth is used effectively. As well as this QoS is responsible for traffic shaping – if bandwidth reduces (for example a reduction in signal strength due to inclement weather) then QoS is able to reduce the quality of the video streamed, selecting a lower quality setting where a lower kb/s bandwidth is requested. When the bandwidth returns to a higher figure, QoS will re-shape the stream allowing a higher quality setting. This is adapted in realtime.

Differentiated Services Code Point (DSCP or DiffServ) is a metric used on Cisco systems used to determine the priority of traffic being sent. It uses a 6-bit field in the IP packet header to classify the type of data being sent and its importance. This operates at OSI layer 3.

Class of service (COS) is also a means of determining the type of data being sent. Here, the payload within the packet is used to determine and to differentiate the traffic being sent. This is a 3-bit field attached to the Ethernet frame header, operating at OSI layer 2.

A **UC Server** (Microsoft Lync Server) provides the infrastructure for enterprise instant messaging, VoIP and video streaming. Users can connect through either ad hoc or structured connections. The UC server will also support wider PSTN connectivity through wither a provider gateway or Secure IP trunk. The role of the UC server is to act as manager and provider to enable clients to connect using UC software (e.g. Lync client) seamlessly.

A **UC device** is any intranet enabled device capable of communicating with a UC server. This may be a wireless VoIP phone or Bluetooth handset connected to a nearby PC, running Lync, Skype or alternative software to connect with the managing UC server.

A **UC gateway** is a PSTN or PBX gateway extension allowing external users to access the UC server, also allowing internal users to dial through to the outside network. This also allows users to connect with non-VoIP users such as phone numbers supplied by terrestrial telecommunications providers. The gateway is usually a dedicated line connecting to the UC server with sufficient bandwidth to take a large number of connecting calls.

1.11

1.11 Compare and contrast technologies that support cloud and virtualization
- Virtualization
  - Virtual switches
  - Virtual routers
  - Virtual firewall
  - Virtual vs physical NICs
  - Software defined networking
- Storage area network
  - iSCSI
  - Jumbo frame
  - Fiber channel
  - Network attached storage
- Cloud concepts
  - Public IaaS, SaaS, PaaS
  - Private IaaS, SaaS, PaaS
  - Hybrid IaaS, SaaS, PaaS
  - Community IaaS, SaaS, PaaS

Virtualisation is the process of simulating a further service which is independent of the host system. This would typically be another host PC, or server providing a service which is not able to be offered on the host system. By using Hypervisor technology it is possible to manage the flow of data to and access of hardware components, sharing resources between a variety of hypervised 'virtual' machines and the host machine. Thus it is possible to run several PCs at the same time on the same physical box.

Virtual machines now exist in two forms:

Type 1 VM is considered an older type. It relied on the host operating system to be active and to manage access to resources for the virtual machine to use.

Type 2 VMs however are quite spectacular. These newer VMs do not rely on the host operating system to be present at all, in fact these Virtual Hard Disks can boot from' cold' if placed into the Boot Manager.

There are a number of services which should not be virtualised:

Domain Controller – if this is not available nobody within your network will be able to log-on. The computers will also be unable to communicate with and authenticate against the Active Directory database.

Network Time server – time on a virtual PC is not strictly linear – the machine may work faster at certain points and as a result clock time will vary. If the NTS is synchronised and only some of the neighbouring PCs readjust their clocks then there will be a time discrepancy on the network. If this discrepancy is over 5 minutes Active Directory will refuse to authenticate those machines until they are re-synchronised with the remainder (and with particularly the Domain Controller)

As the name implies, a virtual switch provides connectivity with all of the created virtual Network Interface Cards and the physical PC. By creating a virtual switch it is possible to control which virtual PCs can communicate with each other, which are stand-alone and also if it is possible to link data through to the physical NIC and therefore to the host PC, or to the rest of the network.

A virtual router allows for a second routing table to exist on the physical router. This allows network paths to be segmented, connecting to different subnets (e.g. to virtual PCs by their separate IP addresses) without the need for further wiring. When referring to mobile devices, especially smartphones the term Virtual Router also refers to software enabling a wireless device to act as a wi-fi hotspot. (Not that dissimilar.)

A virtual firewall is a firewall running on a completely virtualised environment which can be used to monitor the physical network, also for monitoring purposes. Within a sandbox environment Windows Firewall with Advanced Security has to be set up with inbound and outbound rules, also connection rules when creating secure tunnels (e.g IPSec or Teredo). In order to test that the configuration is correct before creating the tunnel in a real live environment and end up potentially causing a service loss, it would be sensible to trial the creation process within a 'sandbox'.

The physical NIC is the actual network card located on the host PC.

The physical NIC can be shared with the virtualised PCs through the virtual switch. The virtualised PCs each have their own NIC, emulating the role of an actual NIC. The virtualised NICs can exist on the same subnet as physical devices allowing virtualised PC. The only limitation is through sharing the bandwidth used by the actual NIC the data transfers for each device are queued through the physical NIC which will also have its own data to send.

Software defined networking is the concept of focussing on the use of the Operating System to focus and manage network connectivity. Hardware and lower level elements of the network and automatically configured through the use of NIC drivers (or virtualised NICs managed by the Operating System through the Hypervisor), DHCP and DNS. Users can now focus on services offered rather than the technical actions needed to configure and operate the device. Storage Area Network is a device attached to the network which offers data storage and data transfer capabilities at the block level. Each data block can be transferred across the network one block at a time. iSCSI is the transfer protocol used to manage the flow of data blocks across the network.

Internet Small Computer System Interface (ISCSI) is used for NIC teaming, clustering and Storage Area Networks, where a fibre optic cable is used to connect the Storage device directly to the network, using iSCSI (a data transfer protocol) to transfer the data. The user only sees the logical device and does not need to concern themselves with the physical device. ISCSI is capable of transferring data blocks across the internal network, a wider area network, or even across the Internet. ISCSI does not use specialist cabling (as is the case with Fibre Channel) – it can integrate seamlessly with existing fibre. Existing SCSI commands are sent across the existing IP network.

Jumbo Frame – as discussed earlier, the Maximum Transmission Unit (MTU) of an Ethernet frame is 1500 bytes. Anything larger than this is referred to as a Jumbo Frame. The Jumbo Frame MTU is usually 9000 bytes. The Jumbo Frame offers far greater performance for file and data transfer, reducing CPU overhead as a file can be sent in fewer packets than a conventional Ethernet frame. Internet Service Providers currently do not support Jumbo Frames, so these are only used for internal transfer.

Fibre Channel was mentioned earlier as a dedicated fibre solution. It is used on large enterprise computers and to connect to Storage Area Networks. Fibre Channel uses its own protocol independent to the Internet Protocol and as such is incompatible with the conventional network. FC is used to connect storage devices (SANs) together and to integrate a SAN to the rest of the network.

Fibre Channel does not use the OSI model. It has its own 5-layer model as detailed below:

FC4 – The Protocol-mapping layer, in which application protocols, such as SCSI or IP, are encapsulated into a Protocol Data Unit http://en.wikipedia.org/wiki/Protocol_data_unit for delivery to the FC network.

FC3 – Common services layer is designed to add encryption or RAID implementation.

FC2 – Network layer is responsible for data transfer on the network and the transfer from port to port.

FC1 – Data link layer is responsible for the signal coding.

FC0 – defines the cabling and connectors used.

There are three fibre channel topologies available:

Point-to-Point (FC-P2P) – here, two FC devices are directly connected to each other. This provides a volume extension, striping or disk mirroring.

Arbitrated loop (FC-AL). Here, the devices form a ring, as will FDDI or Token Ring. Although AL can create a loop with only two devices, AL differs to P2P in that the protocol decides the best route for the data to take, also to manage contention on the loop. One pair of devices (referred to as ports) can communicate at the same time on the loop.

Switched fabric (FC-SW) is the third topology type used. Here, the devices (or the loop) is attached to a fibre channel switch which allows traffic to transfer through the switch. The operation (or failure) of one port will not affect other ports on the switch. SW is used to manage data transfer out to each loop, or connected port.

Network Attached Storage refers to external hard drives, or a dedicated appliance used as a file storage system. They are a convenient way of storing files accessible from a number of networked computers. NAS devices exist as either a USB / e-SATA connection to an existing PC, or a fibre / Ethernet connection to the existing network. In the latter solution control and management of the data comes in the form of a rudimentary system built into the appliance, although it is usual to see NAS devices as a solution managed by a file server.

Cloud concepts – the concept of a 'computer-free' solution has been proposed for a number of years but is now gaining popularity as all of the IT service providers now offer off-site storage, processing and security solutions. What started in the 1990s with externally managed email systems such as AOL, Yahoo or Hotmail, off-site services were extended with file storage available for the user's account, which as with email is accessible from anywhere and from any computer so long as authentication can be met. The services offered have now been extended so that software developers can store, compile their solutions from anywhere, negating the need to have programme editing software on their local host PC. In this way they can work on their projects from any PC. Microsoft Azure is an example of such a solution.

Cloud also offers support with maintenance and deployment of computer images. By storing the installer files in the cloud and using a management system such as Windows Deployment Server or System Center Configuration Manager, an organisation's machines can be re-built discretely across the network and the files stored off-site using a cloud solution. With the movement of IT professionals to Azure and for the service PCs to exist in the cloud, machines can be serviced quickly and easily. Cloud solutions are offered as subscription systems. They are provided as an 'always on' solution. The subscriber pays for a package dependent on the hardware profile of the computer that will be used. Management software owned by the cloud provider will partition a series of cores, RAM and disk space within the virtualised environment to cater for the request out of an existing hardware farm. The customer pays for the service on a 'per use' basis. The customer receives an 'always on' solution and enjoys peace of mind provided by a legal contract ensuring 100% uptime (or as near as can be offered by the provider). With the setup of clusters, it is possible to have a service managed by several cloud computers, so if one in one location is not available, another configured exactly the same way will be able to continue to offer the required service.

Cloud solutions are separated into three distinct categories:

Infrastructure as a service (IaaS) – here virtualised cloud PCs and other virtual 'hardware' offer network devices offered as part of the existing infrastructure, but happen to exist off-site. These may be load balancers, virtual switches, file servers or storage devices.

Platform as a Service (PaaS) – here, virtualised cloud PCs provide specific dedicated services which otherwise would be provided by dedicated servers as part of the existing corporate network. For example Azure with Team Foundation Server, or a Git repository can be used to host software under development and to project-manage its creation across the team, including file versioning. Email servers (Exchange online) can provide corporate email from a cloud email server. Active Directory store can be used to keep a copy of the Active Directory database used for authentication and to enforce rules across the network. SQL Server online can offer existing database services as part of a cloud solution negating the need for expensive, dedicated hardware onsite. A cloud-based IIS or Apache web server can be used to host a corporate intranet, or public-facing internet web site. This may be an ideal solution for a company who does not want to host their site on-premises.

Software as a Service (SaaS) – with this solution, the cloud solution offers a dedicated application for a specific purpose. For example, a virtual desktop may be used for testing purposes. Access to the software is on an 'on-demand' basis. Applications run on the cloud-resident PC and is accessible remotely from any other computer. A common example here is for cloud-based systems to be used for intensive calculations such as Bitcoin calculations, or World Community Grid. The customer can 'remote' into the running PC to use the application on any PC irrespective of the hardware on the client PC.

Public cloud – here, subscription costs are low and often some services are offered for free. The main concern here is that there are no guarantees over the security or availability of any data stored on the cloud subscription. This solution is therefore not ideal for a business solution as data will be visible to the subscription provider and security cannot be assured. The solution may be withdrawn at any time, so business-critical data may be lost. An example of this type may be an Azure account where the customer can provision a virtual PC as a server, or as a test Windows 8.1 / Linux Ubuntu device.

A Private cloud solution is a subscription service offered to business where legal protection is offered – data is kept private and availability is contractually assured. Private cloud solutions are offered to businesses with guarantees of high availability, scalability, high utilisation (such as in the case of thousands of customers viewing a corporate-hosted website) and a lower Total Cost of Ownership than would otherwise be possible as owning and maintaining a complex server would be expensive.

A hybrid cloud is a combination of some systems which are managed in-house by the company and some parts of the solution offered off-site through cloud services. It is usual for a company to host sensitive data internally (such as financial corporate accounts and legal / HR data) whilst other aspects of the company (such as the public facing website / e-commerce solution and stock data) can be hosted and managed by the cloud provider.

A community cloud solution is common where organisations decide to share their resources, where there is commonality across the organisations. A solicitors firm, for example may subscribe to a website where they would be able to look up specific cases, or legal compliance information. If a company are planning to meet ISO requirements they could look up the appropriate information offered by a compliance database. This information would be common to many companies, so all members would be able to access the same data.

All three of the above scopes can provide IaaS, PaaS and SaaS solutions.

1.12

1.12 Given a set of requirements, implement a basic network
- List of requirements
- Device types/requirements
- Environment limitations
- Equipment limitations
- Compatibility requirements
- Wired/wireless considerations
- Security considerations

Network requirements – the most basic type of network you will encounter is two directly connected PCs. They can be connected via a serial cable (or USB). This is encountered when moving a user profile from an old PC to a new PC. In terms of a network, a peer-to-peer (workgroup) network can be created by using a crossover Ethernet cable. This creates a data loop where connectivity can be assured. For more nodes, PCs are connected using a straight-through cable to a switch, or hub.

Hubs are considered an ineffective means of connecting PC together. Hubs replicate the signal coming in on one port and sends the copy out on every other port in the hope that one of the other PCs is the intended recipient. Other PCs cannot communicate at the same time as they are receiving the data frame and so have to wait until the data frame is identified and unneeded and dropped.

A switch however is more efficient. It contains a small rudimentary system and is able to store the MAC addresses of the NIC connected to each port by the sending of a test packet. As the data frame is received, the MAC address the frame needs to be sent to is looked up against the table and the data frame is forwarded onto the correct port. This way, other ports are free to communicate at the same time.

To connect to different network groups (referred to as subnets), each NIC uses an assigned IP address, manually configured. The node also needs to know move out of the subnet onto other subnets, so the IP address of the router (the default gateway) is identified. Routers have two IP addresses – one internal to the subnet and one on the external subnet. Routers examine the IP address of the data packet and can forward to the correct port as it stores a table referencing the port to the respective NIC of the node connected to it.

To connect routers to other routers, we use a crossover cable to establish a data connection. Most modern switches and routers however are auto-sensing and can ensure that the cable, whether straight-through or crossover, can transfer data between the routers.

To manage the type of data being transferred on the network, we use a firewall. This is a dedicated piece of hardware which can disallow packets of a particular type. The firewall operates on the TCP / UDP protocol portion of the OSI model and contains a series of 'gateways' (0-65535 for both TCP and for UDP). These ports are standard on all networks. Ports can be opened, or closed programmatically, or set to allow data in, out or both ways.

In order to manage user accounts, we centralise the user information onto a domain controller. By providing a series of servers which will operate centralised services the user can connect to any PC on the network with the same account. Files are also stored in a central location, making file management and backup easier.

The Domain Controller server supports the Active Directory database of known managed computers and users. This is used to authenticate a user on the network and for rules to be applied on login.

To facilitate management of IP addresses, they can be provided (leased) by a DHCP server. This negates the need for manual IP configuration.

A DNS server is used to remember common shared folders, computers and to invisibly provide the IP address needed for connectivity. By placing a DNS server on the network the user can access a resource by its resource name (UNC path such as : \\computername\share) from any computer on the network.

As you can see with the above centralised managed network we can creating a domain (client-server model).

It is common to find that the infrastructure components are connected by CAT5e, CAT6 or multimode fibre cables (Ethernet cable is the most common). Wireless connectivity is offered by wireless access points either connected to an existing PC, or as a standalone device linked to the switch via an Ethernet cable. A series on wireless access points across the building can allow roaming users to connect if they are within range. To ensure that there is no crosstalk which may interfere with traffic, neighbouring wireless access points are set to transmit on different channels within the available frequency range. WAPs overlap slightly, and power-balanced so that the signal is not available outside of the building, but that the best coverage is offered.

To ensure compatibility of all of the nodes it is common to find that hardware across the network is similar. Also, Operating Systems tend to be of a certain type, e.g. Windows Professional for client computers as this supports domain-level authentication whereas Windows Home does not. It is also worth noting that iOS systems do not support domain-level authentication on their own and it is a complex task to add this to an iOS system. iOS systems tend to connect to NAS devices for file storage and operate as standalone, or workgroup computers. This can cause a partition in the network between the iOS and Microsoft systems. Other similar problems can occur although standardisation has led to the TCP/IP protocol suite as the standard protocol for network communication across a range of OS providers (making Appletalk, Novell Netware or NetBEUI redundant).

In order to ensure that the node is secure we can consider storing centralised services in a lockable cabinet (e.g. a 'rack' cabinet), stored in a highly secure part of the building which itself is locked. By introducing backup servers (e.g. Primary Domain Controller and Backup Domain Controller) we can 'fail over' to another device which is always available.

Data is backed up regularly, usually daily as part of an agreed backup solution (e.g. Normal and differential backups making up a backup set, stored to DAT tape). The backup tapes are stored off-site at another nearby location to ensure that in the event of a serious problem within the building (e.g. earthquake, flood or fire) that the data is not compromised and a rebuild can take place at another site.

Domain 2
Network operations

This domain will consider the practical application of a network and discuss most of the common tools and how to perform specific management and servicing operations on your network. By network from here on we are assuming an enterprise-level complex network with several sites and subnets, configured as a domain (client-server model) network.

2.1

2.1 Given a scenario, use appropriate monitoring tools
- Packet/network analyzer
- Interface monitoring tools
- Port scanner
- Top talkers/listeners
- SNMP management software
  - Trap
  - Get
  - Walk
  - MIBS
- Alerts
  - Email
  - SMS
- Packet flow monitoring
- SYSLOG
- SIEM
- Environmental monitoring tools
  - Temperature
  - Humidity
- Power monitoring tools
- Wireless survey tools
- Wireless analyzers

A **network analyser** (or 'packet sniffer' as it is commonly called) is a software application capable of copying traffic passing into the NIC of a node. The packet can then be examined and analysed in relation to the OSI model. The packet is visually displayed showing the various parts to the packet – header, preamble and encapsulated frame. These can be viewed 'bitwise' showing the data stored therein. If the packet is unencrypted it would be possible to use a 'packet sniffer' to read data sent 'in the clear'.

A network analyser is useful for tracking the expected packet types on a network, e.g. to monitor the flow of DHCP traffic – the DORA process is identified as the 4 packets are sent across the analyser. Packets are determined by their protocol, IP and also MAC address and by so doing it is useful to see if any unexpected traffic is present on the network (e.g. from a port expected to be blocked).

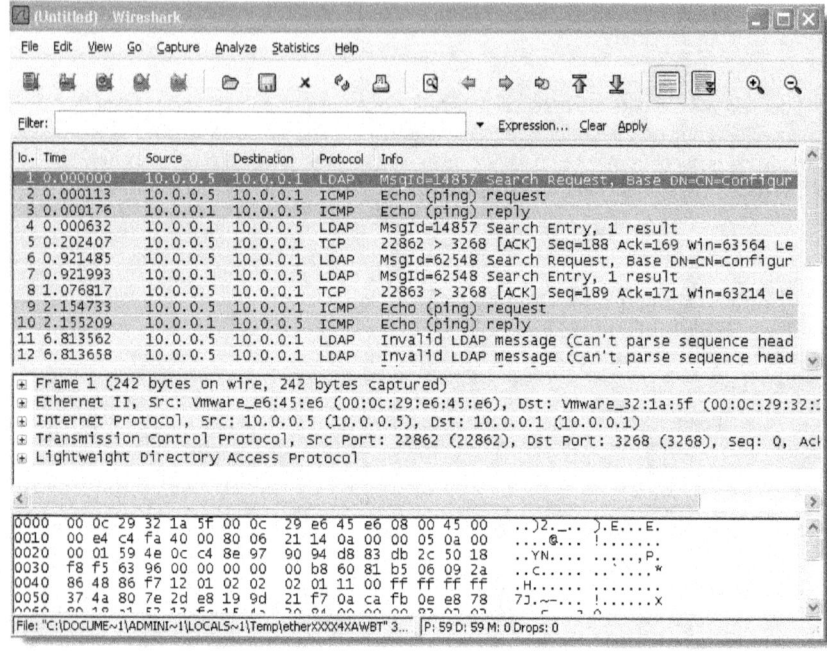

Wireshark Network analyser

Interface monitoring are a collection of tools used to check connectivity and data usage at a particular point on the network:

Bandwidth monitoring tools – these are useful to determine the amount of data bandwidth at a particular point on the network. It is useful to also check if the data has been traffic-shaped and the extent to which QoS has filtered or favoured VoIP data over file transfer traffic (for example). These tools can provide a visual representation of data usage on the network card. An example tool is Task Manager, also Performance Monitor on Windows systems which can give an overview of usage.

IPCONFIG (IFCONFIG on Linux systems) is used to check the configuration of a network card, reporting its IP settings and known configuration information such as:

- if the PC is set to serve on a domain,
- the existence of a DHCP server,
- if the IP address is leased by a DHCP server or manually configured,
- the name of the domain the computer is connected to,
- the DNS IP address of the DNs server,
- the IP address of the default gateway,
- whether the IP address system used is IPv4 or IPv6.

```
[rich@cirrus rich]$ /sbin/ifconfig
eth0      Link encap:Ethernet  HWaddr 00:40:95:2D:05:7D
          inet addr:192.168.1.2  Bcast:192.168.1.255  Mask:255.255.255.0
          UP BROADCAST RUNNING MULTICAST  MTU:1500  Metric:1
          RX packets:259 errors:13 dropped:0 overruns:0 frame:0
          TX packets:133 errors:0 dropped:0 overruns:0 carrier:0
          collisions:0 txqueuelen:100
          RX bytes:29575 (28.8 Kb)  TX bytes:12294 (12.0 Kb)
          Interrupt:11 Base address:0x6000

lo        Link encap:Local Loopback
          inet addr:127.0.0.1  Mask:255.0.0.0
          UP LOOPBACK RUNNING  MTU:16436  Metric:1
          RX packets:10 errors:0 dropped:0 overruns:0 frame:0
          TX packets:10 errors:0 dropped:0 overruns:0 carrier:0
          collisions:0 txqueuelen:0
          RX bytes:700 (700.0 b)  TX bytes:700 (700.0 b)

[rich@cirrus rich]$
```

This information is made available for all cards on the PC.

Packet Internet Groper (PING) – this ICMP tool is used to send 4 test packets to a neighbouring computer on the network to determine that the receiving PC is available and that a route is available. Each packet reports with an acknowledgement specifying the time taken to send the test packet.

PING can also send its test packets indefinitely, flooding the network and is used by people to flood a router, creating a Denial of Service (DOS) attack.

```
Command Prompt - ping www.yahoo.com
Reply from 66.94.230.34: bytes=32 time=9ms TTL=53
Reply from 66.94.230.34: bytes=32 time=11ms TTL=53
Reply from 66.94.230.34: bytes=32 time=9ms TTL=53
Reply from 66.94.230.34: bytes=32 time=10ms TTL=53
Reply from 66.94.230.34: bytes=32 time=9ms TTL=53
Reply from 66.94.230.34: bytes=32 time=8ms TTL=53
Reply from 66.94.230.34: bytes=32 time=9ms TTL=53
Reply from 66.94.230.34: bytes=32 time=11ms TTL=53
Reply from 66.94.230.34: bytes=32 time=10ms TTL=53
Reply from 66.94.230.34: bytes=32 time=5ms TTL=53
Reply from 66.94.230.34: bytes=32 time=8ms TTL=53
Reply from 66.94.230.34: bytes=32 time=12ms TTL=53
Reply from 66.94.230.34: bytes=32 time=9ms TTL=53
Reply from 66.94.230.34: bytes=32 time=10ms TTL=53
Reply from 66.94.230.34: bytes=32 time=9ms TTL=53
Reply from 66.94.230.34: bytes=32 time=8ms TTL=53
Destination host unreachable.
Destination host unreachable.
Destination host unreachable.
Destination host unreachable.
Destination host unreachable.
Destination host unreachable.
Destination host unreachable.
Destination host unreachable.
```

As a basic connectivity test, PING 127.0.0.1 is a loopback test ensuring that the network card of the first NIC connected to the PC is checked and is using the TCP/IP stack.

PING <host IP address> (e.g. PING 192.168.1.22) will perform a loopback test for the local NIC using the IP address it is configured with, so the test will be of itself.

PATHPING is an adaptation of PING, available on server systems which tests the time taken at each hop to reach the final destination. This is used to determine slow routes across an enterprise network of several sites, or for sending traffic to a web server on the internet.

PATHPING of Google site

TRACEROUTE is used to check the route to a specific domain, returning the DNS name of the servers and routers the data packet travels through to reach the destination. This reveals intermediary parties and can be used when planning static routes through a network, or to define a specific web server to facilitate with requests, where many are globally available (e.g. the fastest one, or the most local server).

TRACEROUTE to NetHosted website

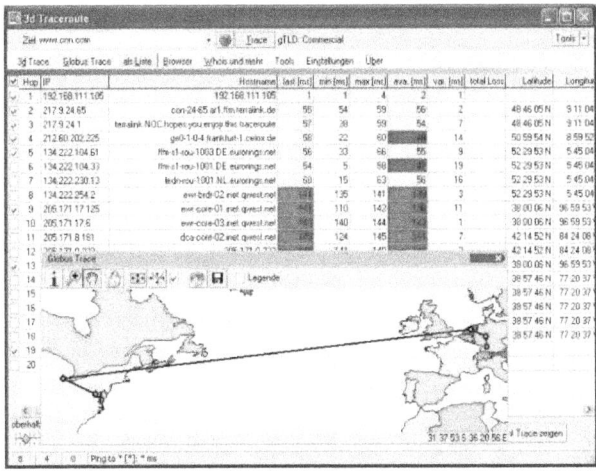

3D Traceroute application

A **Port Scanner** is an application which will probe a device to determine which firewall ports are open. Best practice is to close all TCP and UDP ports other than those needed for common traffic (e.g. port 21 for FTP control, 53 for DNS or 80 for HTTP web traffic). A port scan itself is the use of such a device on the network (or software application) to send test packets on all ports to determine which are open. It is a valid operation for a network administrator to use to test the security of the network, however can also be used maliciously to create additional traffic on the network.

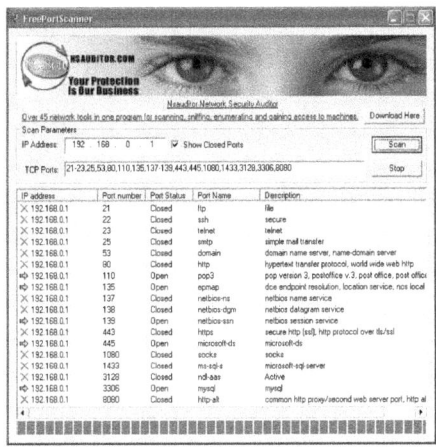

NSAuditor Port Scanner

Top Talkers – On Cisco hardware we can determine which nodes are generating the most traffic on the network with the Top Talkers feature. With the Netflow feature enabled we can see a list of all traffic in order of busiest to less busy. To run the Top Talkers feature we use the command:

```
show ip flow top-talkers
```

A sample session would define traffic on the node:

```
R2#show ip flow top-talkers

SrcIf       SrcIPaddress   DstIf    DstIPaddress   Pr SrcP DstP Bytes
Fa0/0       12.12.12.1     Local    12.12.12.2     06 CODC 0013 1244
```

Listeners – an application or device which will listed for specific network traffic is referred to as a 'listener'. A Network-based Intrusion Prevention Service (NIPS) would block specific traffic known to be a threat. Microsoft Forefront Threat Management Gateway is an example of this as all requests for downloads are checked first by the TMG server.

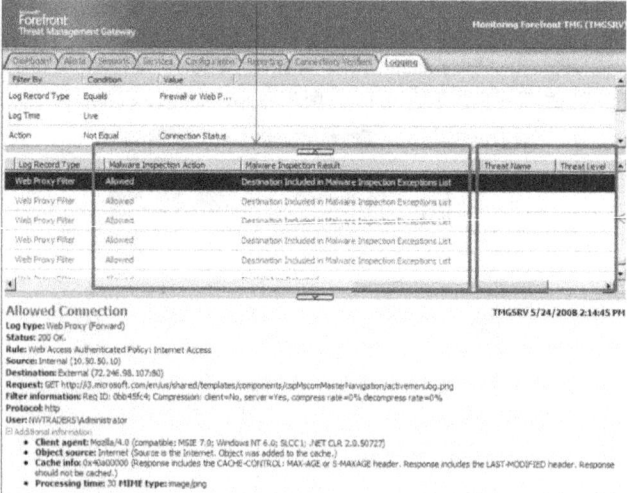

Forefront Threat Management Gateway showing allowed rules and threats.

Listener software is also common with service solutions such as IIS and SharePoint to react to network requests. IIS web services can trigger further actions within a system at the response to specific network traffic.

A SharePoint DWS trigger

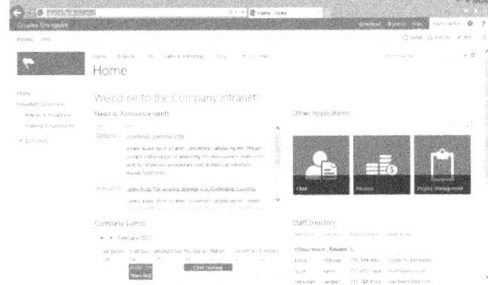

Sample SharePoint site

Simple Network Management Protocol software operate as part of the SNMP layer. SNMP requests can be disabled on the server, but are commonly used to send network management instructions between network devices, primarily between routers, or to remotely control servers. On an internal network SNMP is a useful way of remotely sending commands to other routers across the enterprise, but could be considered a security risk. Extending on from SNMP at the server level PowerShell is used to remotely configure and control other servers on the network.

SNMP sending stations are referred to as the SNMP manager. The receiving PC is the SNMP agent. SNMP uses UDP port 161 to transfer control messages.

Trap – an asynchronous notification from the agent to the manager is referred to as a 'trap' these are used to trigger further actions, such as to run a script.

Get – this command is used to retrieve one or a set of values from the managed device.

GetNext is a variant of the Get command which requests a list of instances from a remote entity and returns the next variable in the Management Information Base (MIB) tree back.

Walk – this command is used to cast several GetNext commands sequentially. It is like a programming script performing many actions within the script. This is a more efficient was of retrieving data from the managed device than sequentially running a series of GetNext commands.

The **Management Information Base (MIB)** tree is a hierarchical database used to manage the nodes on a network. Entities are accessed by using an Object Identifier and data is presented using the common format, Abstract Syntax Notation One (ASN.1).

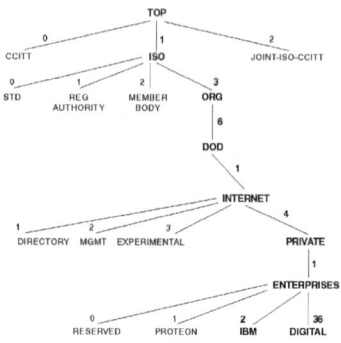

A sample MIB tree

Alerts (triggers) can detect unusual activity on the network and when a specific trigger is met an alert is generated. This alert may simply exist as a new record on a security database (as is the case with Intrusion Detection systems) however more sophisticated prevention systems can programmatically generate and send an **email** alert to the network manager.

An **SMS** alert can also be generated by an IPS device. Though interlinking with Exchange or other similar communications server an alert can be generated causing the Network Manager to know precisely where and when the incident took place and to take immediate remedial action.

Packet Flow Monitoring is the general term used to describe the above 'stateful' monitoring of a node on the network. It is common for a managed switch to contain monitoring software to check each packet before it is delivered to determine if it meets specific network security rules. Equally, a NIPS device will provide stateful protection. A hardware firewall will also support by checking the port used to send the data packet through – if the port requested in the packet is closed and no rule exists to open the port specifically for this packet, then the packet is destroyed.

Syslog is the method used to send event messages to the logging server (referred to as the syslog server because the syslog file resides there). Syslog event data is generated from a number of devices: Managed switches, Routers, firewalls and by sending syslog events to the syslog server we can compile this event traffic in one place, making the network easier to manage.

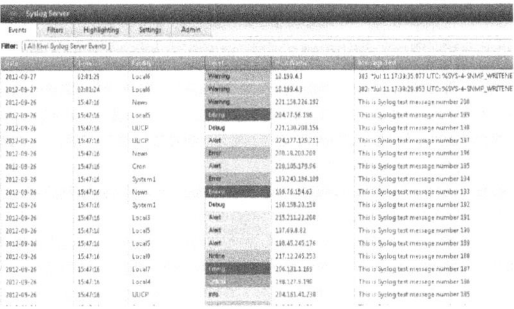

Syslog monitoring software filters messages by type or importance

Security information and event management (SIEM) is the term used to describe software designed to assist the network manager with tracking network events, filtering messages by importance, type or security level. Syslog Monitor, Windows Network Monitor and Wireshark are a sample of some of the software packages available to support with the management and monitoring of network events.

SIEM traffic differs to HIPS software such as Norton Internet Security as it protects the local host and does not broadcast its event traffic to a Syslog server.

The process of managing the power usage, airflow (for rack-mounted servers) or temperature (either the ambient temperature, or that of specific internal components) is referred to as **environmental monitoring**. This also extends to sensors on a UPS device to determine if power is being supplied by the mains supply, or battery. Factors considered by EM sensor equipment are:

Temperature – the main concern is that if a core component temperature rises to above tolerance this may be caused by an overworking server. If the server is conducting a role which causes the processor to overheat, common practice would be to enable throttling on the BIOS of the machine. Throttling reduces the power and therefore the performance of the processor as an overworked processor generates more heat as the processor is required to work at full capacity. By throttling this gives the cooling system sufficient time to reduce the local internal temperature and specifically that of the overheating component. Without throttling, the PC will at first reboot. On a server this is dangerous from a business process perspective as services will be shut down and data will probably be lost. It will also take several minutes of remediation and restarting of internal services before all provided services are available once again. To help with this business service servers are clustered to ensure High Availability. On some systems, the server may shut down completely and suddenly if the core temperature of the CPU exceeds tolerance. Here again the danger is that the shutdown may lose data and leave the system in an unstable state as shutdown was not achieved in a graceful manner. The rebooting system will need to repair any file system damage as well as to re-activate all necessary services before the server is usable again.

Humidity – both resistive and capacitive humidity sensors are available to purchase. These check the level of water within the air (this should be between 35-65%). Low humidity can cause solder paste to dry out creating cracks in the circuitry. High humidity however can cause poor soldering with 'balls' of solder generated and gaps within the solder lines.

More key to the Network+ course is the build-up of static electricity. This tends to occur in cold, dry weather and can cause damage to components if work is done on circuitry without the aid of ESD equipment.

Power monitoring tools are available to determine power usage by the server and other neighbouring devices. As an example the Dell PowerEdge contains its own monitoring software. Dell servers contain power supplies fitted with the PMBus specification – a 2-wire communications link providing power information to the monitoring software. Typical metrics include metrics such as voltage measurement and current level, component temperature, fan speed. Once gathered this information can be used by the system to intelligently throttle or to load-balance server clusters, ensuring that a server is not overworked.

Wireless survey – an important component would be a wireless scanner – a device capable of listing all wireless transmissions within the local area. *inSSIDer* is an example application which will show the channels used by various SSIDs broadcasting in the immediate vicinity.

Linking to Network+, the process of scanning for wireless networks within immediate range without the permission of the person transmitting with an intent to connect to one of these wireless networks is referred to as 'War Driving'. Network analysis software can be relatively basic (such as *Wireless Zero Configuration*) which will display local wireless networks.

Another useful tool is *Wi-Fi Planner for Aerohive Aps* which can provide a 2D map of the building and overlay a 'heat map' of wireless transmissions. This can assist with determining where to place access points to ensure for the widest coverage.

A **wireless analyser** is an application containing a suite of the above features, providing network analysis, scanning and problem detection. It is common that a wireless analyser will contain ping and SNMP command systems so that once a picture of local transmitters has been determined the user will be able to send test packets, or to test the integrity and security of the packets, whether they have a SSID broadcast as part of the packet or not. It used to be the case (in previous Network+ versions) that one way of increasing the security of a network would be to disable the SSID as then the packet would be transmitted but would be invisible to the client. Although this is true more sophisticated applications such as wireless analysers, or even dedicated wireless analysis probes will still be able to read the transmitted packet and perform a 'packet sniff'. An example phone app providing these features is *Network Analyzer Lite*.

2.2

2.2 Given a scenario, analyze metrics and reports from monitoring and tracking performance tools
- Baseline
- Bottleneck
- Log management
- Graphing
- Utilization
    - Bandwidth
    - Storage
    - Network device CPU
    - Network device memory
    - Wireless channel utilization
- Link status
- Interface monitoring
    - Errors
    - Utilization
    - Discards
    - Packet drops
    - Interface resets
    - Speed and duplex

Performance metrics used to determine the effectiveness of a network are categorised as follows:

Baseline – this is the accepted tolerance of the network. This data can consist of latency timings and bandwidth at different key points on the network. It is used as the minimum accepted tolerance of the network and future performance is measured against it.

Bottleneck – an excess of data transfer through one node can cause the node to have problems in sending the large amount of data through. This can be caused by either a narrow bandwidth on an input port into the node, slow data transfer on a cable into the node, dropped packets causing resends and surplus traffic on the network (as would be the case with a hub) or the transmission speed a cable is capable of. Either way, at a key point in the network congestion has occurred which in turn is slowing all subsequent data transfer through the affected node. This is referred to as a 'bottleneck'. It can be relieved by transferring traffic through other nodes to reach the destination, increasing the speed or throughput of the cable into the device.

Log management – by keeping logs regularly backed up and of a manageable size the network manager can keep a record of regular traffic on the network and determine what to expect. With this in mind if any unusual activity is noticed in comparison to older logs it may help to establish that the new traffic is indeed 'exotic' and not within expectations. From this we can then determine when the 'exotic' traffic started to occur and which nodes/devices were involved. From this we can determine how much of the network is affected and from this consider causes of action to take to remediate the problem.

Graphing is the activity of scoping the maximum peak, minimum and standard performance bandwidths of each cable and each device to determine if it would be effective to 'trunk' or to cluster devices in order to improve bandwidth at parts of the network you have control over.

By using visual, graph monitoring software we can determine peaks and bottlenecks. Graphing is the process of attempting to identify and to resolve these.

Utilization – here we are considering what services and types of data we are using the network for. We are considering which business-related activities produce more or less traffic than others and by favouring one service on the network over others, or by denying some services altogether we can reduce additional packets sent on the network, therefore allowing more users to use the network at any one time short of expanding the hardware infrastructure. An example here would be the denial of SNMP or ICMP traffic on the network, or reducing the amount of 'server heartbeats' sent, or the possibility of moving Routing protocols from RIPv1 to RIPv2, which is considerably less 'chatty'. One major consideration we have is the recent integration of communications networks with standard data transfer networks. As both use the IP stack and VoIP traffic is routable through the standard network, although this has reduced the hardware needed for telephony, it has increased demand on the existing network infrastructure. VoIP voice and video traffic can be favoured by the use of QoS packet scheduling but at the expense of file and other network service transfers. **Bandwidth** is actually reduced by the existing network taking on this data-heavy service.

As data transfer rates increase and networks grow network-attached **storage** also increases and the move over to virtualised servers has increased the demand on the network significantly. These servers may store several Tb of data each, allow hundreds of session connections and also need to connect to SAN devices to transfer LUN data (logical blocks of data sent independently of the Operating System) directly across the network. Server 2012 L2 can also trigger SANs to send LUN blocks using the Offloaded Data transfer (ODX) service.

It is also important to realise that one particular node can only work so fast. This is dependent on the network device's own CPU. For example managed switches, routers, firewalls, concentrators, NIDS and NIPS devices all contain a rudimentary computer with its own **CPU** and dedicated small-scale firmware operating system. It can only transfer data through the device as fast as it can transmit down the cable, the speed of the NIC, the throughput of the NIC and the speed of the processor.

As the network device needs to transfer the data from port to port, or to analyse the packet before it is sent on, the data is transferred into realtime memory. The **memory** available can be a limiting factor in the number of packets which can be checked and transferred at any one time. This becomes even more significant with the move over to the new Advanced Format hard drive support 4k blocks and the transfer of 4k at any one time (for the host PC or server) but also across the network with the propensity of Jumbo Frames which are now being supported within the internal corporate network.

We can also see congestion occur if there are several wireless devices connecting to the same Access Point with the same **channel**. Although channels are small areas of the overall frequency available there is a small degree of crossover between adjacent channels, so neighbouring devices physically close to each other and connecting to the same access point are encouraged to not use neighbouring channels (as this will generate some interference) and certainly not to use the same channel (as this will generate crosstalk). The neighbouring devices should be set to channels distant from the neighbour (e.g. 1,3,6,9,12 etc.). This of course assumes that the devices will remain stationary!

Link status – network devices can provide a 'link table' to demonstrate which ports are in use and their state (if they are sending data up (e.g. to the router), down (e.g. to the PC) or offline. A visual representation is also usually available on most switches and routers by means of an activity light which will be lit where there is connectivity between the switch and its end device, also if the correct cable is used (or the device is 'auto-switching'). When the light flashes this proves data is transferring.

Interface monitoring is the process of connecting to either a NIC though a command prompt (usually), or connecting to a managed switch or router by means of a rollover cable, null-modem cable or terminal software. Once connected you are presented on your host device (usually a laptop which can be plugged directly into the device) you can communicate directly with it using a terminal window. The terminal window allows the administrator to authenticate to the main session, but also can ensure that a backup (a 'restore') session is resident on the device. It is possible to switch between these two OS sessions and this is done when updating firmware. In relation to network data monitoring we can check the health of each port on the device as well as adjust its configuration:

Errors can be checked by inspecting the devices' log. Each transaction is recorded in a log so that we can identify the amount and type of traffic but also to determine any system errors or dropped packets to determine if further network changes or device configuration is needed.

What follows is the Cisco logging command help section. As you can see the log can be configured and the extent to which logging occurs can also be set.

```
router(config)# logging ?
  Hostname or A.B.C.D   IP address of the logging host
  buffered              Set buffered logging parameters
  buginf                Enable buginf logging for debugging
  cns-events            Set CNS Event logging level
  console               Set console logging parameters
  count                 Count every log message and timestamp last occurrence
  exception             Limit size of exception flush output
  facility              Facility parameter for syslog messages
  history               Configure syslog history table
  host                  Set syslog server IP address and parameters
  monitor               Set terminal line (monitor) logging parameters
  on                    Enable logging to all supported destinations
  origin-id             Add origin ID to syslog messages
  rate-limit            Set messages per second limit
  reload                Set reload logging level
  server-arp            Enable sending ARP requests for syslog servers when
                        first configured
  source-interface      Specify interface for source address in
                        logging transactions
  trap                  Set syslog server logging level
  userinfo              Enable logging of user info on privileged mode enabling
router(config)# logging
```

Utilisation – by checking the logs for common activities, or data packet types we can determine the propensity of each type of packet and by so doing work out the more popular activities on the network. With this information we can tailor our network to suit. For example, the inclusion of a Lync server and attaching it to exchange will enable Lync calls, video conferencing for all Active Directory members of the network. However, the switch may not be able to cope with the increase of traffic to the Lync server, so a further NIC on the Lync server could be used to handle further requests and this may route to a different switch. The swapping of a CAT5e port with a multimode fibre between two routers would allow for much faster transfer speeds and effective bandwidth if congestion has been identified at this point.

Discards – if packets are being dropped we need to know the cause of this:

- Could it be that packets cannot be handled due to congestion and so the packet reaches its TTL?
- Is the packet important?
- By dropping the packet will this have cumulative effects for the network (e.g. missing heartbeat signals may affect the performance and synchronisation between servers).
- Did we set a rule to deliberately drop the packet if it is encountered on the network? In which case where are they being generated? If we can determine the source we can block the creation of these packets by disabling the appropriate service on the host PC.
- Do we have a routing loop on the network causing congestion? Should we implement Spanning Tree Protocol or an equivalent routing protocol to counter routing problems?

Interface resets – logs can actively report when a NIC, Switch or router was reset, either through power failure, manual reset or hardware fault. From this we can determine the reliability of the network at this point and make decisions on replacing components which appear to be more sensitive to reset, or inactivity. If an area of the network is being attacked by an outside influence (e.g. DoS attack, or Smurf attack) one specific node is targeted (e.g. Router) until it is unable to function. Often at this point safety protocols will cause the device to reset, clearing the problem but causing inactivity for the amount of time the device is rebooting and initialising.

The **speed** of the port can be set within the router itself (Baud rate). Higher speeds however are only achievable if both devices at both ends of the cable are capable of transmitting at the higher speed. Higher speeds also run the risk of an increased number of dropped packets, leading to some congestion, or latency issues.

The **duplexing** mode of the port can be set either to simplex (one way only, such as with an uplink, or a fibre connection on a FDDI ring as this is designed to go in one direction only) and therefore allowing use of the full bandwidth, half-duplex (where half of the bandwidth is used for transmissions in one direction as the other half is used for the other direction) or full duplex (where both directions are possible, full bandwidth, but not at the same time).

2.3

2.3 Given a scenario, use appropriate resources to support configuration management
- Archives/backups
- Baselines
- On-boarding and off-boarding of mobile devices
- NAC
- Documentation
  - Network diagrams (logical/physical)
  - Asset management
  - IP address utilization
  - Vendor documentation
  - Internal operating procedures/policies/standards

Archiving / Backups – it is commonplace to use NAS storage to back up key corporate data such as user accounts and common shared folders, but more recently files are being stored on a SharePoint intranet space. This can facilitate management of the documents held within the organisation however can create another tier of backup as SharePoint also will store social media messages (project feeds and discussions), calendar entries and other collaborative data as well as 'blank' forms whereas the user storage space will typically contain personal data, contact lists and completed forms. All of this data is typically stored to a backup NAS only attached to the network for the duration of the backup, or to DAT tape. A backup strategy such as Normal > Differential is commonly used over the course of a week (e.g. Normal backup on the Monday, Differential backup for the rest of the week) however Differential backups will take longer as they contain all data since the last Normal backup. This will increase the time taken to back up. However, restoring the backup set will only require the Normal tape and the last Differential backup tape, so restoring is relatively quick. On a NAS these are simply two backup files on the drive.

For the reason that we may need to restore business critical data quickly, N-D backup sets area quite popular.

The alternative solution would be to use an N-I backup solution where the Normal backup is again taken on the Monday, but for subsequent days Incremental backups are taken. Incremental and Normal backups clear the archive bit stored on the file which informs the system that the file is now ready for archiving. All newly saved documents are made ready for archiving by default. An incremental backup is relatively small in size because there is no duplication of previous data – the files stored are only those files available which are new since the last N or I backup. Therefore, although the same number of backup tapes are used, the time to backup per session is greatly reduced due to the lack of any duplicated data. This however means that we have no safeguard – for example on an N-D backup, if I am concerned about a file created on Tuesday morning, it would have been captured on Tuesday's but also Wednesday, Thursday and Friday backup sets. If the system failed on Saturday but no further files were made from Tuesday the Wed-Thurs-Fri sets would be identical to Tuesday's set. Any of these tapes could therefore be used. If a mechanical problem occurred and Thursday's tape was damaged, or unreadable, we could use an alternative to retrieve the file. This is not the case with Incremental backups.

On restoring, Incremental backups require all tapes in the backup set to be used sequentially. This increases the time taken to restore the backup and includes more manual labour which tape switching (if not in a DAT caddy system).

Baselining – the purpose of baselining is to measure acceptable working practice for a system. Before purchase, it is customary to look for a machine capable of meeting certain speeds and capacity for business requirements. However, once the machine is loaded with applications and put under the strain of user operation, often without due care or servicing (e.g. Defragmentation, although this is now done automatically by default by Windows 7 and above) our question now is 'to what extent has the user's configuration altered the machine from acceptable working metrics as defined by our baseline?'. Baseline data is collected when the machine is first imaged and is checked to be error-free (in the error logs). At this point there may well still need to be software and driver updates added but we can use this moment in time to consider the machine as in a 'good' state. Any changes to the performance of the machine can be noted against this baseline data. Companies often will buy in bulk a number of the same machine make and model within the same hardware specification and with the same image loaded. Therefore they can rely on the fact that all of the machines should theoretically work the same way and to the same standard.

System Information is an OS tool which can provide a detailed report of the specific hardware and configuration of the machine. Other third-party System Information tools such as *Everest* or *SiSandra* also supply links to the hardware manufacturer site where you can download the latest drivers for the component.

Reliability monitor can provide a 'health chart' of the machine from an OS perspective, over time and produce a reliability index, a number between 1 and 10 which also shows any application, device, driver or other failure which may have impacted on the reliability of the machine over time. A high score shows a reliable machine, but not necessarily a fast one.

Performance Information is a slightly different baseline where each key hardware component is graded in relation to known other hardware stored in the Microsoft hardware database. Each hardware component has been graded and the machine being analysed is compared to these known components. A score is returned for each area: Processor, Memory, Graphics, 3D graphics, Hard disk transfer rate. The score is a number between 1 and 7.9 where 7.9 is high. The overall system score is a subscore from these areas - the lowest number forms the overall score (It is not an average).

Mobile device on-boarding – a common dilemma facing enterprises at present is how to react to the popularity of mobiles within an organisation. Years ago, the use of a mobile phone for personal reasons at work was frowned upon to the point of taking disciplinary action but with the propensity of the internet and also working from home outside of normal work hours, those lines have become blurred and companies are now more accustomed to embrace the mobile smartphone as an office tool. What started with the urge to supply sales reps with company phones has moved to considering a member of staff to obtain limited access to the corporate network to carry out their duties. The concept is split into two different approaches:

Bring your own device (BYOD) – here, the individual can access internal documents after joining the smartphone as a managed device to the domain. The user adds a certificate file to their phone which causes the phone to be a managed computer on the network, therefore subsequent to Active Directory rules. However when the phone is detached from the network (the user actually has to agree to disjoin the network) the phone's operation returns to normal and any files stored on the device are wiped.

Choose your own Device (CYOD) – as a solution to the ownership problem, in acceptance of some of the benefits of being contactable and working outside of the office many companies choose to provide staff with their own company phone so that they can continue to engage in work matters whilst keeping the personal / corporate divide. Usually one make and model of smartphone is purchased for all staff to facilitate management across the organisation.

Mobile device off-boarding – the key aspect here is that when the phone is disjoined from the domain there is a complete removal of organisation settings and files to protect the security of the organisation.

Network Access Control (NAC) – this is a network security concept where the connecting computer has to meet specific 'Health' criteria before it is allowed access to the network. In the case of a remoting individual connecting to the network via a VPN remote link, it is possible that their laptop has not been virus scanned recently, may not even contain the most recent virus definitions, have a virus scanning software which is not recognised by the company's software policy (and therefore may be perceived to be inadequate), may not have the latest software updates therefore leading to vulnerabilities. The presence of a Network Access Control – System Health server is to interrogate the connecting computer's health by commuting with the endpoint reporting module (in the case of Windows systems, *Action Center*). Action Center's report is referenced against the defined system health policies and if the connecting computer is found to require further maintenance it will not be allowed to connect to the wider network, rather DHCP is set to also manage a second 'quarantine' scope – the connecting computer will receive an IP address in the quarantine scope and not receive a standard IP from the main DHCP network scope until maintenance has been completed and the SHS reports that the system is ready to connect to the network.

Documentation is held to assist with the management, design but also maintenance of the network:

Logical network diagram – this document details the connectivity between subnets, listing IP address ranges and the location of network devices, switches and routers. It focusses on the flow of traffic across the organisation and often does not take into account the physical layout of the building or buildings which comprise the network. Due to its logical nature, groupings may be by project, or department as well as site.

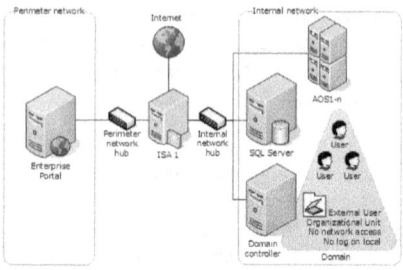

Logical network diagram with perimeter network

Physical network diagram – this is a 'blueprint' or 'floor plan' detailing the exact layout of the building showing where specific cables and components are laid. Metrics here are the port number of the socket, its respective port in the patch panel, which port the panel port connects to in the switch, the distances of cables, the type (and therefore speed) of cables to be used. This is used by an engineer to ensure that the layout of the actual cables is accurate.

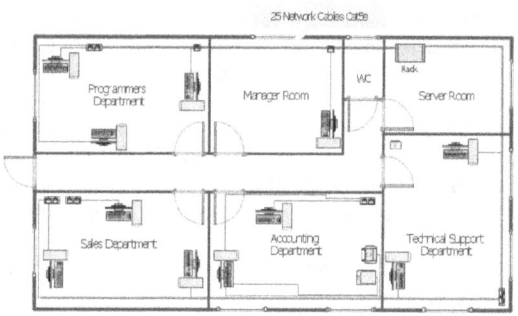

Physical Network layout (floor plan)

Asset management is the process of listing (on a database) and tagging devices owned by the company for the purposes of audit tracking. As capital has been realised as an asset (e.g. the company has bought a laptop), although it is depreciating the asset still holds value and may need to be sold. The asset is tagged 'as is' so one asset number also relates to the respective components which make up this item. For this reason it is common for companies to purchase PCs as ready-made systems and not as separate components. Not only would this complicate the asset management but the purchase of a built machine 'complete' allows the company to enjoy warranty protection and assurances by a named brand. If a component fails the entire system is sent back for replacement.

The only caveat to the above is with hard disks. A Hard Disk will contain company sensitive data and should be wiped, or also destroyed after it has reached the end of its life to stop anyone else from stealing corporate data. Until recent legislation there have been many instance within the UK where public sector bodies have retired PCs simply by throwing them into a skip, to be disposed of by a third-party company for recycling, but either the machines were not being properly disposed of, were being donated to charities with hard drives intact (and therefore access to data stored on the drive as well as free Windows licences) or the components were being stolen by passers-by ('bin-dipping').

IP addressing can create a real problem for network managers. With the propensity of virtual machines the amount of IP addresses needed within the organisation is far greater than previous, where one IP would be sufficient for one machine. We are at a position where the number of publicly available IPv4 addresses has now run out and there is a deliberate move towards upgrading company systems to embrace IPv6 which has a vast number of available IP addresses and negates the need for discrete IP management. However, it is still accepted practice to plan a specific number of IP addresses for each subnet using IPv4 and we will look at this here.

Classfull addressing is the process whereby we use a private address within the available range within the class A, B or C network.

Class	Address Range	Number of IPs
A	10.0.0.0 – 10.255.255.255	16,777,216
B	172.16.0.0 – 172.31.255.255	1,048,576
C	192.168.0.0 – 192.168.255.255	65,536

We will often wish to split the range into discrete sections and for this we use the CIDR system (Classless Internet Domain Routing). We start with a classful address (e.g. class C as above) but decide to 'borrow' a bit so that the subnet mask does not fall at /24 but at /23. By doing so we have effectively halved the number of subnets we can have, but doubled the number of PCs available in each subnet. Within a class C system there are actually 256 IPs available within the subnet as follows:

There are 32 bits in an IPv4 address. The first 24 are used to denote the subnet and the last 8 are used to denote the IPs within the subnet.

2^8 = 256 IPs. Of these the lowest (0) is used to refer to the subnet and not to a specific host. Also the highest (255) is used to specify all of the hosts on the network (a 'broadcast').

So in the class C example where we are using /23, our new subnet mask becomes 8+8+7 as:

11111111 . 11111111 . 11111110 . 00000000 = 255.255.254.0

We are now using 9 remaining bits and there are two IPs we can't use in the range, so $2^9 - 2$ = 510 available IPs (512 hosts, or IPs within the subnet).

If we were to AND 192.168.1.1 as our starting IP address:

192.168.1.1:   11000000.10101000.00000001.00000001

255.255.254.0: 11111111.11111111.11111110.00000000

Result: 11000000.10101000.00000000.00000000 = 192.168.0.0 is the Network IP

Host bits: 00000000.00000000.00000001.00000001 = from 0.0.1.1 upwards

This subnet is therefore from 192.168.1.0 – 192.168.2.255. The next subnet would therefore start at 192.168.3.0

Virtual switches – *Hyper-V, VMWare , Virtualbox* and other hypervisors are able to connect the virtual PC to other virtual PCs and to the host by means of a virtual switch. This acts just like a real switch allowing access to the host. The switch can operate in internal mode (virtual PCs can only talk to each other), public (can stare with the host only but not the wider network), or public (is part of the wider network).

Vendor documentation – one of the most important things to consider is where to go for up to date information. Although a CD is often provided upon purchase of a hardware component, and the diver therein may well be digitally signed, this may not be up to date because the component has been lying on a shelf for several months. The best solution therefore is the manufacturer's website where the latest fixes, driver updates and documentation can be found. Most vendor websites now also have ActiveX software capable of determining the make and model of your component and will select the correct driver for you.

It is worth noting that there is an upgrade order. Windows systems now use an enhanced and more secure boot, audit and analysis module which loads at the early part of the bootstrap and replaces BIOs for key system information. UEFI (Unified Extensible Firmware Interface) is able to provide more information to the Operating System than the BIOS ever could and forms an integral part of the security and encryption of the system, providing initial information for Bitlocker drives and other initial information. However, changes to the BIOS firmware after the OS has been installed may render the OS unusable as the system will think that there has not been a major upgrade, but a replacement of key parts, so either may not run at all, or may require re-activation. This is normal.

Internal operating procedures, policies and standards – the company will hold a Standard (standing) Operating Procedure which determines the correct procedure to follow to perform a series of actions. This procedure has been produced over time and of research of how the company has performed in order to address regular problems and concerns, either to eliminate them, provide alternative approaches or workarounds, or to perform quality measurement benchmarks for staff to follow. These standards are quite detailed and exacting, for example in the Pharmaceutical industry it is necessary for a clinical researcher to read a series of Standard Operating Procedures before working on any clinical trials to ensure that action undertaking are done so in a measured and compliant way.

In relation to network administration there will be a series of tasks which the network team are expected to carry out:

- Remote maintenance of servers and routers
- Configuration of Active Directory
- Backups

- Servicing printers and end devices
- Password and account problems
- Software support
- Training of other staff

Each of these will be detailed in policy document which state the position of the team on the task, the contractual obligation the team will have to the company and to its end users. Other staff are perceived to be internal customers and any work undertaken will be audited against a series of agreed targets and metrics detailed in a contract. Penalties will be given if these metrics are not met.

2.4

2.4 Explain the importance of implementing network segmentation
- SCADA systems/Industrial control systems
- Legacy systems
- Separate private/public networks
- Honeypot/honeynet
- Testing lab
- Load balancing
- Performance optimization
- Security
- Compliance

SCADA systems – an industrial control system is a network strategy where a centralised approach is taken to oversee other industrial systems. SCADA stands for 'supervisory control and data acquisition'. The concept is that a central computer will gather operational performance data from a variety of different production systems and will be able to control the output of each of these connected systems. For example, a SCADA system in a power plant may be linked to the management computers for each reactor. If one reactor demand rises (e.g. it is a well-known fact that an advert break in the middle of a programme watched by a vast majority of the population at the same time, such as a live event) will cause a surge in demand. This can be anticipated by the SCADA system and as a result each of the reactor cores can increase their production to cope with demand. The SCADA system can also communicate with other connected systems at other sites, such as a capacity bank storing over-produced energy from earlier in the day. This energy can also be added to the grid to cope with the expected demand.

Example SCADA system: PlantIQ waste water treatment system.
URL:https://www.youtube.com/watch?v=ZSFdOjxB-1I

Legacy IC systems – here, we are referring to an old, outdated or unsupported system. It is highly likely that the system will have proprietary, bespoke software built for a specific purpose and will be unable to communicate with a centralised system, therefore control of the system requires an intermediary step, either 'bridging' software or the direct control of a member of staff where centralised requirements can be interpreted and production output adjusted accordingly. Legacy systems tend not to be updated and are often expensive to maintain if serviced under a long-standing agreement. If the original servicing company is no longer on the market highly specialised programmers are needed to understand how to communicate with the system.

Conversely some legacy systems have a small total cost of ownership. For example, if the company is an industrial manufacturer who can see no means of updating a process within the factory and the original (now legacy) system is still productive but the code was written decades ago, it may serve to simply hire a programmer as part of the company and provide a decent salary for the person to service the system. An example here would be of a LISP, or COBOL system running a program which will perform a series of actions. There is no need to change the initial requirements and the machine has no need to communicate on the network at all.

The separation of public and private networks goes far beyond the scope of the user. The initial concept was as follows:

Public users can see the internet-hosted (public facing) webpage where they will view non-sensitive information, be able to place orders or look for general information. As rival companies may be looking to gain an advantage by stealing or acting on information available the information presented is often limited.

Private users consist of members of staff, trusted contractors and partners. Information is highly sensitive so is separated based on the individual's role within the organisation (separation of duties). Here, a SharePoint intranet solution and file shares may form access to this sensitive data. A Dynamics or Sage dashboard may also build on form this to show corporate performance, track workflow or which member of staff is working on which project.

Externally-connecting staff can also access an 'extranet' – this is a separate website showing some company sensitive information such as presentation data, sales data, marketing reports and tools so that staff working off-site can still use some key documents.

Home-working, remoting staff will be able to access the internal site as if they are present within the building through the use of a Virtual Private Network (e.g. a DirectAccess system) where their session in actuality runs on a server inside of the network and the user is in fact remoting into this server. If the connection is lost, the session is still running, so when the user is able to re-establish the connection the session can continue from where they have left. Documents are stored internally avoiding the problem of documents being taken outside of the building. This is an important consideration for public sector bodies, lawyers and charities working with sensitive data (e.g financial, legal or safeguarding data).

This brings us to the concept of a perimeter network. This is an interim space in the network design located between two firewalls where we can place public-facing services and resources allowing some limited access to the corporate network. Some companies choose to host their websites within the perimeter network allowing the public to view only the public-facing data. Other more sensitive data is housed behind the second firewall and other additional safeguards. The reason for this approach is where the public data hosted within the perimeter firewall changes regularly due to data from within the internal network.

The perimeter network is also a gateway into the internal network. To deter unscrupulous activity it is common to find a file server to be located within the perimeter network containing files which may seem to be attractive to a would-be competitor, or hacker (this is appropriately called a **Honeypot**). The fileserver is also configured to log access (e.g. the visitor's IP address) and will report the details of a person attempting to access the resource where further action may be taken. By doing this the company builds up a reputation for securing their systems from would-be attackers and this serves as a deterrent.

A collection of Honeypots on the perimeter network is referred to as a **Honeynet**.

A **testing lab** is an environment where the software under development can be put under stringent testing to ensure that it meets the outlined specifications. We use the Input > Process > Output model, where 'process' refers to the software under development. Testing falls into three different categories:

White-box testing – here, every facet of the system is known to the tester. We can see at every stage how input data is passed through the system, through various modules, how it is adapted by module code until the output is formed.

Black-box testing – here, we cannot see any of the system, merely provide inputs and check expected outputs.

Grey testing – some general aspects of the software are known to the tester, but access is not provided to all of the code, rather a general overview of the process is provided.

A **sandbox** network is a specific type of network completely separate from the main corporate network. User accounts and computers are not subsequent to the corporate Active Directory rules and any software used within the network stays within the network. There is usually no bridge between the sandbox and the production environment.

Sandbox networks are used to check that the configuration of software is exact before releasing the changes onto the live production environment. An example here may be the configuration of a Dynamics CRM system before adding the managed package onto the live system.

Within educational establishments such as colleges and universities there are often limitations on the type of licenced software you are allowed to run on the main network. A Sandbox network can avoid some of the limitations imposed by policy and with management agreement it will be possible to run Open Source, or Freeware software for specific purposes as long as the software licence agreement is upheld.

Another more prominent type of testing environment is a '**dirty lab**'. This is used in the teaching of Cyber security where a network security researcher learns how a virus works and can see it in action on a completely isolated network, but also can revert the systems (usually through re-imaging back to a 'good' point before the virus was introduced to the dirty lab) in order to carry other further testing.

NB: The **National Cyber Security Centre** in Malvern, Worcester work with QinetiQ, GCHQ and other cyber security companies in the area to offer training through the use of their dirty lab. http://www.cyberskillscentre.com/

Load balancing is the process of ensuring that all systems offering the same service within a cluster are able to share the demand equally. This is common practice where a website may be visited by thousands of visitors at the same time. Each visitor would expect the same experience and if served by only one IIS web server new visitors may experience timeout errors, or delays in accessing pages. A load-balanced site forms a management bridge between the IIS systems and equalises the load so that each system takes an equal proportion of the connections, sharing the load across the systems. As long as the systems are in contention and are not hampered by other activities, but are dedicated to the take in hand then this works fine. With this, we are maximising the available throughput and reducing access time for every visitor.

Load balancing can lead to advanced clusters, even to Grid computing where the rendering requirements to render the scenes for a 3D movie can be shared across an array of computers. Pixar have a grid setup used to render the cinema-resolution frames for their films. Adding in a variety of computers and batch-processing the job can reduce production time considerably.

Performance optimisation is the process of comparing current performance with the baseline and finding ways to achieve optimal performance after maintenance and upgrades have taken place. It can involve factors such as:

- Stopping and disabling unnecessary services on the PC
- Offloading services onto other servers to free up processing capability, or RAM
- The use of a RAID system to reduce latency through striping (e.g. RAID 6)
- The use of a iSCSI fibre to transfer files at the data block level rather than having to resolve them into the OS for conversion as part of the transfer
- The addition of more, or faster RAM to increase system scope.
- The use of NUMA (non uniform memory access) to share hardware capacity across several virtual PCs.
- The updating of virtual hard drives from VHD to VHDX in order to break the 2 Tb limit to much larger drive sizes.

System security can be increased as follows:

- Ensure that the software firewall is active for all profiles.
- Create rules to open a firewall port for a specific application, rather than leaving the port number in question open.
- Consider opening some ports for sending 'out' only, or 'in' only as required.
- Use dynamic port mapping on the firewall (e.g. port 21 for FTP control is open, but 20 is closed. Both systems agree to use a dynamic port other than 20 (the default) and the port is opened temporarily for the transfer and closed immediately after the session has concluded).
- Switch off ICMP (e.g. Echo or PING) requests on the network as these can be used to generate additional traffic, even to stop services.

- Switch off SNMP traffic to servers or end devices as these generate unnecessary traffic. Focussing use for SNMP between routers however is desirable.
- Use a less chatty protocol for large networks, e.g. RIPv2.
- Implement a hardware firewall at the proximity of the network. This will add a further layer of protection.
- Implement a NIDS to log any anomalies, or a NIPS (more complex and expensive) to actually deny access to exotic packets.
- In addition implement a HIDS / HIPS (e.g. Norton Internet Security) on every end device.
- Deploy a NAC (Health) server on the network along with an updated DHCP server with a quarantine scope so that remoting users and laptops not usually connected to the network can be checked before being granted access.
- Ensure that devices are managed by Active Directory.
- Ensure that users log on with Active Directory accounts.
- Disable local administrator accounts on end devices.

Compliance can be met by putting in place trackable workflows where the activities undertaken by the member of staff can be monitored against metrics and following the Standard Operating Procedure. Embed procedures into training and ensure that management can use these to determine the performance of the individual.

From a technical perspective do not introduce any non-standardised devices onto the network and if there is a need to run these, the software is to be run on a sandbox, or in a virtualised environment where it cannot alter or harm normal process. A machine is also compliant from a System Health perspective if it meets the requirements of the Health server. This process can be automated, but the ramifications of a production machine dropping in to quarantine could be severe for the normal operations of the company, so the scope of assessment, or the scope of machines inspected by the Health server can be adjusted and usually this would apply to laptops only, or remoting devices and not to internal production machines (e.g. on the factory floor).

2.5

2.5 Given a scenario, install and apply patches and updates
- OS updates
- Firmware updates
- Driver updates
- Feature changes/updates
- Major vs minor updates
- Vulnerability patches
- Upgrading vs downgrading
    - Configuration backup

OS updates – this can now occur as a relatively straightforward process for the end-user to implement (e.g. upgrading from Windows 8 to 8.1) however a transition from one architecture to another (e.g. XP to W7 or to Linux) would require significant changes. This would require for files to be backed up using a profiling tool such as User State Migration Tool, or Windows Easy Transfer, for the backed up profile to be stored on a temporary storage location, such as an external hard drive, for the machine to be upgraded (the machine will first be shut down and booted from a bootable upgrade disk so that system resources normally locked to the OS are freed) and then finally for the profile to be re-added (assuming that the old profile was not readable). For example the upgrade from XP to 7 requires Windows Easy Transfer to be run from the Windows 7 installation DVD, with XP running. The backup file is then moved to a temporary storage device and as the architecture is quite different it would be usual to restart the PC, booting into the Windows 7 installation disc and to perform not an in-place upgrade but a 'wipe and load' meaning that the entire contents of the local hard drive are wiped and a clean installation is undertaken.

With the development of Windows Deployment Services, it is possible to now customise images with various permutations based on departmental need. The process of installing can be performed across the network and in a staged manner. If a new updated version of the installation file becomes available it can be swapped into the WDS deployment stack, ensuring that the latest available installations are used.

With an existing system it is customary to regularly check for system updates from the vendor website. With Vista onwards, there is no need to visit the website – the OS can now periodically check and report back on any updates it has found and let the technician decide which are relevant. On an enterprise network the involvement of a WSUS (software update service) server centralises updates by auditing all required updates and to which machines the updates need to be sent. The updates are downloaded from the Windows Update website and stored in a central location on the corporate network. The file only needs to be downloaded once, reducing external network traffic. WSUS then rolls out the update to all machines which need it and automatically manages the process of adding the update.

Updates typically do not require a restart and can be added whilst normal work operations are taking place. A collection of updates is referred to as a Service Pack – these are released periodically (usually every 18 months) and can be added manually by the technician to simplify the updating process. These files are usually changes to core OS files and architecture.

Firmware updates – this is an update to software stored on the controller chip which manages a component of the system. An obvious example would be a BIOS firmware update – this is a binary file which is added through a small application also provided by the vendor. The data is written to the BIOS and will undertake the update upon reboot. The BIOS version number will be updated and additional functionality may be made available, or system stability should be improved. Be careful to only install the correct firmware update for your exact model – there is no margin for error here. Although the updating process only takes a few seconds, if the system hangs, or there is a power outage during the update, the part-written file will leave the system in an unusable state (commonly referred to as 'bricking the system') and the component will have to be replaced (e.g. a new motherboard).

Firmware updates are also available for graphics cards to obtain better performance from the GPU.

Updating the firmware for hardware routers is quite common, although it is recommended that you save the new version to the second partition on the router (most have one and you can swap between the partitions), also that you save the current configuration and reload it onto the new router OS.

Driver updates – driver files have been checked and digitally signed by the vendor to assure that they will work as expected with the Operating System used. However new code is released improving the hardware throughput of a device, making it more stable, or offering additional features. It is therefore advisable to check for updates on a regular basis. Driver updates that are digitally signed will appear within the Windows update check, but for other systems (e.g. Linux) the updating process is quite manual – you have to download the correct TAR file and extract it, or replace the current installer module (RPM) with the more recent RPM file. Once the driver folder is extracted there will be an information file with instructions of how to add the file to the system. As this is a system change you will need to operate this with an elevated privilege (e.g. SUDO as ROOT).

Feature changes – a server will serve a variety of operational services. These are split into two categories: Roles and Features. A Role is a service the server can perform (e.g. IIS server, Active Directory Federation) whereas a feature is an underlying software module, component or protocol which can enrich the system (e.g. TFTP, Remote Assistance, Background Intelligent Transfer). By adding features the performance of the machine may increase and the machine can be tailored to server a particular role (e.g. the IIS server requires security, internet and networking features in order to perform its role).

The removal of features will conversely free-up system resources. It is quite common to find that an end-user has added all available features expecting to use them all, only to find that some of these are now running in the background as background tasks and are using up resources as they wait to hear from other (often for the home network) non-existent services on other computers on the network. This increases local resource demand but also network traffic as the machine is trying to contact other servers which may not exist on the network.

Features and updates - we make a distinction between features and applications – applications may be stand-alone and will operate on the OS using their own code and resources, but often not requiring the use of OS-specific features. Applications also may require updating as regular revisions to the underlying code may be released which can make the application more responsive, or stable. In some cases applications were designed to operate with an earlier OS version and compatibility issues may be present which are resolved by a recent update.

Major and minor updates – Major and min or refer to the revisioning of software development. Each iteration released received an increment. The increase in the Major revision refers to a significant change of functionality of the product. The Minor increment is added when there are only small discrete fixes (e.g. bug fixes, or code clean-up).

A **vulnerability patch** is an update usually released very quickly in response to a problem which has occurred after release. For example a major update of an application may have left it susceptible to attack from a virus. A vulnerability patch is an adaptation to the underlying application source code which would close this vulnerability. The problem with a vulnerability patch is usually it is in response to a known threat and often will shut down a service or some functionality offered by the application rather than completely correct the fault. It is designed to allow the end-users to have a stable application and not to damage the reputation of the application as a product, or of the product manufacturer/software development team.

Upgrading v Downgrading – as mentioned earlier a common problem is that the end-user will install a variety of applications they do not commonly, or rarely use and their presence on the system may take up system resources. The transfer of non-essential files to a storage device and from the local hard drive, for example will free up disk space. The operation of clean-up software such as Pifiform Ccleaner will remove unused cookies and temporary files which could be cluttering the hard drive. The action of completing a defragment of the local hard drive will increase performance on a mechanical disk (with SSD drives this is not necessary as access time should be the same across all RAM blocks).

By auditing the system and only installing applications and background services that are absolutely necessary the performance of the machine can be increased.

Upgrading a machine is often the first, not the last resort. If a machine is working well, there should be no need to upgrade it unless there is a significant demand caused by new software. For example the company may decide to keep a stock database using SQL server. They decide to dedicate one existing server as a SQL server and remove its other roles. However, the architecture required for SQL server is quite demanding for good performance, often with many cores, a 64-bit architecture, a minimum of 32 Gb and up to 2Tb of available RAM (depending on the size of the database and amount of people connecting to it) and also the (as an example) the relicensing of the server to Server 2012 R2 datacenter edition (from Standard).

Configuration backup – all of these changes could have a severe impact on the machine if the machine were to fail during the upgrade phase. Given that an upgrade will require further hardware and for the OS to also be upgraded, there is a likelihood of a degree of failure. To avoid this we can first take a backup of the existing configuration, is in a worst-case scenario the configuration can be re-loaded, or manually reconfigured. This may be as low-level as exporting the registry entries, or noting the settings of specific applications or server roles should the server have to be wiped, reinstalled 'from clean' at the updated state and then the configuration re-entered.

2.6

2.6 Given a scenario, configure a switch using proper features
- VLAN
    - Native VLAN/Default VLAN
    - VTP
- Spanning tree (802.1d)/rapid spanning tree (802.1w)
    - Flooding
    - Forwarding/blocking
    - Filtering
- Interface configuration
    - Trunking/802.1q
    - Tag vs untag VLANs
    - Port bonding (LACP)
    - Port mirroring (local vs remote)
    - Speed and duplexing
    - IP address assignment
    - VLAN assignment
- Default gateway
- PoE and PoE+ (802.3af, 802.3at)
- Switch management
    - User/passwords
    - AAA configuration
    - Console
    - Virtual terminals
    - In-band/Out-of-band management
- Managed vs unmanaged

In this next section we will consider Switch management, starting with switch configuration to meet the following actions:

Configuring a VLAN – The following steps detail how to configure a VLAN on a Cisco router:

```
Switch1>enable
Switch1#configure terminal
Switch1(config)#interface vlan 2
Switch1(config-if)#description Finance VLAN
Switch1(config-if)#exit
Switch1(config)#interface range FastEthernet 0/1 , FastEthernet 0/12
Switch1(config-if-range)#switchport mode access
Switch1(config-if-range)#switchport access vlan 2
```

In this demonstration we are enabling admin mode. We are then entering configuration mode as admin. We are requesting a VLAN (in this case it is the second VLAN to be built on this switch). Next, we enter a description for the VLAN. Exit is used to exit the configuration interface. Still within the configuration of the VLAN, we configure a range of ports (ports 1 to

12). Within this range we're specifying the access mode, assigning this range of ports to the VLAN.

Switch ports can connect to other switches. This cable connection will carry bulk data frames and is referred to as a 'trunk port'. The Ethernet standard **801.q** allows the data to be directed to the appropriate VLAN configured on the switch. Switches will share management and tagging information to direct traffic accordingly.

A native VLAN – any untagged data frames are sent to the VLAN on the switch marked as the 'native VLAN'. The native VLAN is the VLAN designed to handle untagged frames.

A default VLAN – this is VLAN 1 which is already in place on the switch. The default VLAN is mandatory and cannot be deleted. The default VLAN automatically has all ports assigned to it and acts as a management structure. If the switch is not connected to any other switch (as far as the VLAN is concerned) the ports themselves are considered 'untagged' as they are not connected to a VLAN group spanning several switches. By default a standalone switch sending frames out to its own ports would be considered to by sending 'untagged' data.

VLAN Trunking Protocol (VTP) – This is a Cisco-specific communications protocol used by managed switches to propagate VLAN information across the network. VTP information is sent to other switches through trunk ports as advertisements. With VTP configuration changes to VLANs are made to the first switch and then this information is propagated to all of the other switches which will reconfigure themselves with this change. This eliminates the need for the administrator to duplicate the configuration task on every switch.

One disadvantage of VTP is that bridging loops can still occur, so the process is not completely automated – the administrator will still have to check and to 'break' (reconfigure) any loops.

Spanning Tree (802.1d) – this protocol is used to combat routing loops on the network. This of course is also evident with switches (switching loops) as the data frame could be passed form switch to switch using the closest port and end up never reaching its destination. Repeating frames from the same source would cause congestion leading to a more serious network Denial of Service on the network if the switch can no longer handle the traffic.

STP would typically take up to one minute to achieve full convergence due to the time taken to send initial 'handshake' information between switches ('hello' traffic).

If an active link fails Spanning Tree Protocol records and makes use of alternative links which are also available and will switch traffic to this when the man (preferred) link is not available.

The switch ports are referred to as 'bridges' and each is given an identifier. The network topology from the switch to its immediate neighbours is used to create a 2D map of the network. The starting point of this topology is referred to as the 'Root Bridge'. The root bridge is the bridge (port / node) with the lowest ID. **The first key stage therefore is to determine our starting point – the root bridge.**

Each connection to another node is assessed and given a cost value. This may be calculated based on speed / bandwidth, availability, latency or other metrics. The path which has the shortest cost is the 'preferred path'. **The second key stage therefore is to determine the least cost path from the root bridge.**

Once the designated path has been established, all ports which form part of the path are designated paths. All other ports are blocked.

A switch port can have one of the following port states:

- **Blocking** – if the port were used and might cause a switching loop, it is blocked by STP. If other links fail in the case of an emergency blocked ports may still forward frames on to other neighbouring switches, but Blocking is used to stop routing loops from occurring.
- **Listening** – If a port has been opened from the blocking state it is said to be in 'listening' mode as may receive an instruction for it to return to Blocking state. In 'listening' mode it does not forward frames, or update the MAC table.
- **Learning** – at this stage the port cannot forward frames, but does learn the source addresses from incoming frames and adds the information to the switching database. The MAC address table is populated in this stage.
- **Forwarding** – this is normal operation for the port. STP can still send information to block the port.
- **Disabled** – although not carried out by the STP protocol a port may be manually disabled.

Rapid Spanning Tree (802.1w) is an enhancement of STP developed in 2001. It is able to send configuration data faster and to achieve stable state (convergence) in a much quicker time. RSTP is backwards compatible with STP. It is seen as a replacement for STP.

We now use the following new RTSP bridge port roles:

- **Root** - A forwarding port that is determined to be the best port to the root bridge.
- **Designated** - A forwarding port which is part of the path.
- **Alternate** - An alternate path to the root bridge.
- **Backup** - A redundant path to a segment where another bridge port already connects
- **Disabled** – as before, a port may be manually disabled.

RSTP switch port states:

- **Discarding** - No user data is sent over the port
- **Learning** - The port is not forwarding frames yet, but is populating its MAC-address-table
- **Forwarding** - The port is fully operational

> For further information on RSTP please refer to the Cisco page URL:
> http://www.cisco.com/c/en/us/support/docs/lan-switching/spanning-tree-protocol/24062-146.html

Flooding – if a switching loop occurs, the packet will be sent around the same path in a loop. Other frames will also be sent using part of the same affected path, so parts of the network will become congested. As the frames build up, traffic increases to a point where the switch can no longer handle further traffic on the port leading to the situation of a blocked port (the port is flooded with the same packets going around in a loop, stopping new packets from using the same port). In some switches this may even cause the switch to fail, or to reset. This can only be avoided by blocking the last leg of the loop which otherwise would return the frame back to the loop starting point. This is the purpose of STP. When the network realises that this circular loop is broken it will not send traffic that way but use an alternative, therefore avoiding the loop.

Bridge protocol data unit – this is the metric used to calculate the effective route between switches.

BPDU Filtering – this is the process of using the BPDU to filter the sending and receipt of BPDUs on a switch port. If a port is configured instead to 'PortFast' then BPDU data is not needed. Blocking the receipt of BPDU data on a switch port can effectively take the port out of the STP calculations.

Portfast – if a switch port is configured to PortFast, it is taken directly to Forwarding mode, bypassing the listening and learning states. This is usually used we care connecting directly to an end device.

Interface configuration - what follows is an example of how to set up configuration using Security Manager v4.1, taken from the Cisco support website at:

http://www.cisco.com/c/en/us/td/docs/security/security_management/cisco_security_manage r/security_manager/4-1/user/guide/CSMUserGuide_wrapper/rtintf.html

Defining Basic Router Interface Settings

When you define an interface or subinterface for a Cisco IOS router, you name it, specify how it is assigned an IP address, and optionally define other properties, such as the speed, maximum transmission unit (MTU), and the encapsulation type.

Note Basic interface settings are always local to the device on which they are configured. You cannot share this policy with other devices. You can, however, share advanced interface settings. For more information, see Advanced Interface Settings on Cisco IOS Routers.

Related Topics

- Deleting a Cisco IOS Router Interface

Step 1 In Device view, select Interfaces > Interfaces from the Policy selector.

The Router Interfaces Page is displayed.

Step 2 To add a new interface or subinterface, click the Add Row button to open the Create Router Interface dialog box.

To edit an existing interface or subinterface, select it in the Interfaces table, and then click the Edit Row button to open the Edit Router Interface dialog box. Refer to Create Router Interface Dialog Box for descriptions of the fields in these dialog boxes.

Step 3 Select Enabled to have Security Manager actively manage this interface or subinterface. If this option is deselected, the interface/subinterface definition is retained, but the interface/subinterface itself is disabled (or "shutdown").

Step 4 Choose Interface or Subinterface from the Type list.

Step 5 If you are creating an interface, enter a name for the interface. You can click Select to open a dialog box that will help you generate a standard name based on interface type and details about the interface's location, such as card, slot, and subinterface. For more information on using the dialog box to generate an interface name, see Interface Auto Name Generator Dialog Box.

Note When naming a BVI interface, use the bridge group number as the card number. Deployment will fail if you configure a BVI interface without configuring a corresponding bridge group.

Step 6 If you are creating a subinterface, provide the following:

a. Parent—Choose the parent interface for this subinterface.
b. Subinterface ID—Enter a number to identify the subinterface.

Note Security Manager configures serial subinterfaces as point-to-point, not multipoint.

Step 7 To specify a Layer Type, choose a Level 2 (data link) or Level 3 (network) option from this list.

Step 8 Choose a method of IP address assignment for this interface/subinterface, then provide additional information, as required:

- Static IP—Provide an IP Address and Subnet Mask.

- DHCP—No additional information is required.

- PPPoE—No additional information is required.

- Unnumbered—Provide the name of the interface from which an IP address is to be "borrowed."

Note Layer 2 interfaces do not support IP addresses.

Step 9 Define additional properties of the interface/subinterface:

- Use the Negotiation check box to enable and disable auto-negotiation for the interface.

Auto-negotiation detects the capabilities of remote devices and negotiates the best possible performance between the two devices. When Negotiation is enabled, the Fast Ethernet Duplex and Speed options are disabled.

Note Auto-negotiation is available only for Fast Ethernet and Gigabit Ethernet interfaces on ASR devices.

- Choose a transmission mode from the Duplex list. If you choose Auto, be sure the network device to which this interface is connected is set to automatically detect the transmission mode. (Auto is not available on ASRs; use auto-negotiation instead.)

Note   You must configure a fixed speed to define the duplex value. Tunnel and loopback interfaces do not support this setting.

- Choose a transmission speed from the Speed list. If you choose Auto, be sure the network device to which this interface is connected is set to automatically detect the transmission speed. (Auto is not available on ASRs; use auto-negotiation instead.)

- Enter the maximum transmission unit (MTU), which defines the largest packet size, in bytes, that this interface can support.

Note   Certain interface properties are set automatically, or are unavailable, depending on the interface type and the underlying port type. For example, the Speed options are available for Fast Ethernet and Gigabit Ethernet interfaces only.

Step 10   Choose an encapsulation method from the Encapsulation list:

- None—No encapsulation; no additional parameters are required.

- (Ethernet subinterfaces only) DOT1Q—VLAN encapsulation, as defined by the IEEE 802.1Q standard. Provide the following VLAN parameters for this subinterface:

– Enter a VLAN ID to associate with this subinterface.

Note   All VLAN IDs must be unique among all subinterfaces configured on the same physical interface.

– If you are defining the 802.1Q trunk interface, select Native VLAN.

Tip   To configure DOT1Q encapsulation on an Ethernet interface without associating a VLAN with the subinterface, enter the vlan-id dot1qcommand using CLI commands or FlexConfigs. See Understanding FlexConfig Policies and Policy Objects, page 7-1. Configuring VLANs on the main interface increases the number of VLANs that can be configured on the router.

- (Serial interfaces only) Frame Relay—IETF Frame Relay encapsulation. Provide a data-link connection identifier (DLCI) for the subinterface.

Note   Frame relay must be configured on the parent interface.

Note   IETF Frame Relay encapsulation provides interoperability between a Cisco IOS router and equipment from other vendors. To configure Cisco Frame Relay encapsulation, use CLI commands or FlexConfigs.

Step 11   (Optional) Enter a description of up to 1024 characters for the interface.

Step 12   Click OK to save the interface/subinterface definition and close the dialog box. The new interface is displayed on the Router Interfaces page. Subinterfaces are displayed beneath the parent interface.

Port trunking – this refers to the increase of bandwidth between two nodes (such as two main-line switches) in order to meet higher demands on the network at this point. This is done through a process referred to as 'link aggregation' which effectively means that two or more switch ports are associated to each other so that frames can be sent using one or more than one of these ports at the same time. The connections operate in parallel, allowing for multiple frames to be sent at the same time. This combined series of cables is referred to as a 'trunk line' because of the large volume of data it can handle.

In telecommunications, the term 'trunk' has historically referred to a large cable capable or transmitting a very high bandwidth and is used to pass bulk data. The term 'trunk call' was used to refer to a phone call routed through the trunk line. This would typically be a long-distance call between exchanges within the same country.

Port bonding (LACP) refers to the use of the **Link Aggregation Control Protocol** (a software protocol within the switch) is to bond switch ports together to form a 'trunk'. LACP can also auto-negotiate the bundling of links by sending LACP frames to another switch or other device which also support LACP. In this way neighbouring cables which currently are operating independently but are connected to the same node as the first port in the intended trunk can be added to the trunk when demand increases and then removed 'on the fly'.

When we consider the connection of multiple NICs on a server to perform link aggregation we refer to this as 'bonding'. In the Linux world, a bonding driver is used to connect NICs to form a bonding group. With Microsoft systems this process is referred to as 'NIC teaming' and again can be used to increase bandwidth through aggregation.

Port mirroring is the process of using an otherwise unused switch port to copy traffic from one other port, discretely without interrupting the flow of data on the selected port to be mirrored. This is used by Network managers to monitor traffic on the network by checking a sample of traffic on various key ports. Mirroring negates the need to break the link and to add in a monitoring PC as a 'man-in-the-middle' and so normal operation is not affected. The mirrored port can then be used by network analysis software such as a Network Intrusion Detection System, *Microsoft Network Monitor*, or *Wireshark* to examine precisely what traffic is being sent on the network as well as to diagnose errors or to debug data frames.

The above description describes the usual use of Port mirroring referred to as **Local Port Mirroring**. It is however possible to send the data frame to a remote location where the data can be debugged. This is referred to as **Remote Port Mirroring** and can be set up as detailed below:

(Taken from URL: http://kb.juniper.net/InfoCenter/index?page=content&id=KB10878)

Configuring Port Mirroring for Remote Traffic Analysis

To mirror traffic that is traversing interfaces or a VLAN on the switch to a VLAN for analysis from a remote location:

1. Configure a VLAN to carry the mirrored traffic. This VLAN is called remote-analyzer and given the ID of 999 by convention in this KB:

[edit]
user@switch# set vlans remote-analyzer vlan-id 999

2. Set the uplink module interface that is connected to the distribution switch to trunk mode and associate it with the remote-analyzer VLAN:

[edit]
user@switch# set interfaces ge-0/1/1 unit 0 family ethernet-switching port-mode trunk vlan members 999

3. Configure the analyzer. Choose a name and set the loss priority to high. Loss priority should always be set to high when configuring for remote port mirroring:

[edit ethernet-switching-options]
user@switch# set analyzer employee-monitor loss-priority high

Specify the traffic to be mirrored- in this example the packets entering ports ge-0/0/0 and ge–0/0/1:

[edit ethernet-switching-options]
user@switch#set analyzer employee-monitor input ingress interface ge-0/0/0.0
user@switch#set analyzer employee-monitor input ingress interface ge-0/0/1.0

Specify the remote-analyzer VLAN as the output for the analyzer:

[edit ethernet-switching-options]
user@switch#set analyzer employee-monitor output vlan 999

4. Optionally, you can specify a statistical sampling of the packets by setting a ratio:
[edit ethernet-switching-options]
user@switch# set analyzer employee-monitor ratio 200

When the ratio is set to 200, 1 out of every 200 packets is mirrored to the analyzer. You can use this to reduce the volume of mirrored traffic as a very high volume of mirrored traffic can be performance intensive for the switch.

Port speed – the speed of each switch port (measured in MBps) can be set individually, as follows:

```
SwitchA>en
SwitchA#config t
Enter configuration commands, one per line. End with CNTL/Z.
SwitchA(config)#int f0/1
SwitchA(config-if)#speed ?
  10    Force 10 Mbps operation
  100   Force 100 Mbps operation
  auto  Enable AUTO speed configuration
SwitchA(config-if)#speed 10
SwitchA(config-if)#
```

Port duplexing refers to the mode of the port – can it transmit Up, Down or both? On Cisco switches the duplexing options are **Full**, **Half** or **auto** (auto negotiate). If a duplex mismatch exists on a link, this may occur as one side of the cable (switch port A) is set to a different duplex mode to the other end (switch port B), causing a duplexing mismatch.

IP address assignment – the switch itself needs an IP address so that the administrator is able to access the management web dashboard across the network. The Switch also needs to know the default gateway so that it is able to communicate across the network higher than OSI layer 2.

Before remotely accessing the switch, for basic configuration you first need to connect to the switch using a console port connection and physically connect to the switch locally by connecting the switch directly to your laptop with the Terminal connection. On some switches there is an RS-232 serial port for terminal connection, whereas with others port 1 serves as the terminal port.

To set the management IP and default gateway please refer to the following instructions from the Cisco catalyst configuration guide located at URL:
http://www.cisco.com/c/en/us/td/docs/switches/lan/catalyst2950/software/release/12-1_19_ea1/configuration/guide/2950scg/swipaddr.html#wp1037806

Beginning in privileged EXEC mode, follow these steps to manually assign IP information to multiple switched virtual interfaces (SVIs) or ports:

	Command	Purpose
Step 1	configure terminal	Enter global configuration mode.
Step 2	interface vlan vlan-id	Enter interface configuration mode, and enter the VLAN to which the IP information is assigned. The range is 1 to 4094 when the enhanced software image is installed and 1 to 1001 when the standard software image is installed.
Step 3	ip address ip-address subnet-mask	Enter the IP address and subnet mask.
Step 4	exit	Return to global configuration mode.
Step 5	ip default-gateway ip-address	Enter the IP address of the next-hop router interface that is directly connected to the switch where a default gateway is being configured. The default gateway receives IP packets with unresolved destination IP addresses from the switch. Once the default gateway is configured, the switch has connectivity to the remote networks with which a host needs to communicate. Note When your switch is configured to route with IP, it does not need to have a default gateway set.
Step 6	end	Return to privileged EXEC mode.
Step 7	show running-config	Verify your entries.
Step 8	copy running-config startup-config	(Optional) Save your entries in the configuration file.

VLAN assignment – to assign a switch to be part of an existing VLAN, we need to change the management VLAN for the switch to be part of an existing cluster. This can be done as follows, as is detailed at the following URL:

http://www.cisco.com/c/en/us/td/docs/switches/lan/catalyst2950/software/release/12-1_9_ea1/configuration/guide/scg/swvlan.html#wp1290598

	Command	Purpose
Step 1	configure terminal	Enter global configuration mode.
Step 2	cluster management-vlan vlanid	Change the management VLAN for the cluster. This ends your Telnet session. Change the port through which you are connected to the switch to a port in the new management VLAN.
Step 3	show running-config	Verify

Power over Ethernet – this is used to supply power using switch ports and Ethernet cabling. This is commonly used as a strategy to power devices such as webcams or CCTV cameras directly from the switch negating the need for external power supplies. This is extremely helpful in situations where cabling to devices needs to be tamper-proof, or hidden from the elements (as CCTV cameras are used often externally).

Other devices which make use of PoE are PTZ cameras (motorised cameras with Pan, Tilt and Zoom motors built onto the camera – the camera is mounted onto a gyroscope gimbal and can be remotely controlled. These are often used within TV studios (e.g. 'Big Brother').). IP phones and remote Ethernet switches can also be PoE powered.

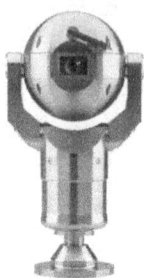

Figure 1 A 'Big Brother' style, gimbal PTZ camera

The cable can be used to provide both data and power to the end device. PoE allows us to transmit power over long lengths making this a good solution for CCTV and a better solution than USB which has a limited range.

Twisted pair cabling uses differentiated signalling which has the effect that power for not cause interference to the data being transmitted.

The switch would ace as the PSE (Power Source Equipment) and the end device to be powered is referred to as the Powered Device. The Powered device is able to request its power requirements and power can be increased to the requirement. With PoE (IEEE 802.3af-2003) 15.4 W (with an assured 12.94 W) is available for the device.

Power over Ethernet+ (IEEE 802.3at-2009) is an update to the PoE standard. It allows for up to 25.5 Watts, although all 4 pairs within the Ethernet cable cannot be used to supply power. A theoretical 51 Watts can possibly be transmitted.

Switch Management – As with other OSI network hardware, a switch is a rack-mounted device designed to be operated remotely by a network administrator. There are very few user accounts, usually one 'management' or 'admin' account and any changes to the system can only be done in 'admin' mode. By default, when a user access a switch you are not in 'admin' mode and there is a requirement to switch out of admin mode to normal mode to test your configurations.

Switches typically contain two firmware OSses (one as a backup) and it is possible to install firmware updates onto the reserve and then to switch to and from the reserve. This ensures that configuration information can be loaded from the old to the new OS quickly without the need to reconfigure the router from its default state every time the administrator wishes to upgrade the switch. The switches typical state is to service the network and to send data on, so this cannot be interrupted for maintenance without causing major disruption to the network. Configuration changes are often made at the switch port level, so that only one link at a time is affected (the rest of the switch operates as normal).

Examples earlier in this chapter use the concept of switching into 'manage' or 'admin' mode before changes can be made, also focussing the configuration onto the specific aspect of the switch which will be changed.

The admin account will have a default password set 'at the factory'. It is highly recommended that this is changed and that a different password for the admin account and normal user logon account is used. This can often be changed through the web management portal.

Switches use the **AAA** security principle – Authentication, Authorisation and Auditing. In this fashion a user is scoped to the extent to which they can make changes to the system, once their credentials have been established. All changes are logged so that all staff who can access the log can see who made the change and when this occurred.

Console view is the primary means of connecting to a switch. In the initial configuration it is necessary to connect directly to the switch from a laptop using a terminal cable (or patch cable, depending on the type of switch). Here, using a terminal window we can access, authenticate and provide basic configuration settings for the device. Once set, we can access the device remotely through the web dashboard.

Virtual terminals – a virtual terminal (or virtual console) is a text-based screen displayed to give configuration and status messages when the Operating System is booting. On a Linux system this is referred to as 'stage 1 boot'. A virtual terminal forms one of many terminals and each can be configured to display different information. On the Linux system we can alternate between the different graphical workspaces within **X window** and each of these is referred to as a **virtual console**. Setting the virtual console in use focusses the Operating system to send keyboard data to the selected terminal, also to receive output from this terminal. It is worth noting that some high-level switches which are integrated can work with a terminal emulator (a console window) to provide different displays for each switch which form part of a cluster. When we connect to a terminal session through Telnet or PuTTY we can specify which virtual terminal we wish to see.

In-band management – this refers to the management of the local device, where data flow for managing the device uses OS resources which are part of the device itself.

Out-of-band management – this refers to the management of a remote device where data flow for managing, viewing and controlling the remote device is separated from the data flow used by normal operations. For example, a dedicated line may be set up to allow remote access to a switch, rather than 'piggy-backing' remote management through the normal switch ports used for internal network traffic. This way normal operations are not hampered by the additional remote management traffic.

Managed v unmanaged switches – there is a degree of confusion over the terms 'managed' and 'unmanaged' switch as some of the protocols used on unmanaged switches operate on layer 3 of the OSI stack. Traditionally an unmanaged switch was a simple device capable of automatically self-configuring at layer 2 of the OSI model and required no configuration. It has a built in MAC database and updated switch port information based on communications frames.

Conversely, a managed switch has to be managed – there is a user account, an administrator account and a portal allowing access to the device by the use of an IP address. The Managed switch itself needs to know the Default Gateway of the subnet in order to communicate with other switches which may form part of a cluster. As the switch has an Operating System and communicates using the IP information, therefore at the layer 3 stack (although IP packets are not strictly sent – this is the job of a router) it is said to be a 'managed device'.

2.7

2.7 Install and configure wireless LAN infrastructure and implement the appropriate technologies in support of wireless capable devices
- Small office/home office wireless router
- Wireless access points
  - Device density
  - Roaming
  - Wireless controllers
    - VLAN pooling
    - LWAPP
- Wireless bridge
- Site surveys
  - Heat maps
- Frequencies
  - 2.4 Ghz
  - 5.0 Ghz
- Channels
- Goodput
- Connection types
  - 802.11a-ht
  - 802.11g-ht
- Antenna placement
- Antenna types
  - Omnidirectional
  - Unidirectional
- MIMO/MUMIMO
- Signal strength
  - Coverage
  - Differences between device antennas

- SSID broadcast
- Topologies
  - Adhoc
  - Mesh
  - Infrastructure
- Mobile devices
  - Cell phones
  - Laptops
  - Tablets
  - Gaming devices
  - Media devices

SOHO router – this is a multifunction device which contains the following components are services: built-in ADSL modem (or connection to one) Wi-Fi access point, router, DHCP server, firewall, demilitarised zone. These devices are typically provided by Internet Service Providers to be a 'catch-all' solution for the home user. Home devices can connect through the (usually up to) 5 Ethernet ports available and are typically used to connect to a Satellite box for interactive services, a HDTV for interactive services, home PCs, printers and gaming consoles. Laptops can also connect through a wired connection, but it is more common to see the Wi-Fi connectivity be used for smartphones and laptops.

The router has a management console, usually based on IP address 192.168.1.254 This has a login password which can be changed, will measure uptime and is also store the ADSL connection information. A firewall can block standard ports, or be used to allow specific ports to be used to create a 'tunnel', enabling a port to be used specifically by a commonly known application or product (e.g. Xbox, or Steam account for internet play). The rudimentary DHCP server can provide all connecting devices with a leased IP address, negating the need for manual IP configuration. The Wi-Fi access point will have been set up at the factory with the MAC address of the Wi-Fi NIC, default SSID and a password. Both are printed on a detachable label which clips onto the reverse of the device and can be used to pair devices for Wi-Fi connectivity.

A BT HomeHub v5 front and rear

Wireless Access Points (WAP) – as discussed in the previous section, a WAP is a device which will broadcast a radio signal within the local area, usually limited from 10 to 100 metres depending on the protocol used and the transmission power. They are a small box with an omnidirectional antenna, so broadcast a circular range from the base station. Transmission occurs on a defined channel (1 to 16 can be used) and this channel has to be set in advance. The WAP can be configured to broadcast or to hide the SSID (the Station packet ID) – once other end devices have been configured to connect to the WAP the SSID can be hidden to stop any unwanted neighbours from finding and connecting to your network.

Wireless NICs (known as a **Wireless Controller**) are typically in-built into end devices. They can work in ad-hoc mode (to make a direct connection to another end device for the purpose of a simple file transfer and therefore creating a small Personal Area Network), or in Infrastructure mode where authentication and security are greatly improved. End-devices can also use 'Wireless Access Point Traversal' in order to hop to the strongest signal or closest WAP.

Wireless Access Point Device density – this refers to the number of connecting devices (or rather packet sessions) a WAP can handle at any one time.

Roaming is the ability for an end device to remain connected across the network. If the connection with the Wireless Access Point becomes weak the device will switch sending packets to another supporting Wireless Access Point with a stringer signal. Packets are sent using the same end device IP address, but the receiving station must communicate across the network to pick up additional information about the (effectively) new device (from the perspective of the Wireless Access Point). Roaming is for the end user a seamless transition from one wireless station to another.

VLAN pooling – a VLAN pool is a collection of VLANs, each with its own subnet. It allows us to have a large number of users whilst also keeping the amount of subnets/broadcast domains.

Lightweight Access Point Protocol (LWAPP) is the name of the protocol used to control several Wireless Access Points at once. As well as sending configuration information to several WAPs we can also monitor traffic on specific WAPs. LWAPP is implemented on a central server and can manipulate and monitor several Wireless Access Points at the same time. LWAPP works on OSI layers 2, 3 and 4.

Wireless bridge – this device is used to extend the physical network by passing wireless frames on to a further access point. The bridge itself does not change the wireless frame but retransmits it onto a neighbouring Access Point. It is used to forward data onto a WAP which is out of range from the host Wireless Access Point alone (e.g. to reach a neighbouring building), thereby extending the wireless network.

Site surveys are the process of performing an audit of the relative distances and power strengths for each Wireless Access Point The range of each WAP is mapped onto a site floor plan to determine where overlaps occur, also to ensure that there are no areas within the building where there is no access to the network. Conversely, WAP transmission power can be reduced to ensure that there is no 'signal bleed' – that the range does not extend beyond the boundaries of the building leaving the network prone to outside attack through 'War Driving'.

A 'heat map' is a visual representation of the amount of traffic per channel, also can be set to show the WAP data density and this data can be mapped to the 'floor plan' so that we can determine physical areas of high demand where further wireless acess points could reduce the load on the network. The aim is to use the heat map to remove areas of congestion, ensuring that all requesting users can connect to the network and stay connected whilst they roam throughout the building.

There are two key frequencies used by common wireless protocols:

- **802.11a** - used from 1999, this earliest protocol transmits with a peak data rate of 54Mb/s using **5GHz**. It was highly susceptible to signal interference from walls.
- **802.11b** – this early protocol can transmit longer distances than 'a' and is less susceptible to signal interference from walls or objects. Its peak data rate is slower at 11Mb/s. It transmits at **2.4 GHz**.
- **802.11g** – more recently 'g' has supposed 'b' as the main wireless protocol for public use. It can transmit long distances and provide the stability benefits of 'b' whilst providing peak data rates of 54 Mb/s. 'g' uses the **2.4 GHz** band.
- **802.11n** – this makes use of a Multiple Channel system (usualy 2 but can be up to 4 antenna within the station). It can transmit on either the **2.4 or 5 GHz** bands offering peak data rates of 600 Mb/s.

Channels – a wireless channel is a specific range used for transmission. The channel is set on the WAP and devices will determine the best channel to use (although some end device wireless NICs allow the user to also set the channel which will be used). The range is 22MHz, so is quite a narrow band. The bands are numbered and each overlap slightly. Channel centre frequencies in the 2.4 GHz range start with channel 1's centre frequency at 2.412 GHz, up to channel 14 at 2.484 GHz.

Goodput – wireless packets are considered 'good' if they can be used by the end device (the system). A weak packet may mean that not all of the information is received, equally interference or crosstalk may affect the transmission, leading to the packet having to be dropped and sent again by the sending WAP. Goodput is the throughput (at Application level of the OSI model). It is a measurement of the quality of data transmission based on the efficacy of the data transfer (in that it can be used by the system).

If we were transferring a file with high goodput, there would be no need to resend corrupt data packets, so file transmission speed will be only as long as would be expected through the confines of the hardware and protocols used. We sometimes express the goodput as a percentage of the best possible time taken to transfer the file divided by actual time taken to transfer the file. Typically however Goodput is represented as a ratio between the delivered amount of information and the total delivery time. We are aiming for the ratio to be low, or as close to 1:1 as possible.

802.11a-ht. This refers to a wireless adapter with the Physical Type referred to as High Throughput (high successful data delivery) and using the 802.11a protocol.

802.11g-ht. This refers to a wireless adapter with the Physical Type referred to as High Throughput (high successful data delivery) and using the 802.11g protocol.

Antenna placement is very important when configuring the network as each WAP needs to be able to provide the greatest range possible with the transmission power selected. An antenna, as with an FM radio is a metal pole raised from the WAP allowing airborne transmission of the radio wave. It also is able to receive other radio transmissions and to pass these to the WAP for processing.

When attempting to connect a trunk line between two Wireless Access Points, the antenna has to be placed so that both antenna are transmitting within each other's range. A Unidirectional (Yogi) antenna is used to direct the signal to the receiving WAP station.

An **Omnidirectional** antenna provides an equal range in every direction.

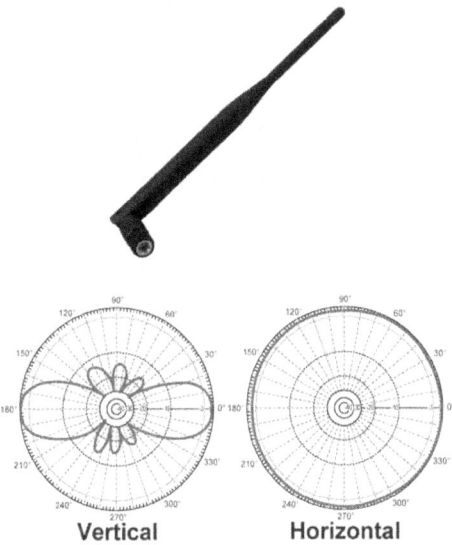

Vertical   Horizontal

An omnidirectional antenna. Range diagram of the antenna.

A **Unidirectional** antenna provides a highly focussed arc, able to achieve slightly longer distances, but generates the signal in a specific location (as with a microphone).

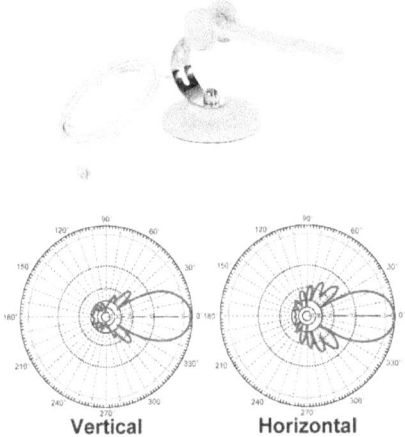

Vertical   Horizontal

An omnidirectional antenna. Range diagram of the antenna.

MIMO stands for **Multiple-input and Multiple-output**. Multiple antennae work as a group to transmit and receive data packets at the same time. There are three functions for MIMO:

Precoding – the same signal is transmitted from each of the antennae in such a way that the signal power is maximised as much as is possible at the input receiver. This is referred to as beamforming and can improve signal gain.

Spatial Multiplexing is the technique whereby the high-rate signal is split into multiple lower-rate streams and each stream is transmitted from a different transmit antenna in the same frequency channel. As these data signals have been sent from antenna which are slightly spatially different, the input receiver will be able to separate the streams into multiple separate channels. This allows us to be able to send more data in areas of higher signal-to-noise ratio (e.g. lots of interference) and increase the chance of getting readable data.

Diversity coding is a special technique used where there is no channel knowledge at the transmitter. It is able to work alongside the other two elements. The signal is mathematically augmented with a signal processing coding technique and the augmented signal is sent on the additional antennae. The receiver is able to use the difference between the 'clean' and the augmented signals to determine and to separate data from background noise.

Multi-User MIMO uses a suite of technologies to send the signal from an array of different independent antennae and access points. MU-MIMO uses an extended version of the space-division multiple access algorithm to allow for separate signals to be combined and sent within the same radio band.

MU-MIMO - several streams communicating at the same time

Signal strength is a measurement of radio transmission in dbm (decibels per metre). It is usually displayed to the end user as a percentage, or using 5 'bars' to grade the signal. The signal represents the strength to a specific connected endpoint (e.g from the laptop through several wireless bridges and to a wireless router). The 'strength' is quite a general measurement and does not take into account the signalling technologies or algorithms used, only is a measure of strength and of dropped packets. Usually when the 'bar' rating drops to 2, wireless starts to become intermittent as dropped packets are quite frequent, so file transfer time will slow as 'goodput' quality reduces.

Coverage – as mentioned earlier this is the area covered by the Wireless Access Point where a usable connection can be made.

SSID broadcast – as discussed earlier in the section, the SSID is required to be able to establish the connection to the end device. The SSID is broadcast from the wireless router to determine which router you wish to connect to. The SSID name can be changed by the network administrator.

> *Exam tip:* On its own disabling the SSID will not make your wireless network completely secure. It is however one of the steps one should take to make the network more secure as it can deter war driving, or unsolicited connections from neighbours. If you have the option to also suggest WPA2 and WEP, or are on an enterprise network and have a certificate system in place then these are much better solutions to choose.
>
> A **MAC Access Control List** is also a good idea as with this solution only wireless cards with a MAC address present on the list will be accepted by the router. However, if the MAC address of an existing device can be obtained by a hacker, then it is possible to adjust their own MAC address to 'spoof' a 'known good', so again on its own this is not a complete solution.

Three wireless topologies are currently in use:

Ad-hoc – as discussed earlier, the casual direct connection of two peers (end devices) is considered an ad-hoc network. No or little security is in place to allow the users to communicate with each other as the users would have given their consent (or in the case of a Bluetooth connection have used a shared PIN code).

An ad-hoc network

A **Mesh** is a mixture of different connected networks, usually all Infrastructure but may share trunk lines such as metropolitan radio masts to widen the network. It is likely that the Internet in some form and the provision of this through various service providers will form a part of a Mesh solution.

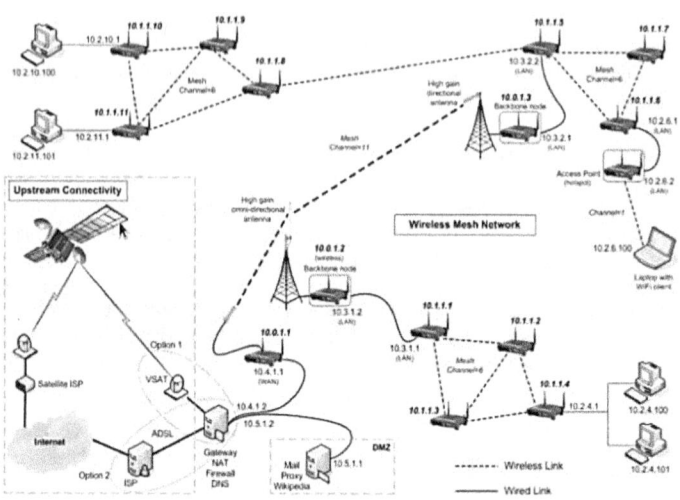

A sample mesh network (cited from Wikipedia)

Infrastructure – This mode requires a more complex security system using all layers of the OSI model. Here, we use encryption of the packet, authentication of the computer and user and integration with Active Directory and network services.

Mobile Devices also have their own built-in wireless transmitter and and perform the same functions by connecting across the wireless network. They differ more on the Application layer in how the network is used:

Cell phones – these are used to access the internet, GPS data to track movements or to find your way to where you are travelling to, use of Apps such as FourSquare to log and report your current location to other internet users, to send SMS text messages, emails and also to make telephone calls (over VoIP or satellite). They are also commonly used for PAN networks ad-hoc) for file sharing with friends.

Laptops can now provide all of the features of standard PCs and quite often are as powerful as office PCs. They are mobile and can allow connectivity to different networks at different locations. They are designed for infrastructure access.

Tablets work on the same principle as both cell phones and laptops. As with Cell phones most tablets on the market today use the Android OS and perform much the same functions as a cell phone. They are a versatile device, but are often used more for gaming, also for customers to make selections. For example restaurants have now dispensed with the old-fashioned pen and notepad to instead use a tablet, or cell phone connected to an in-store app to add the meal requests from each table direct to a database and from here immediately to the kitchen. Deciphering shorthand scribbles is now a thing of the past!

Gaming devices tend to be dedicated platforms such as the Xbox, Wii or even PC console. They are often customised to ensure that they perform well for gaming, so often have high-end processing capabilities and response times, particularly with the use of GPU graphics processing, by using high-end graphics cards. As internet games are currently very popular a dedicated tunnel through the existing internet connection needs to be established – modern SOHO routers now have the ability to provide a hole in the firewall for gaming tunnels. In order that gameplay is not affected, the network connection needs to provide realtime responses across the network. The gaming platform also often uses an IRC (Internet Relay Communication) messaging / chat facility with other gamers so interactivity is not only within the gaming world but also within the real world.

A **media device** such as a media server is used to store home movie files, audio and images for use on all of the devices within the SOHO network. It used to be the case that a wired connection was needed, but the development of faster data transmissions is comparable to the resolution which can be displayed across the local internal network wirelessly. Earlier 802.11b networks did not have the throughput to provide High-Definition quality however later wireless systems are able to support this. Media streaming is also now extremely popular – anyone can set themselves up as their own radio station from the comfort of their own home with simply a PC and access to the internet. It is worth mentioning that media end devices (e.g. iPods) and smartphones now support Near Field communication, so you are now able to download an album within a matter of seconds from the media server simply by walking past it.

Domain 3
Network Security

In this domain we will consider techniques to strengthen the security of the network, as well as common threats and vulnerabilities found on a network and how to combat them. From a management perspective we will consider risk concepts and how risk can be mitigated by introducing further supporting equipment and procedures. We will then compare different types of network vulnerabilities and threats to the network (e.g. attacks). Given specific scenarios we will consider how to harden the network, protecting it further from attack. We will then consider the use of physical security controls, we will consider factors pertaining to the use of a firewall and will look at restricting use by the implementation of an access control model. Finally we will consider forensic controls and techniques.

This section works intimately with the CompTIA Security+ exam. Content for the Security+ exam would be relevant as further reading. As a starting point I recommend the Professor Messer video series on Security+ to accompany this chapter.

http://www.professormesser.com/security-plus/sy0-401/sy0-401-course-index/

3.1

3.1 Compare and contrast risk related concepts
- Disaster recovery
- Business continuity
- Battery backups/UPS
- First responders
- Data breach
- End user awareness and training
- Single point of failure
    - Critical nodes
    - Critical assets
    - Redundancy
- Adherence to standards and policies
- Vulnerability scanning
- Penetration testing

Risk is a measurement of the likelihood that an event might occur. A high-risk action will be quite likely to occur. When we talk about actions being dangerous, or high-risk we are referring to the impact it will have on the person as well as the extent of failure (e.g. performing hardware maintenance with electrical equipment while the machine is still powered is high risk because of the likelihood of electric shock to the operator and damage to the components.) We therefore take action to minimise, or 'mitigate' the risk so that the action can be performed safely. In the above example, power would be turned off, the machine gracefully shut down, backups of data taken, the machine removed to a suitable workbench, ESD equipment used, the machine isolated from the network and the correct tools used to work on the machine. A standby machine is put into effect, so that continuity is present on the network – services offered by the original machine can still be offered by the 'failed over' or 'backup' machine.

Disaster recovery – this refers to specific actions which can be taken to recover from a disaster. This will include the restoration of data from backups, the introduction of failover hard drives (a powered hard drive already in a rack ready to take over if another disk in the rack should fail), the introduction of a fault tolerance strategy, the inclusion of backup power solutions to ensure high-availability.

Disaster recovery became an important aspect of data control and management in the 1970s as mainframe computers were in fact one very costly computer system – all data input was carried out on punch card entry machines (teletype typewriters) and data storage was critical. If the mainframe was inoperable, work would have to stop until the problem was resolved. This was inefficient and led to the inclusion of multiple parallel systems, then again focus returned to centralisation of resources. As this was the case we needed 'backup' or 'failover' solutions to be ready to automatically sense when a service was not being offered. Focus has been primarily around backup and failover of the Active Directory database by the inclusion of a Backup Domain Controller, however we are now looking to private or hybrid cloud solutions negating the need to focus on complete network replacement in the event of a disaster.

Disaster recovery procedures are agreed upon in advance of the disaster (the incident) and are documented by corporate policy so that every member of staff knows the extent to which they are responsible to support in a disaster situation. For example, it may be the responsibility of end user staff to ensure that they save their documents to the network share (e.g. a 'H:' home folder will re-route any document saved to the 'my documents' folder instead to their own respective folder on the network share. Files are stored centrally and caught in the backup solution, negating the need to back up individual local machines.) Moreover, end-users may be restricted by Active Directory policy as well as by corporate policy documentation from saving any files locally.

Starting with site definitions:

Hot site – a separate building with machinery already wired in simply waiting for users to arrive is in place. If the main building is unusable (e.g. through flood, fire, earthquake or other disaster) the staff can be taken to another nearby building. Data can be loaded from recent backups, or is already available within a private cloud so the simple action of arrival and authentication is all that is needed. Suspected downtime will be considerably low – perhaps only a matter of hours as the majority of network tasks have already been performed. The company have been leasing this second building as a 'ready to go' backup for some time.

Hot sites are commonplace – companies will buy into contracts to make use of business space at business development centres and pay for the rooms on a lease at reduced price. This provides peace of mind that in the event of a disaster the workforce can simply relocate.

In the case of a college, there may be a problem with a classroom, so the class relocates to another assigned classroom also domain-joined. Learners can log-in to their same domain account from the alternative room and get virtually the same experience. This could be considered a 'hot site' in its most basic form.

Warm site – similar to the above, but key specific services, machinery and configuration will have to be done before the site is ready. Often this will involve setting up the basic network, or arriving to a site which has key components already installed, but further work is needed, particularly if specialised machines or systems need to be moved into place. For example, a copy of the main network Domain Controller is present, but a SQL database server may need to be initialised and made active replacing the one at the disaster site before other systems dependent on it (e.g. Dynamics CRM) could be used. Downtime will be in the range of days rather than hours as more complex systems will need to be restored from backups and end-user workstations fitted. Again, the site is leased by the company at reduced cost.

Cold site – this refers to an empty site. The site is leased on a long-term contract, but there is considerable downtime as support staff will need to set up new, or move existing equipment from the disaster site (if this is possible), or to make ready replacement servers and put in place the entire network infrastructure, restore data form backups and install applications. The downtime is often measured in days or weeks. Most office buildings deliberately leave floors empty but in reality these floors have been bought for contingency purposes on a long-term lease for use as a cold site. Network 'plenum' cables from sockets through to the patch panels are usually already in place – only the company-specific equipment is missing.

Business continuity refers to procedures and secondary systems in place to be used to 'fail over' to in the event of an incident. Business continuity planning is the process of documenting, requesting, purchasing and maintaining these secondary systems which will be available the moment a problem occurs. In the case of a power failure two items of equipment are vital for continuity:

An **Uninterruptible Power Supply (UPS box)** is a rechargeable array of batteries and a DC/AC inverter capable of providing Ac power to a server for a few minutes, or with some even up to an hour. The metric we use with UPS is the kWh – a typical server may need 500 – 800 Watts of power and the battery array will be able to keep supplying power for a limited amount of time.

The UPS batteries are rechargeable and all mains power is passed through the recharging unit, therefore a degree of line conditioning is taking place. In the event of a blackout and mains power stops, the batteries will still supply AC power through the built-in inverter giving the Network Administrator sufficient time to save any work and to shut down the server gracefully.

When a UPS box is missing AC power and if powering a device, an alarm beep will sound to alert the Network Administrator of the problem. Some advanced boxes can even send an SMS text directly to the Network team to alert them of the problem. The UPS also has a USB or serial data cable 'tether' to the server, reporting back the charge state of the battery array and advising how long the UPS box will be able to sustain the server in the event of power loss.

In the event of a long-term loss of power (e.g. several hours), to maintain availability of power and therefore service to the network a generator is required. **Generators** are often diesel or petrol powered and will supply a lifeline of AC power to equipment, but are a temporary solution. Generators need to be placed outdoors and a feed cable is run into the building.

The **First Responder** is the first person to reach the incident. In IT terms, they will assess the damage and consider what courses of action can be taken to make safe the environment. There may be the need for a forensic examination of the affected incident area (e.g. in the case of an explosion, or fire) and priority must be given to saving lives before retrieval of data. In medical terms, the First Responder is a medically trained member of staff capable of giving medical help in the event of an emergency. Each team will have a member of the department who is trained in basic First Aid in the Workplace, however may not be suitably qualified to handle a first response situation. They may be trained in basic first aid and cardio-pulmonary resuscitation, but their role is to assess the situation, make the area safe if they possibly can and to treat any casualties until more qualified help arrives.

As part of the training certified first responders have a 'duty to act'. All emergency workers such as Police Officers, firefighters and ambulance staff are trained 'certified First Responders'. Wikipedia details Certified First Responder training as dealing with the following areas – "First responder courses cover the human body, lifting and moving patients, legal and ethical issues, patient assessment, medical and trauma emergencies, cardiopulmonary resuscitation (CPR), automated external defibrillator usage, oxygen administration, suctioning and airway adjuncts, spinal and bone fracture immobilization, and EMS operations."

This is in variance with 'first responders' in the case of an IT incident who may simply be the closest person to the event at the time. This person may be required as part of a detailed investigation to give a detailed testimony of events leading up to the incident and also an eyewitness account of the incident site, providing technical details of faults noticed which may be relevant, or may have led up to the incident.

Data breach – this refers to the breach of security surrounding the protection of corporate data. A breach may occur if the data falls into the hands of people outside the company, such as a person working for a rival company, the press, or to the public. For corporate sensitive information a breach may occur whilst still internal to the company by a member of staff without the sufficient clearance level viewing data which they are not supposed to see.

Breaches may be intentional (e.g. for personal gain) or unintentional (a memory stick unintentionally left on a train). Key points here are that the data may be viewed, copied, transmitted, stolen (whether used by the thief or not) and that the thief is unauthorised to carry out the act.

A **'black hat' hacker** is a person who maliciously and deliberately attempts to and succeeds in breaking through corporate security with a view to obtaining, or at least reading sensitive corporate data.

End user awareness and training – most incidents can be avoided through effective training. To this end the end user must be vigilant to ensure that they adhere to company policy, particularly when data security is concerned. It is human nature to find 'short cuts' but these may have unintended consequences. As an example, an end user is working on corporate sensitive data. They plan to continue working on the document at home but do not have a pen drive to hand. Company policy allows working on documents at home, however the user decides, due to the absence of a pen drive, to email the document to themselves. However as they cannot access their work email at home via a corporate web portal or an email client, they decide instead to use a public web-based email service (e.g. Hotmail / Outlook, Yahoo, AOL or Google mail). This means that a corporate-sensitive document has been uploaded, without encryption and is being stored in an environment unmanaged by the company and therefore outside of their control. If the service providers' email accounts are 'hacked' (or even if another member of the family viewed the data whilst the member of staff was working on it at home) they may gain sensitive information that they are not privy to.

End user training is not always a formal process, although there are a number of courses which will educate staff of the dangers inherent in these actions. However end users should be encouraged to support each other – to watch for unauthorised staff on-site, to feel confident enough to be able to challenge any visitors not wearing an ID badge, to challenge any contractors or visitors who are near to company sensitive information, to correctly support visitors attempting to obtain access to the network by checking first with the IT department that they should indeed have access.

Other low-level actions and standard policies may include:

- Locking the PC before you move away to make a cup of tea, or to use the restroom.
- Use a glare guard and keep your monitor turned away from open spaces so that other people cannot easily see what you are reading.
- Encrypt documenting using company-provided certificate-based encryption, or Bitlocker.
- Maintaining a complex, strong password with at least one character, one capital letter, over 8 characters in length and one symbol.
- Not to use default passwords.
- As a network administrator do not log in as the Domain Administrator but instead use a restricted network user account. For actions requiring administrator approval, use the 'Open As...' or 'Run As...' option and allow the one application elevated privileges. This also reduces the attack surface area should your system be compromised by a virus.
- On a corporate network, set User Account Control security to 'High'. The user will be prompted before any key system changes can occur.
- Disable or delete the guest account on an enterprise network as guest access will have the same level of privilege as a user account, but will be difficult to audit. Any visitors or contractors should receive their own account connected to a highly restricted Active Directory group.
- Avoid every using the Enterprise Administrator account unless you (the Network Manager) are trying to create a trust between two domains.

- Avoid use of the root account on Linux / UNIX systems unless performing major changes to the system. Run commands with elevated privileges with the SUDO command.

Single point of failure – where only one device or system is providing a service on the network we refer to this as a single point of failure because if the device were to fail there is no backup or 'failover' strategy in place. The service will therefore not exist on the network. This is undesirable, therefore alternate routes and devices are added to the network not only to reduce load, but also to provide a secondary provision of the service. An example would be two switches working as a cluster – if one fails the other is configured to continue to offer the same routes across the network. Another example may be a Backup Domain Controller which will take over if the Primary Domain Controller were to fail, offering Active Directory authentication and rule-based control to the network.

Critical node – this refers to a unique device on the network offering a specific service not emulated by any other device on the network. If the device fails, the service (or data provided by this node) will not be available by the system.

Critical asset – this refers to key components on the network which if unavailable, damaged and inoperable, would cause the system as a whole to be severely impacted, or perhaps even unusable, affecting production and normal operations. The failure of a DNS server would be an example of this as this would negate the ability to access other computers on the network by their given Fully Qualified Domain Name. A more severe problem would be the failure of the Domain Controller which (if configured to disallow local logins of cached credentials) would disable any client from logging into their workstation, or to access other network-based resources which will require authentication. The critical asset is often an expensive item (e.g. a main server).

Redundancy refers to the presence of another duplicate service, or of a critical component on the network (e.g. In the above example the presence of a DNS server cluster made up of several DNS servers, also of a Backup Domain Controller would help to continue the availability of the service to the network.)

Adherence to standards and policies – through end-user training, management analysis of network activities and the highlighting of errors, or breaches is an active process requiring compliance by the end user to follow standards which have been produced to ensure the integrity of the corporate network. Disciplinary procedures may be followed, dismissal, fines, or legal action may be put in place for workers who have not adhered to policy and by so doing caused harm. In order for the workforce to follow the standards, they are required to read and to acknowledge that they have understood them. With Standing Operating Procedures, the worker / end user is required to read and adopt practices detailed in the document. Worker operations will be assessed by management in line with these processes to ensure consistency. Conversely policy should not be designed to be overly complex but efficient, practical and sensible explaining why each process should be followed in the prescribed manner.

Vulnerability scanning is the process of hardening the network as a whole, also by hardening key systems by checking for known flaws in the current network. It is an active process of looking for key areas where a hacker may obtain access to, or limit the operation of a system. Vulnerability scanning uses specialist software to attempt to attack the network and to report on any successful breaches in network security. It can be both hard and soft: vulnerability scanning can also involve testing the security consciousness of the workforce by involving shoulder-surfing, obtaining the confidence of employees, socially engineering people to obtain passwords or information about the network structure, or of corporate information.

For 'hard' testing, software used can be categorised as follows:

- *Microsoft Baseline Security Analyser* can be used to perform sweep of the network for weak passwords, PCs which have not been updated for a time, unsecure databases on the network, virus software not updated, machines in quarantine and virus scans not completed for some time. As an extension to this *Intune* can be used to remotely report on and to remediate these machines, as can *System Center*.
- A Port scanner is an application which will report on all uncommon, open firewall ports (e.g. *Nmap*).
- *Nessus* is a common network vulnerability tester which will perform a number of network analysis and attacks to determine further hardening actions which can be performed.
- Web applications may not be secured – these can be hardened by the addition of token, or session-based security such as to interlink the IIS server's hosted sites to Active Directory. *Nikto* is a common application capable of checking the security of web servers.
- *Scuba* is a common database scanner which will determine if a database is encrypted, password protected and also the extent to which it is secure across the network (e.g. HTTPS links to the database).
- To check host machines specifically, *Ovaldi* is a common application which will determine if further action needs to be taken.

There are other checking applications which are used, often performing specific functions (e.g. to check for vulnerability to the Heartbleed bug).

Other collections of virus code are available as 'exploitation software packages' such as the *Metasploit* suite. These are not intended for use on the network 'at large', rather an image of the workstation is taken and tested in a secure, isolated environment.

The above software is available to both White Hat (staff deliberately looking for security flaws in the network with a view to reporting these and remediating the problem) and Black Hat (malicious hackers attempting to exploit the network with a view to either damaging it, or performing an illegal act)

Penetration testing is the process of checking the security of the network by discovering exploits and testing the extent to which the exploit will affect the network.

> NB: The Professor Messer Security+ course features several network security flaws and how penetration testing software such as Cain and Abel, or the Metasploit framework can be used.

3.2

3.2 Compare and contrast common network vulnerabilities and threats
- Attacks/threats
  - Denial of service
    - Distributed DoS
      - Botnet
      - Traffic spike
      - Coordinated attack
    - Reflective/amplified
      - DNS
      - NTP
      - Smurfing
    - Friendly/unintentional DoS
    - Physical attack
      - Permanent DoS
  - ARP cache poisoning
  - Packet/protocol abuse
  - Spoofing
  - Wireless
    - Evil twin
    - Rogue AP
    - War driving
    - War chalking
    - Bluejacking
    - Bluesnarfing
    - WPA/WEP/WPS attacks
  - Brute force
  - Session hijacking
  - Social engineering
  - Man-in-the-middle
  - VLAN hopping
- Compromised system
- Effect of malware on the network
- Insider threat/malicious employee
  - Zero day attacks
- Vulnerabilities
  - Unnecessary running services
  - Open ports
  - Unpatched/legacy systems
  - Unencrypted channels
  - Clear text credentials
  - Unsecure protocols
    - TELNET
    - HTTP
    - SLIP
    - FTP
    - TFTP
    - SNMPv1 and SNMPv2
  - TEMPEST/RF emanation

In this section we will consider a variety of network attacks and explain how each of these will impact on the network.

An **'attack'** (also referred to as a 'threat') refers to the possibility of attack, not that an attack is taking place presently. It refers to a security vulnerability which may be exploited in the future.

A **Denial of Service** (DoS) describes a service on the network which, for some reason is no longer working. For example, the flooding of a router with data may cause it to shut down, or restart. For the period whilst the system re-initialises the service offered by the router, namely data transfer from the subnet, is not available.

A **Distributed DoS** refers to the fact that multiple machines act to flood or otherwise attack the same device on the network, increasing the likelihood that the device will fail. An example of this is a 'Smurf' attack. This is where one workstation is infected with a virus or malicious code and due to its connection on the subnet is able to automatically pass on the code to its neighbouring machines, which also pass on the code to their neighbours and so on until all of the workstations are infected. These PCs (referred to as 'Zombies') send ICMP packets (e.g. a repeating PING) all to the same router with the intention of causing the router to become flooded to a point where it cannot handle legitimate network traffic, or even for the router to shut down.

In the last section I referred to a Zombie as an infected computer which is, unbeknownst to the user, sending out malicious code, spam or is attacking the rest of the network. The term '**Botnet**' (robot network) is also used to describe such an infected computer.

A **Traffic Spike** refers to a sudden and unplanned increase in data transmission which in itself may seem harmless, but could affect normal operations. In order to counter a sudden surge of system usage, redundant systems form a cluster to be able to deal with additional load. This is extremely important when we consider website traffic- a publicity event or advertisement may cause a rush of visitors to the site at the same time. Network cabling leading traffic from the internet to the web server cluster must be capable with handling the load as must the web servers to be able to allow, authenticate and service user requests by rendering specific pages as requested by the user.

This blog contains key information from Google concerning actions you can take to mitigate your system from a traffic spike:

http://googlewebmastercentral.blogspot.co.uk/2012/02/
preparing-your-site-for-traffic-spike.html

A **coordinated attack** is a deliberately planned offensive action to affect a strategic, key system. An example of this would be recent attacks of web servers in an effort to bring down a public-facing website by the 'Anonymous' group. Websites associated with the World Cup, including Bank of Brazil's and that of the country's military police have been targeted:

http://www.ft.com/cms/s/0/5ec411c0-f1a7-11e3-a2da-00144feabdc0.html#axzz3BrmymyEG

Distributed, Reflective Denial of Service Attacks (DRDoS) consist of an attacker sending instructions through key systems (referred to as Masters) which each manage a portion of the network we are trying to infect. The infection spreads in a hierarchical fashion from the Masters, through the network. A line of attack is created in the form of a series of 'slave' Zombie / Botnet systems.

In a DRDoS attack, master zombies send a stream of packets with the victim's IP address as the source IP address to other uninfected machines (known as *reflectors*). This causes the reflector system to connect with the victim's system. By using reflectors, the attack is exacerbated by the use of uncompromised machines (the reflectors themselves are no infected, but are increasing traffic to the victim's PC), which mount the attack without being aware of their action. This is otherwise referred to as an **'amplified attack'** in that the denial is caused by two separate actions – infection through flooding caused by infected machines, but also reflection caused by flooding from uninfected machines.

For further reading please refer to the Professor Messer Network+ series for further information on ARP poisoning, and other DoS attacks.

http://www.professormesser.com/n10-005/denial-of-service-attacks/

Domain Name System (DNS) is a dynamic role provided by a dedicated server on the network. Its function is to resolve name requests to IP addresses. This is referred to as a 'forward lookup'.

Imagine that you wish to contact another computer on the same domain. It could be located anywhere, geographically, but it exists within a site, within the domain, within the forest. For example, I want to view a shared folder on PC1 located on the network called *Corporation.com*. The Fully Qualified Domain name would therefore refer to the computer on the domain so:

<Computername>.<domain name> / <Shared folder>

So: ***PC1.Corporation.com/MyShare***

The problem is that in terms of the OSI model and the sending of data packets, I don't precisely know the IP address of PC1. (Users tend not to learn or to use IP addresses – it is more convenient to use computer names.)

As my computer has no record in its local cache of PC1 (as it has never visited this computer before), it needs help to reach PC1. DNS is a centralised 'phone book' of known computers on the network and will provide the IP address associated with the requested computer name. Once known this information is stored locally on your host PC's DNS cache should the user wish to contact the same computer again in the future, negating the need to query DNS names every time the user wishes to access the resource. Once the IP address is known, the computer communicates directly to PC1 via its IP address.

The *DNS server* is a collection of text files – a rudimentary database with different record types, serving the following functions:

A *SRV* record denotes the name and IP address of a DNS server on the network. It is normal to have several DNS servers, each servicing a portion of the network and for server records to be shared between them.

A *SOA* record denotes the starting DNS server in the cluster. The server identified as SOA (Start of Authority) is the lead server in the cluster.

An *A* record is a specific record referring to a computer by name and the IP address associated to it. In order for a computer name to be resolved the requisite A record must exist on the DNS server. DNS entries are created and updated automatically by Active Directory if this has been configured. Every computer on the network will have at least one A record.

An *AAAA* record is the same as an A record, however an A record is intended for use with IPv4 addresses and AAAA recorded are used with IPv6 addresses.

A *CNAME* (or Canonical Name) is a 'shortcut' or 'nickname' for a computer already identified on the network. For example, a web server may have a complex computer name such as : IIS7-AD_Pub_SharePoint_FS-12.Corporation.com which is difficult to remember or to type, but within the network administrators may need quick access to the machine so have 'nicknamed' it 'Charlie'. The CNAME of 'Charlie' would point requests instead to the actual name of the server. It is used to facilitate administration, although services may also refer to a server by other names programmatically – the changing of the computer name would mean a rewrite of code, however the use of a CNAME as an intermediary step would negate this need ad the CNAME would be automatically updated when the A record is updated.

An *MX* record is used to denote the location of the Mail Exchange server, so that email can be routed across the network.

Reverse lookup zones can also be created with perform the opposite role – once given the IP address the name of the computer associated to it is returned. This is not as useful on a network unless you wish to determine which NIC in a server is handling data, if the server forms part of a cluster of servers each performing the same role. A common occurrence of this would be a web server farm where one website is hosted by several load-balanced web servers. The DNS 'reverse lookup' would by used to provide the location and name of the hosting server.

DNS servers tend to be configured as different types:

- A *DNS forwarder* is a DNS server which will forward DNS queries for external DNS names to DNS servers outside of the network.

- A conditional forwarder is a DNS server set to forward to specific domain names, for example if you wish to send traffic to a specific site on the network where the request will be handled by the site-specific DNS servers.

The DNS structure is hierarchical. A DNS server can be configured to either be a forwarder to other internal DNS server, or otherwise to use Root Hints. Root Hints are the primary DNS server databases hosted and managed by the Internet Assigned Numbers Authority (IANA). These 'root' databases are the '.co.uk', '.com', '.info', etc. databases and act as starting points for traversal to other networks. A URL is in fact a Fully Qualified Domain Name. For the URL: http://www.bbc.co.uk/DrWho we are really asking the following: *"Please check with IANA's root database covering companies in the UK that a network domain called 'BBC' exists. Once we have found the IP address for the gateway to the BBC domain, we will look in a shared folder on the network called 'www' (this is hosted on the web server). Within the 'www' folder there will be a subfolder called 'DrWho'."*

We start by querying the root hint database for '.co.uk' which reports back the gateway IP address of the BBC public domain. Our PC communicates with the BBC domain by using this IP address. The external-facing router in the BBC network is configured to forward requests to the web server. The request to access the 'www' folder is granted and then within this the child folder 'DrWho'. Within the child folder will be a starting file (e.g. index.htm or index.asp) which will start the rendering process and the page will be rendered, part on the server (dynamic data rendering) and part sent to the client for local rendering (static rendering).

The BBC Dr Who home page and its source code showing dynamics and static data.

With reference to attacks, **DNS poisoning** (**DNS spoofing**) is the augmentation of a cached DNS entry on the local DNS cache. By directing the uninfected PC from its gateway to instead connect to a web-based server external (or potentially a known infected PC the client is being directed to) can then pass on the infection / malicious code. In essence, the client PC is directed from the correct resource to a fake server where it will be prone to attack.

DNS poisoning can be used as a security trap by network administrators. By adding known websites as empty new zones in the DNS server (e.g. www.Facebook.com) the client computer will always try to resolve a web name locally before attempting to communicate on the internet. As it finds a local zone on the internal DNS server, it will respond to provided instructions which stop it from looking further and therefore the legitimate facebook.com site cannot be accessed by internal staff. This technique is sometimes used within colleges and schools in addition to more complex proxy servers (e.g. *Smoothwall*).

The **Network Time Protocol (NTP)** is a key consideration for an Active Directory Domain. When a computer authenticates on the network its system time must be within 5 minutes of the Active Directory Domain Controller otherwise the client PC falls 'out of scope'. The client PC cannot authenticate until this is resolved. Common causes for repeated NTP problems could be simply the on-board lithium battery which powers the BIOS / CMOS chip when the PC is off if running down.

An NTP server is a dedicated time server linked to an internet-available atomic clock. Time packets are sent out across the network to all clients so that all machines are synchronised with the NTP server and subsequently all PCs are showing the same time. However, the presence of a second NTP on the network broadcasting a different time would accept the working of client computers connecting to the 'rogue' server and these client PCs will fall out of scope.

Smurfing is the process of infecting neighbouring PCs and causing them to run malicious code against one computer, or device (usually against a Router) with a view of flooding the device and causing it to be unable to respond to genuine traffic. The malicious code runs as a background service, but also spreads to other nearby computers in the subnet.

DNS can also feature as part of a smurf attack – the DNS TXT resource record can be padded with additional "attribute" data, creating a very large packet without fragmenting. When the DNS server is asked to resolve the affected record's address, the reply is much larger than the request, causing a delay in service.

Friendly DoS refers to the action of causing a Denial of Service by a local user request and poor performance in communicating the request. For example, a client may be attempting to download a very large file using Wi-Fi and the Wi-Fi network may have a weak signal between a Wireless Access Point and a connecting client node and large packets are being sent over this link. The packet will be retried several times and as the WAP attempts to service the request for other packets of the downloading file, but congestion builds up. It just so happens that other users also are trying the same thing and all are waiting an unacceptable amount of time to download their files, causing the service to become slow or even unusable.

A DoS attack can also be generated by overuse of the PING command. A PING – t will send not 4 test packets but an infinite stream of test packets to the device being tested and is an easy way to affect the service offered by the device.

The above DoS is considered 'friendly' as it was generated by users with no malicious intent to disrupt the service. A data spike caused by a sudden popularity of a web site can generate too much for one web server to cope with, causing the web server to be unresponsive to some of the people attempting to connect.

Physical attack refers to the malicious act of sabotage. This may be simply by switching off the device rendering it incapable of servicing the network, but at other extremes may include the violent act of attacking the device. A natural attack such as a flood or fire rendering the device unusable would also constitute a physical attack. A powr spike may cause the device to 'fuse' rendering it inoperable.

Some physical attacks are not malicious and easy to cause – if a network is precarious in its physical nature, for example in a test state and cable management is poor, a staff member may trip over a cable, dislodging it. If this is a trunk cable it would stop the router form uplinking to the rest of the network. To avoid this cable plugs contain locks to keep the cable firmly in place in the socket (the port), or may be screwed into place (e.g. BNC or F-type coaxial connections).

Permanent DoS – DoS attacks tend to be transient in nature and often caused by a client PC. If the malicious code can be removed with Antivirus / Security software and the DNS local cache wiped, the machine will again use the DNS server as it was intended and return to normal operation. A permanent DoS (also referred to as **phlashing**) would mean that the damage to the system as so severe that it would necessitate the repair or hardware, or the re-building of a system image onto the PC as core components within the OS are affected and the damage cannot be reversed. It is customary to keep a generic image of office PCs on the network and allow the transfer of the image to a PXE-enabled NIC. The affected PC can instead boot using the NIC, receive a temporary IP address for the repair and then receive the image in a matter of minutes. A WDS server is used where the build is more complex or has to be customised based on the use of the computer (e.g. part of the sales department so needs specific additional software to be installed as well). Again, the process can be automated and the PC rendered 'good' within a matter of minutes or within the hour.

Some **phlashing** attacks are quite severe, even rewriting the BIOS, in which case the repair may be hard to implement.

ARP cache poisoning (spoofing) refers is similar to the DNS cache poison attacks but operates at a lower level. The ARP cache is a table if IP addresses and the known MAC address it is assigned to. An ARP request is the process of querying the cache with a view to sending a data frame to the receiving NIC. Usually ARP is an invisible process allowing the NIC to do its job and to sned the data across the network as a data frame. However, it is possible to adapt an entry in the cache, pointing traffic to an intended IP to a completely different MAC address.

A '**man-in-the-middle**' attack is an ideal example of ARP poisoning. Here, a monitoring PC poisons the ARP caches of both the sending and receiving computers, establishing itself as the recipient of traffic. It is able to then forward data frames onto their intended host by augmenting the MAC address in the data frame and then sending the packet on its way. In this way the 'man-in-the-middle' can seamlessly sit between two nodes and copy all traffic sent through the 'middle' device.

The ARP protocol has no security associated with it. By using interpretation and poisoning software such as *Cain and Abel* (available at: http://www.oxid.it/cain.html) we can adapt frames as they are being sent. It is however worth noting that ARP traffic does not traverse subnets.

(It is also worth noting that *Cain and Abel* can also record passwords sent in the clear within IP packets.)

First, the 'middle' man communicates with the end device (e.g. the router) with an ARP request. The router's IP and ARP are recorded in the cache. The 'main in the middle' then sends an ARP instruction to the 'client' to update the ARP cache so that its record for the router is augmented, sending traffic intended for the router to the 'man in the middle' instead. Cain and Abel on the 'man in the middle' will augment packets and send them out to the router – the client and router do not realise that there is a problem. When the hacker has finished, the *Cain and Abel* software can 'tidy up' and repair the cache on both ends, making the monitoring process quite invisible. Network administrators must be vigilant by checking router logs for unusual ARP activity over a short timeframe.

Packet abuse refers to the use of the network for purposes not defined by corporate policy (e.g. the downloading of illegal files using a *BitTorrent* client). Software such as *Wireshark* (available from: https://www.wireshark.org/download.html) can monitor network activity on a particular point of the network (node) and filter by protocol and by so doing determine the IP and therefore which computer is using the unauthorised service (e.g. *BitTorrent*). Once the IP address is identified, Wireshark can also resolve and list the websites being visited by this user.

In broader terms packet abuse also refers to the augmenting of a packet in order to mask the original sender, or by using a legitimate IP address to redirect to a 'spoof' or 'fake' node on the network:

Wireless packet abuse opens up a new realm of possibilities as a device such as a smartphone could be programmed to operate as a 'spoof' device and draw network traffic to it with a view of a hacker gaining more information about the structure of the network, or to capture data being sent across the network:

Evil Twin – this refers to a rogue Wi-Fi access point which is broadcasting a legitimate SSID and appears to the user to be legitimate. In reality it is intending to eavesdrop on data being sent on the network – the 'evil twin' will be connected to the network already but will act as a 'man in the middle', able to read sensitive data from packets being sent into the device.

To combat an evil twin on your network you will have to implement MAC filtering and also perform RF sweeps to check for newly added devices.

A **Rogue Access Point** is the more general term for an access point installed onto the network without the knowledge or authorisation of the Network administrator. An 'evil twin' is an example of a rogue access point.

As referred to earlier in the course, **War Driving** is the process of walking (or driving) past a building with a known Wi-Fi network and performing an RF scan in an attempt to audit, or even to connect to network with a view to obtaining sensitive corporate information. Software (e.g *NetStumbler*) is available to perform War Driving scans. Games such as Metal Gear Solid and Treasure World feature war driving as part of the plot, or even contain war driving applications built into them.

War Driving evolved from 'War Dialling' – the process of using a model and telephone line to call a variety of telephone numbers where a computer network was connected at the other end, with a view to finding an 'open' system which could be communicated with. Whilst war driving appears unethical, even illegal when we consider corporate data, the practice of connecting to other networks with a view to forward data is exactly how the internet works, so is not technically unethical. A number of cafes and shops host Wi-Fi hotspots and encourage users to connect to their public Wi-Fi offering not only to allow access to the internet whilst using the facilities, but also to provide advertising of store products and features whilst you are connected.

War Chalking is the drawing of symbols to inform other Wi-Fi users able to interpret them of the type of Wi-Fi network (and its associated security) at this location.

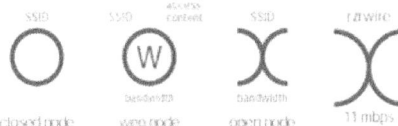

Bluejacking refers to the practice of 'hijacking using Bluetooth' – the act of sending unsolicited messages to other nearby mobile phone users using Bluetooth. The sender would typically be sitting within 10 metres from the victim, making this more an advertising tool than a serious threat to the network, but for a while was a problem within schools as was an easy way to perform cyber bullying.

Bluesnarfing is the use of Bluetooth to obtain information to personal data stored on the phone the attacker has connected to. This may refer to the copying or theft of image files, calendar information, or the viewing of emails.

Wireless security attacks (Aircracking): by capturing the wireless authentication handshake and then attempting to crack the pre-shared key used by both devices to secure the communication channel. Systems using the *BackTrack* image (a Linux distribution with a variety of network hacking software installed) are typically used to be able to crack the pre-shared key once the authentication handshake data has been captured.

Wi-Fi Protected Access (**WPA** and **WPA2**) contain checking systems and TKIP encryption which is different for each packet. The use of a pre-shared key known to both the sender and recipient's computers can further secure the connection. However, if the passphrase is weak, it can be easily cracked. WPA was designed to be an additional layer of security onto the WEP system.

An Exhaustive Key Search (**Brute Force Attack**) is an attempt to crack packet encryption by guessing the pre-shared key and trying every possible combination until the correct one is discovered. By increasing the cryptographic key size the number of possible combinations has grown to a situation where it may take not minutes, but years to 'crack' the code.

A **session hijack** is an attempt by another user (the hacker) to impersonate the victim's current session. As part of the authentication process, once the computer and user account have been successfully verified and authenticated, a session token file is generated on the server and sent to the client. (In the case of a local session, the local SAM database is used to authenticate and to create the session token.) The session key (token) is a piece of information containing the session ID and other data which identifies the active session. In the case of websites, a user authenticates and the web server generates the session key, which resides on the client PC's browser cache as a cookie.

Injection code on the web server can reveal the session ID where it can then be copied and used by the hacker. A session hijack is covered in the Professor Messer video:

http://www.professormesser.com/security-plus/cookies-header-manipulation-and-session-hijacking/

Social engineering refers to the process of gaining a person's confidence with a view to tricking them to reveal corporate sensitive information which will give the recipient a better understanding of the configuration of the network. Most social engineering is subtle and general conversations will reveal software installed, the placement of servers and so forth, but also key personal information may be revealed (e.g. birthdays) which may help the 'engineer' to gather enough information to attempt to guess a password.

Listed are several social engineering tools and methods in use:

Pretexting – using a contrived scenario obtain the trust of a person, tricking them into revealing accurate information. For example, a contact centre receive a call from a person claiming that they work for the company's IT department, need to check a few details on their machine and need their password to do so. A variant of this is **'Quid Pro Quo'** in which the attacker, claiming that they are able to provide technical support do try to fix a technical problem, but in the process would need access for them to be granted so that they can perform the fix. Once access has been granted, they also inject malware onto the system.

Diversion theft is the process of convincing a delivery person to send the delivery somewhere else (not the intended address) where the delivery can be intercepted. In IT terms this may be a false web address which may actually install spyware or other monitoring software.

Phishing – the act of sending a genuine-seeming email formatted to look like it could be from the actual business but in reality any links will take you to a web server where spyware may then be installed on your system, or adverts may run. It is called 'phishing' because of two reasons:

- To obtain personal information from the victim.
- To verify that the email address is 'live'. Email addresses can then be filtered and sold on to other advertising companies and other 'phishing' agents.

Vishing is the sending of legitimate-seeming automated calls asking the caller to log into a telephone banking site using their phone PIN. The PIN used will be the correct one, but the action will be rejected by the automated system, causing the victim to try again. This way the attacker has logged the actual PIN and verified it. They can then separately use this information to log into the victim's bank account for themselves. Vishing is so-called as it is a shortening of 'Phishing using Voice over IP'. Vishing tends to occur on corporate systems such as a customer service phone bank.

Baiting is the process of leaving a CD-ROM, or USB key, or perhaps even giving these out at a trade show, by a seemingly-legitimate company. The key would contain a virus or other such malware which will automatically install when the victim attaches and mounts it to a corporate computer. Malware can often spread across the network and report back 'to base' (usually a collecting web server hosted by the attacker).

Returning to focus on wireless attacks, Social engineering would be in an attempt to obtain access to the pre-shared key where this key can be memorised, or copied by the attacker.

A 'man in the middle' attack using wireless would require the victim's computer to instead send its wireless data packet to the 'false' wireless router instead of the genuine router. The 'false' wireless router would then augment the MAC address as with a wired MIIM attack and forward the packet on to the genuine router.

For this to work, the 'false' wireless router must be in range of both other nodes, also the client would need to reconnect to the false router, so the SSID of the 'false' router would need to be enticing (e.g. usually it is the same SSID as the genuine router, but the signal strength is stronger due to close proximity, so the victim chooses the stronger router by default.) The problem is that the data within the packet is still encrypted, so further work would need to be done to be able to 'crack' the packets.

VLAN hopping is the process of obtaining access to resources stored on a virtual LAN. As we have discussed it is possible for switch ports on different switches to work together to form a group. Normally only traffic intended for the VLAN can access the VLAN.

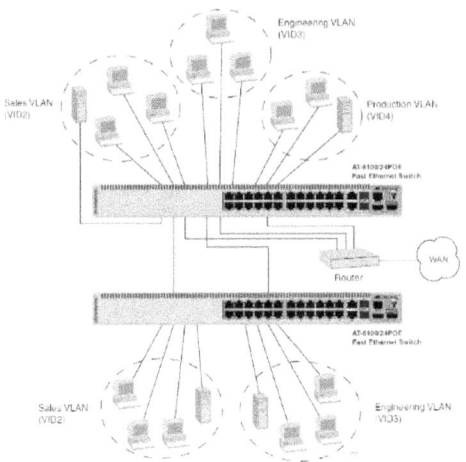

Several VLANs across 2 physical switches

There are two attack types used:

Switch spoofing – here, the attacker's computer pretends to be a trunk switch and sends information to the real switch group in order to obtain access to a VLAN.

Double tagging – this can be found where VLANs exist on an Ethernet network (using 802.1q). Two VLAN tags are added to the packet. The first tag contains information about the VLAN the attacker is connected to. The packet is forwarded then without the first tag. The second false tag is read by the second switch within the group which indicates that the packet is intended for a host located from this second switch. The packet then reaches its target host. Further configuration may need to take place to allow the target host to reply to the attacker.

The term **'compromised system'** refers to an infected computer, or group of computers, or a part of the network. Services may not be available as a result of the infection, or the technical team may need to deliberately remove the affected computers from the network to stop the further spread of infection but also to repair the damage. It is usual due to the generic nature of images on a corporate network to be able to repair a system through a complete wipe of the hard drive and rebuilding of the partition from an image. Another alternative would be simply to boot to the WDS server and allow a deployment to rebuild the system layer by layer, adding software in sequence as instructed by the WDS server. The term 'compromised' comes from the fact that critical data may have 'leaked' to the outside world but we now use the term to refer to an infected or misconfigured PC.

Malware is a very broad, general term for any software which can cause 'bad' (*French: 'mal'*) things to happen. This software may not be in itself damaging, but may cause poor performance, or affect the workflow of the user through the presentation of advertisements, or even cause the PC to shut down unexpectedly. The effect of malware from a network perspective is that services offered by affected servers may run slowly, if at all, therefore not only affecting one user but all users connecting the service.

An **insider threat**, or **malicious employee** refers to the deliberate sabotage of the network system by a member of staff who has clearance to work on the network. This may be due to a grudge and as a means to inflict harm on the company. Data may be lost and may need to be recovered, or in some cases hardware may need to be replaced. The most problematic aspect is that the employee would have the opportunity to know the whole system and may know its weak points. They may also be able to remove a component from the system which is hard to locate, or may not be the obvious cause of a fault and by so doing the repair team may be concentrating on the wrong area in order to effect the repair. This will have the impact of extending the inactivity of the affected service.

An insider threat may also refer to the compromising of data security such as through the use of a **'mole'** (an agent working within the company who would pass sensitive information on to a third party, usually for financial or political gain).

A **zero-day attack** refers to an attack to a system which the original programmers did not anticipate and as such no 'patch' or 'fix' currently exists. Zero-day refers to the face that the programmers have had no time to fix the fault.

Other vulnerabilities may cause the network to be insecure and as such need to be considered and remedial action taken:

Unnecessary running services either on client machines or servers have the effect of having other communications and data transfer protocols 'live' and therefore these can be used to exploit the network. By limiting the protocols and services in use to those which have been actively secured we can ensure that we have control of our network. Additional services should only be started when they have been tested in a Development environment first to ensure that their operation will have no adverse effects on other running and required current services. Secondly, additional services will increase the RAM footprint of the system, causing the system to behave slightly slower and may lead to a performance drop. The RAM-resident data may also be accessed by an attacking PC on the network and this data may contain sensitive information which may be accessible.

Open firewall ports can lead to exotic data transfers unbeknownst to network management staff as they may only be checking common ports. Good practice is to only allow a port to be opened when a specific application is run. Also, with the use of Dynamics ports, we can change the port number which will be used each time the port is opened, or the application run, thereby making it harder for an attacker to determine the port being used.

Legacy systems no longer supported by the technical team, or with an old Operating System may still be in use within a company as business process relies on software which will only work on this particular system, or the company has bought computer-aided machinery and the PC is embedded into the machine (e.g. a guided lathe) and cannot be upgraded. Business process dictates that the lathe will only be upgraded as a complete entity when its operational life ends. Therefore other systems have to adapt to communicate with the legacy system. This may involve the inclusion of now very old ('archive') protocols which may be insecure. Where legacy systems are using unpatched, early operating systems (e.g. the original edition of Windows XP) vulnerabilities may still exist which are normally fixed through the inclusion of a patch or service pack. These systems may not be able to be patched because, in a development environment the legacy system was found to become unstable or unusable after the patch was added, so the patch has had to be removed. Also where a legacy system is not connected to other network devices there may be no obvious need or even method to patch the system. If the legacy system contains bespoke firmware, rather than a standardised Operating System, it may be difficult to patch. If the manufacturing company wo supplied the system in the first place are no longer in business, there may be no way of supporting the system.

A good example is an unpatched XP system attacked with buffer overflow caused by a module from the Metasploit framework as is detailed in the Professor Messer video:

http://www.professormesser.com/security-plus/buffer-overflows/

An **unencrypted channel** poses the danger of surveillance monitoring where the packets received can be read 'in the clear'. These packets may contain sensitive data including user passwords allowing an attacker to then impersonate the user. The sending of user authentication data without encryption is referred to as **'Clear text credentials'**.

It is worth noting that users are often unaware that not every protocol automatically encrypts data. The following protocols are often used on a network although some of these are now retired as have been replaced with secure protocols instead:

- **TELNET** is a very powerful console protocol allowing administrators to send command instructions to other PC on the network. The problem here is that the TELNET user has to authenticate to the remote PC and so a username and password is sent across the internal network, in the clear. TELNET has been superseded by PowerShell, which sends its commands as encrypted data.
- **HTTP** is also an unencrypted protocol. Secure data is sent instead using HTTPS (an encrypted 'tunnel' between both endpoints relies on certificate encryption on both the web server and client). HTTPS is often used for the transfer of sensitive data such as credit card data, or bank account login details.
- **SLIP** (Serial Line Interface/Internet Protocol) is an internet / interfacing protocol for the sending of IP data over a serial cable. SLIP is now replaced by the Point to Point Protocol (PPP) for modem connections which can support encryption.
- **FTP (File Transfer Protocol)** is a protocol used to transfer files across the network. It can support authentication to an FTP file server but, server permitting, can also support anonymous connections. FTP packets are checked for errors, but are not encrypted. **FTP Secure** is a separate extension to the FTP protocol which provides encryption.
- TFTP (Trivial File Transfer Protocol) is similar to FTP but does not perform error checking. Data is sent from the server but if the client misses part of the file, the part is not resent.
- **Simple Network Management Protocol (SNMP v1 or v2)** is used to send management data to other routers and managed switches. The SNMP suite supports a range of hardware, including servers. Version 3 is secure, so this is now used. The earlier versions (v1 and v2) do not encrypt the data sent.
- **TEMPEST** Emission Security refers to the act of analysing wireless and radio traffic within a building, also audio sounds to determine if any are present in areas where they are not intended to be. As an example, a wireless access point near to the edge of the building may send out an RF signal which could be accessible from outside the building, which clearly leaves the company open to war driving. Protecting equipment from spying involves consideration of distance, shielding, filtering and masking techniques and methods in place across the company. Some of the TEMPEST standards are classified, but part of the TEMPEST standards are available for public use. An example of this would be 'Red/Black' classification and separation. Red areas refer to non-encrypted transmissions, where Black are encrypted areas.

3.3

3.3 Given a scenario, implement network hardening techniques
- Anti-malware software
    - Host-based
    - Cloud/server-based
    - Network-based
- Switch port security
    - DHCP snooping
    - ARP inspection
    - MAC address filtering
    - VLAN assignments
        - Network segmentation
- Security policies
- Disable unneeded network services
- Use secure protocols
    - SSH
    - SNMPv3
    - TLS/SSL
    - SFTP
    - HTTPS
    - IPsec
- Access lists
    - Web/content filtering
    - Port filtering
    - IP filtering
    - Implicit deny
- Wireless security
    - WEP
    - WPA/WPA2
        - Enterprise
        - Personal
    - TKIP/AES
    - 802.1x
    - TLS/TTLS
    - MAC filtering
- User authentication
    - CHAP/MSCHAP
    - PAP
    - EAP
    - Kerberos
    - Multifactor authentication
    - Two-factor authentication
    - Single sign-on
- Hashes
    - MD5
    - SHA

The use of **anti-malware** software within the corporate environment requires the use of a central server to manage threats by checking downloaded files before they are sent to the client. Microsoft Forefront Threat Management Gateway is an example of this (http://technet.microsoft.com/library/ff355324.aspx). It is a **server-based** solution.

Host-based solutions are installed on every client on the network. These work in the background offering 'real time protection' by performing a heuristic analysis of files, looking for data patterns which may be similar to those of known viruses. The concern with Host-based solutions is that they are very process-intensive and have a tendency to slow down a client PC. If the client system is built with hardware capacity only sufficient for user tasks, the system performance will drop considerably. Also, application will often need to be trained – new applications need the confirmation of the user that the application, or file is actually safe. However, it is quite common for less IT-savvy users to not understand the messages, either ignoring them or setting everything to be blocked by default. An example of a host-based solution may be Norton Antivirus (http://uk.norton.com/antivirus/). Whilst 'real time protection' can be turned off and virus scans run at times when the user will not be using the PC, this leads to a lack of management on the part of the user who is unaware of the application findings. The software often reports back with alerts if RTP is turned off, confusing the user who believes that the system is not safe.

Our third solution is web/cloud-based solutions, such as web scanners available on the Norton or MacAfee site. These will often only check common file locations and may not contain all of the features available from the loaded product. The cloud solution is often useful for a 'quick sweep' but some web-based scanners may in fact provide false positives or intend to encourage the user to purchase the client product.

One interesting note is the use of Microsoft Intune – a cloud based solution where the network manager can get a top-level view of system health and perform fixes remotely. (http://www.microsoft.com/en-gb/business/products/windows-intune)

Switch port security refers to the tools and methods we can deploy to secure a switch port.

DHCP snooping – The DHCP process for a new PC is 4 stages: Discover, Offer, Request, Acknowledge. On returning PCs hoping to renew their IP lease only stages 3 and 4 (RA) are sent. With the DHCP snooping feature enabled, ACK(nowledgement) packets travelling on ports that are not trusted are dropped.

ARP inspection is then deployed. This feature limits the number of ARP packets which can be sent on a port, per second, therefore countering the ARP poisoning of a port.

MAC filtering is then used on the switch to restrict data frames sent through the switch to only known good MAC addresses. The two methods which can be used are 'blacklisting' (the blocking of traffic from specific MAC addresses), or the more secure 'whitelisting' (the blocking of all traffic except for those MAC addresses on the list).

VLAN assignment is the process of separating traffic into different virtual LANs. This is not usually based on physical location but tends to be logical in nature. On the previous VLAN diagram we saw the groups *Production, Engineering* and *Sales*. These exist across the switches on the network. Members of Production would be able to access the *Production* area on the VLAN – this usually an extended area of the general network with services and files pertaining to this group. It is also possible to create a *Sandbox* environment – a separate area of the network separated from the main network so that any work that takes place within this secured area does not affect normal operations.

Network segmentation is typically into managed zones based on the level of security, or the extent to which the user within this area needs access to corporate data. In the earlier diagram of a **Demilitarised Zone**, we saw a public area (the **Internet**), a semi-public area where externally-connecting staff could gain access to non-sensitive corporate data (e.g. newsletters, marketing material and blank forms). A dedicated area for externally-connecting staff to obtain this information is referred to as an '**extranet**'. The DMZ is a perimeter network separating the **public** and **private** zones. The third is the **intranet** – the internal network. This is heavily secured and is intended for corporate staff only, usually connecting locally (within the physical network), but by 'tunnelling' remote workers can gain access to the internal network, sending their data through an encrypted 'tunnel'. This **tunnel** is considered to be unbreakable and so we consider it to be safe across the internet, particularly as the data stream is heavily encrypted and relies on Active Directory authentication as well.

A **security policy** within Network+ exists within two contexts. It is a management document which determines the measured which have been put in place to secure the network. It details procedures which staff should follow to ensure that the network remains secure, also protective corporate data. The second context refers to **Active Directory policies (Group Policy Objects)** which are specific restrictions and their scope. Through **Windows Management Instrumentation** filtering I can also apply different GPOs to laptops.

We have already discussed the need to **disable network services** currently not required and to make any changes to the network including the addition of new services part of a change management process. This way network managers can retain control of services, guarantee performance is maintained and ensure that other unwanted protocols are not being abused on the network.

Secure Shell is a secure protocol designed to allow encrypted, secure connections to remote computers. Example SSH applications as *Microsoft Terminal Services Client* (known as *'Remote Desktop'*), or *PuTTY* which uses OpenSSH.

As mentioned earlier, **SNMPv3** is able to encrypt any management commands and data sent across network devices.

Transport Later Security with Secure Socket Layers (TLS/SSL) provides a secure tunnel between the web server and client machine. It is commonly associated with accessing secure ('padlocked') web pages. **HTTPS** refers to secured website data traffic using port 443.

As discussed earlier, **SFTP** extends SSH enabling FTP traffic to be secured.

In addition, the **IPsec** protocol is used to authenticate and to encrypt each IP packet sent across a secure tunnel.

An access list is a list of known good computers, or users which are allowed access on the network, however the term can also refer to any form of security list on the network which restricts access to resources, or the extent to which the user can interact with the item, or file.

An **Account (Access) Control List (ACL)**, is a list of users able to access the resource (e.g. a shared folder on the network). On Microsoft systems, an ACL contains two lists – *Allow* and *Deny*. The principle used is one of 'least privilege' – the group or user in the list should only be given sufficient access to the resource and no further. This way each user's access level can be managed with a highly granular management scope. A Network Administrator may have full access (referred to as Full Control) to the file, whereas a user may only have Modify rights (they can open and save changes to the file, but are not the file owner – the Network Administrator can take control of the file and assign other users and groups to access the file.

To set the extent to which the user can access the file, we set the Allow list to just enough for them to perform their duties. We do not use deny other than to create special security combinations, or as a way of overriding the allow list. The security permission can also be cascaded to its child folders.

Another type of access control list would be a **web/content filter**. **Web filtering** is a 'whitelist'/'blacklist' approach of banned sites, or (more restrictive) the only allowed sites. This site list can exist on the client, but to ease management and to ensure that a consistent approach is used, a web proxy server (e.g. *Smoothwall*) can be used for web filtering.

Content filtering is the process of disallowing access to web pages based on specific words present on the webpage. Again, this can be centralised by using a proxy server.

Port filtering is the process of enabling / disabling specific firewall ports within the TCP and UDP list based on need. The connection makes use is a 'socket' – the combination of an IP address and the port which will be used to send the data through the firewall. The ports are opened and closed at the request of the client application. Firewall advanced security rules can be used to open and close the port.

IP filtering is the process of only allowing a series of IP addresses to be available. As with web proxy 'whitelisting' we can define only a specific series, or specific IP addresses to be accessible from this location. The IP address within the packet header is inspected and if it does not match an IP address on the allowed list, the IP will be ignored.

Implicit Deny refers to the fact that we have to specify who can access a resource on the Access Control List. If the user (or a group to which the user is a member) does not appear on the list, then the user cannot access the resource. This is an 'implicit deny'.

> *NB: Microsoft recommend to disable the guest account and to not use the 'Everyone' group, ensuring full enumeration and specific management of the resource.*

There are different scenarios where we may want to use different types of wireless security. **WEP** is used to provide a cypher encryption of wireless data packets by the use of an encryption key. On its own WEP is relatively insecure and can be 'cracked' quite easily (referred to as 'aircracking'). Once the key has been determined by a hacker, the complete system is open to attack. WEP is the initial choice available on all wireless routers. WEP is commonly used in either infrastructure mode (for use on domains), or for 'ad hoc' mode (used when two laptops, or smartphones directly connect as a PAN style network.)

WPA can be added to provide an additional layer of security to and existing WEP system. WPA1 was intended to be an intermediate step.

WPA2 supports AES encryption – this is a very strong encryption standard used on a corporate domain. WPA2 with AES is the de facto standard and the most secure option we have.

In WPA2, **Personal mode** is used for home and small business (SOHO) networks. We use a standard password set on both the Wireless Router and client. **WPA2 Enterprise** mode makes use of a RADIUS authentication server, using the username and password as it appears on the Active Directory database. WPA2 Enterprise is known as 802.1x and is typically certificate-based.

To support WPA, Temporal Key security (TKIP), as discussed earlier will encrypt the data packet using a timestamp. However, if the base time is known across the network an attacker may be able to emulate the time within the augmented packet they attempt to send.

AES, the **Advanced Encryption Standard** uses a cipher known as 'Rijndael' (after the names of the standard authors). It is a symmetric key algorithm – the same key is used for encrypting and decrypting the packet. The ciphering process undertakes 10 to 14 'rounds' in which the packet is augmented by the cipher. AES has the approval of the US government through the National Security Agency (NSA). It is considered stronger than 3DES which is a 3-round cryptographic process.

Transport Layer Security (TLS) is considered to be the successor to SSL. It is designed to provide security for data across the internet. It is an asymmetric cryptographic system and also makes use of certificates. TLS is commonly used for web browsing but also for other activities:

- SSL-secured transactions on an e-commerce site
- Client authentication on an SSL-secured Web site
- Remote access (e.g. with Remote Desktop)
- SQL access to the SQL server database
- E-mail via Exchange.

TLS has one drawback – it was designed for a wired network and in itself does not offer particularly strong encryption.

Tunnelled Transport Layer Security (TTLS) is an EAP method which encapsulates a TLS session. There is a 'handshake' phase, then a 'data' phase. The server is authenticated (or both are mutually authenticated to each other) and a secure tunnel is created to then send the data. During the data-send phase, an authentication mechanism exists within secure tunnel which may be EAP, PAP, CHAP, MS-CHAP or MS-CHAPv2. This provides legacy authentication systems whilst also keeping the encryption secure.

TTLS is used for the creation of secure tunnels such as for remote workers wishing to VPN to the network. DirectAccess (Microsoft's recent implementation of a VPN by using a dedicated server hosting the remote session within the intranet, not on the remote client machine).

MAC filtering is a common technique used on wireless routers to only allow specific wireless NICs to access the router. However, MAC addresses can be spoofed if the attacker is able to obtain a legitimate MAC address on the local network. Through a little trial and error, it would be quite easy to find one MAC address on the list.

User authentication in the process of allowing only recognised user accounts on the network. This is performed by authenticating against a Domain Controller (for internal users), or a RADIUS / TACACS+ server (for external-connecting users).

Password Authentication Protocol (PAP) is a legacy protocol where a password is supplied and used for authentication. The protocol is not able to encrypt the packet, so should only be used where no other options are available.

CHAP and **MS-CHAP** are challenge handshake protocols used on legacy systems. MS-CHAPv2 was introduced in Windows NT SP4 and has been added also to Windows 98. It is used to authenticate modem connections.

CHAP and **MS-CHAP** are useful for protecting against replay attacks. The identifier and challenge regularly change, so authentication is periodically challenged throughout the session. The plaintext of the secret (local code used to create as part of the authentication process) is present on both the client and the server. The secret itself is not sent across the network.

CHAP is considered to be a stronger authentication system than PAP.

EAP, the Extensible Authentication Protocol is used for wireless and point-to-point connections. There are several different types of EAP – they define the message format. EAP messages are encapsulated within the protocol it is working with. EAP is therefore an authentication framework.

Kerberos is Microsoft's authentication process. It is named after Cerberus (the three-headed dog guarding the gates to the underworld in Greek mythology). The Kerberos protocol uses a series of 'tickets' to securely provide identify information from the client to the server and back. It provides mutual authentication – both sides have to authenticate the opposite node therefore making it very secure and as with CHAP, replay attacks and 'man-in-the-middle' attacks cannot be made.

Kerberos is the default authentication standard from Windows 2000 onwards.

Multifactor authentication refers to the need for the user to provide two different sources of information before they are granted access to the system. One factor may include:

- Username and password together
- Chip and PIN code
- ID card present in keyboard reader / swiped
- Picture gesture
- Password.
- Retinal scan

- Fingerprint scan

Multifactor refers to 'more than one' method before access is granted. **Two-factor** authentication is commonplace on corporate domains for staff to log on to their client PCs where two authentication items are needed. They can be:

- Something that you know (e.g. a password, or special date)
- Something that you have (a key fob or ID card)
- Something that you are (member of the Network Administrators group)

Single sign-on refers to the use of one authentication token across multiple sites and services which require the use of the same authentication. For example, logging onto my Hotmail / Outlook site with my Microsoft Account would allow me to access my email, but then if I change the website to the Microsoft Partner centre, MCP / MCT site, Microsoft e-learning site, Microsoft Virtual Academy, Microsoft Labs online or any other sites which form part of the Microsoft family, I obtain access to the site and am automatically logged in. There is no need for the user to re-authenticate when they change from one site to another within the same family. These sites are connected as they form part of the same domain, or trust relationships between the domains allow access for the user.

On a domain, **Lightweight Directory Access Protocol (LDAP)** enables the user to authenticate to various resources hosted on the domain.

A hash is a piece of data generated by passing the source data from a file through an algorithm and a result is produced. The product (referred to as the 'hash' or in its simplest form a 'checksum') is stored and the same 'hash' will always be produced. If the file is changed in any way, when the file is run through the algorithm, a different hash result will be generated. The generated hash is compared to the known hash output stored by the system. As the two differ, the system can realise that the original file has been altered.

Hashing is used with data validation and also within password checking systems. The algorithm used in this example is the 'Pretty Good Privacy' protocol (PGP).

AppLocker is a feature offered by Windows Server 2012 which manages access to specific files by file name, by path (which can be easily broken if the exe file is a standalone simply by copying the file to a different location) or other data. The Hash of a file can be used to confirm the integrity of the file.

A **Message Digest 5 (MD5)** hash is a common hashing algorithm used to verify data integrity. The hash function produces a 128-bit hash value, stored as a 32-digit Hexadecimal number.

MD5 is not suitable for use in combination with SSL certificates, or digital signatures. Although it was been a robust system from 1992 to 2004, research over the past 10 years have found several flaws with MD5.

MD5 is widely used as a checksum hash to check file integrity. File download sites will often publish the hash of the file to ensure that you are downloading the legitimate file, or for you to determine if your file has been altered during transit.

Secure Hash Algorithm (SHA) is a suite of hash functions developed by the National Institute for Standards and Technology (NIST). SHA blocks are usually quite large at 32-bit (SHA-256) and 64-bit (SHA-512).

SHA-2 encryption supports certificates and is accepted by systems with OS Windows XP SP3 or later.

3.4

3.4 Compare and contrast physical security controls
- Mantraps
- Network closets
- Video monitoring
    - IP cameras/CCTVs
- Door access controls
- Proximity readers/key fob
- Biometrics
- Keypad/cypher locks
- Security guard

This section will consider some of the various corporate physical security controls.

Mantrap – this is an 'airlock' style area within a building separating two security zones of different security levels. Typically there are two security doors – one to enter the 'airlock' and the other to leave it. Each of these have an access code however the code is usually different for both doors. Within the 'airlock' section is an observation window where a security guard in the adjoining room can check to see who is in the 'airlock'. If the visitor is not able to open the second door, the guard can 'lock down' the area until help arrives.

Network closet (also referred to as a network cabinet, or wiring closet) – servers are typically rack-mounted. They are lockable cabinets and keys are only available to select members of staff. Access to servers however is usually by Remote Desktop – access to the cabinet is only required if the backup tape recorder, is located there, if hard drives need to be replaced or hardware servicing needs to be performed.

Video monitoring is the process of using electronic surveillance to record and to view activity in key locations of the building. The recording is held digitally, such as on a hard drive, or video recorder. A time code can be added to the recording with a time and date stamp imprinted onto the recording. Recordings can last for several days – some systems recycle data and only extract sequences to keep or to use as evidence.

An **IP camera** is a form of Closed-Circuit TV surveillance where a webcam is mounted in a key location. The data is transmitted across the internal network as IP data. The camera generates IP data packets. Each camera has its own IP address and data packets are sent on the corporate network – there is no need for dedicated data cabling, although some smaller CCTV systems to supply data cables to the main recorder.

A **door access control** is a form of electronic lock which is connected to a central security database. The control can operate using Near Field Communication to take an RF signal from a **Proximity Reader (a key fob)**, or an access code can be typed to unlock the door.

Knowing the access code itself is not sufficient – the person attempting to obtain access must also present the code within 'opening hours'.

Mentioned above, a **Key Fob** is a small field transmitter able to send a weak RF signal a short distance. The received data will be an ID code unique to the fob. On the centralised security server the fob is registered against a specific employee – based on restrictions on the fob or on the employee and also time constraints on the access group used (e.g. the member of staff may be a shift worker and only able to access through the door during the hours they are expected to be on-site).

Biometrics refers to a scanner or reader which makes use of the individuality of parts of the human body. Code patterns are made up from uniqueness of the individual's body. Typical parts of the body associated with biometric scans are:

- Fingerprint scan
- Retina scan
- Facial recognition (using position and sizes of various elements of the face).

Cypher locks are now quite common for banking transactions. In order to obtain access to a banking site, multifactor authentication is used – the site visitor must answer a series of questions, present a username and password, but also use a cypher lock. This is a battery-operated, small calculator-type device which, when the saved PIN code is entered, a session unique code is generated. This is usually a 6-digit number. It is random in nature, but can only have been generated from the PIN as a base element. This generated number must also be entered to allow access to the site.

The cypher lock is also used when the site user wishes to conduct a financial transaction, or to set up a standing order.

A **security guard** is a person employed to preserve the integrity of the existing corporation, including its hardware. They are tasked with responding to incidents and would be the first responder in a security incident. Guards would validate visitors and also ensure that people stay within the security zones to which they are allotted access to.

3.5

3.5 Given a scenario, install and configure a basic firewall
- Types of firewalls
  - Host-based
  - Network-based
  - Software vs hardware
  - Application aware/context aware
  - Small office/home office firewall
  - Stateful vs stateless inspection
  - UTM
- Settings/techniques
  - ACL
  - Virtual wire vs routed
  - DMZ
  - Implicit deny
  - Block/allow
    - Outbound traffic
    - Inbound traffic
  - Firewall placement
    - Internal/external

Operating at layer 4 of the OSI model, a firewall is a protection layer designed to only let specific data through into the network. A Firewall divides parts of the internal network into security zones, but also can be used to separate the external network (the internet) from the internal network.

A 'Perimeter network' consists of a logical security zone walled by two firewalls. In reality this may just be one physical firewall separating traffic into these separate security zones.

A firewall is a hardware device, rack-mounted and actually quite expensive. The device analyses the IP packet to determine if the traffic should be allowed through the gateway, or not. There are 65535 different ports (doorways) for TCP and also the same for UDP. Common port numbers are used globally, so that traffic can be managed based on the type of data we are sending. Common port numbers are:

- 20 – FTP data (traditional. This is not used for data if Dynamic FTP has been assigned)
- 21 – FTP control (for connection handshaking)
- 22 – Secure Shell (SSH) is used with Remote Desktop connections, also for port forwarding.
- 23 – TELNET. Not used (not encrypted data traffic)
- 25 – Simple Mail Transfer Protocol (SMTP) – email out, also Mail server communications traffic between email servers.
- 53 – DNS
- 67 – BOOTP (Bootstrap Protocol for network imaging and deployment), also for DHCP – server end.
- 68 – BOOTP (Bootstrap Protocol for network imaging and deployment), also for DHCP – client-side.

- 69 – Trivial File Transfer Protocol (TFTP)
- 88 – Kerberos traffic
- 110 – Post Office Protocol (POP3) for email 'in'.
- 123 – Network Time Protocol (NTP) – to synchronise time across the network.
- 143 – IMAP (web-based email)
- 500 – ISAKMP
- 520 – RIP
- 546 – DHCPv6 client
- 547 – DHCPv6 server
- 666 – Initially used as an 'open window' for LAN games matches (e.g. Doom), but now is connected with Aircracking activities. Best left closed.
- 691 – Microsoft Exchange routing
- 3389 – Remote Desktop data.

A **host-based firewall** is installed onto the client. It is a software application, either a third party application, or a service provided by the OS. With Windows systems, both a simplified firewall and an 'advanced security' version where rule sets can be configured.

The difference here is that a **network-based firewall**, as described in the earlier section is a dedicated device screening all traffic entering this section of the network. Corporate rules may differ on specific client machines, but the network-based firewall will corporately allow and block based on specific ports.

A **software- based firewall** has the disadvantage in that it is software – it is a combination of a frond-end client management application and a background service. Both of these can be attacked by a virus, or by outside configuration (even a rogue PowerShell script sent to your client PC could disable the background service if the credentials are correct). It also is heavily reliant on the processing power provided by the client PC as well as the existing OS architecture to allow it to function. A network-based firewall has its own Firmware OS and it dedicated to performing its one task only.

A **software-based firewall** can be configured to operate as an **applications firewall**, namely that use of a specific application can temporarily open a specific port, just for the use of this application. When the application is closed, the port is also closed. Software-based firewalls also allow the user to create an IPsec tunnel to secure a dedicated VPN connection into the network. The same tunnel has to be configured at both endpoints. When a firewall opens based on the use of a **specific application**, or due to changes to the system brought about by the running of an application (e.g. starting Skype may then start services pertaining to QoS, Video conferencing and audio VoIP calls) this is said to be a **context aware** firewall solution. Context is also used to refer to the connection profile used by specific rules – when the laptop is connected to a Domain, domain-specific rules are applied but when at home, Private rules apply.

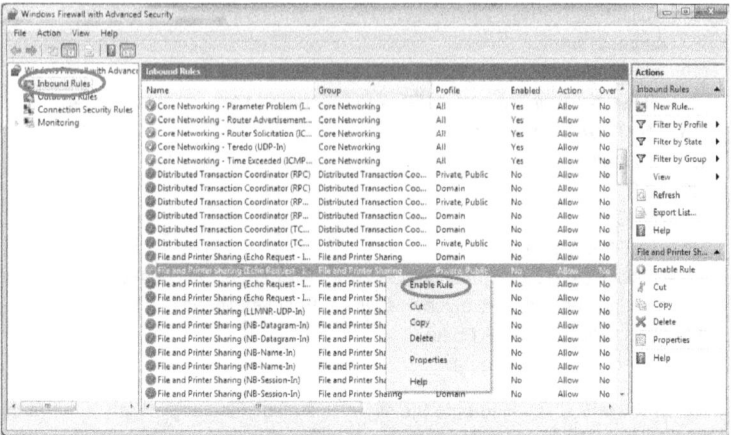

Windows Firewall with Advanced Security

A **SOHO firewall** is a role of most 'all in one' home ISP solutions provided by your Internet Service Provider. The firewall is designed to block ports, but has an application-blocking / opening facility often used by gamers to allow Xboxes to 'tunnel', sending game-specific data to the gaming arena so that internet gaming matches (e.g. *Warcraft*) are possible.

Stateful Inspection - packets intended to be sent on the specific connection are allowed through the switch port on the firewall whereas packets with port numbers which have been blocked on the firewall's ports table will not be allowed through. The process of inspecting the packets is active – packets are dropped or allowed as the connection is being sent. However, stateful can do much deeper in its inspection of the packet to determine not only the port number but which application will be using the data. Therefore a Stateful inspection is said to traverse all of the layers of the OSI model (as it considers the application which will be using the data. If this application is allowed to use the data, the data can be sent on).

Stateless inspection does not inspect the packet at the deeper level. The port number is read from the header of the IP packet and checked against the list of allowed / blocked ports. If the number corresponds to an allowed port, the packet is allowed through, otherwise the packet is dropped.

> Tip: There is a very good animation called 'Warriors of the Net' originally designed some years ago now and is heavily used as a starting point with Cisco training to describe the journey of a web packet through the corporate network and out onto the internet. There is a good sequence within the film describing a stateless inspection corporate firewall.
> https://www.youtube.com/watch?v=PBWhzz_Gn10

Unified Threat Management (UTM) was mentioned earlier in our discussion of Microsoft Forefront – Threat Management Gateway. The idea is to have a primary network gateway defence solution – a single 'first stop' for all incoming traffic to be analysed, thereby reducing the need of configuring other systems with a large number of blocking rules. The UTM device is typically a high-performance server capable of acing as a security gateway, performing antivirus sweeps of data sent through as well as firewall regulation. Client requests to access sites would be sent to a proxy server and checked that they meet corporate policy before allowing potentially unsavoury traffic onto the internal network. By working with the proxy server the download takes place away from the client machine and if the download is acceptable to security policy the downloaded file is then copied across to the client. To the client the process does not seem to change from a normal download, however client requests are being dealt with 'by proxy'.

Several techinques are available for us to consider to use:

The **Account Control List** refers to a security list of allowed resources, but may also be used to restrict who can access the internet, or other network zones, and also the extent to which they can interact with these other zones.

A **virtual wire** is the process of using two physical cables either side of a firewall (one in each of the adjacent security zones the firewall is connected to), paired together within the firewall configuration to form a single logical wire. From the perspective of the router or switch at the other end of the cable in either of the security zone, the firewall in the middle of the 'wire' is invisible. The firewall will however be able to forward allowed packets into the other security zone.

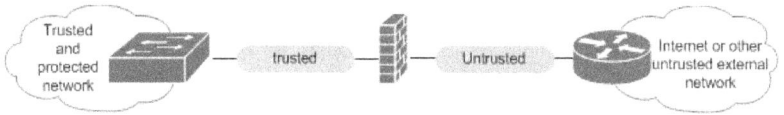

A virtual wire connecting two security zones.

The difference with a **routed connection** is that a router will augment the IP header information in order to resend the packet into the other domain. A 'virtual wire' acts more like a bridge in that the initial packet sent from the switch in the first security zone is not altered in any way by the firewall.

We have earlier described the use of a perimeter network and how it can be used for public access to corporate resources which are not confidential in nature. A Demilitarised Zone is a form of perimeter network security zone where services offered are screened from accessing the internal network. A **DMZ** is considered to be the logical 'space' between two firewalls both performing stateful inspection and restricting access through into the more secure internal network.

DMZ zones are also often used with virtualised environments and with virtual switches to create separated areas from the internal network and by so doing can run experimental networks separated from the main infrastructure and therefore causing the main internal network no harm. An example of this may be to test a WDS deployment which also houses a DHCP server. The DMZ would screen broadcasts from a new 'blank' PC which is about to receive its image. This broadcast will be responded to by the DMZ's DHCP server and not by the main corporate intranet DHCP server.

An **implicit deny** is the default state for a firewall – if no other rule is present on the port table, or Access control list, then the traffic should be blocked by default.

To 'block' refers to the deletion of the data packet as it is being inspected by the firewall, not allowing it to travel beyond the firewall and into the next security zone.

'Allow' refers to the process of inspecting the packet and based on information in the packet conforming to a rule configured on the firewall, the packet is allowed through and into the next security zone.

Outbound refers to any data packets travelling from the host machine we are working on (or from the zone we are connected to, e.g. the internal corporate intranet), past a firewall and onto another security zone (e.g. the Internet).

Inbound traffic refers to any data attempting to access our network from an external security zone also connected to the firewall.

NB: Ports can be set to allow inbound traffic, allow outbound traffic, to allow both, or to block both.

The **firewall placement** is between two logical security zones. In reality placement is by CAT5 / CAT6 cable between two switches, or two routers each of which servicing a different part of the organisation (e.g. different security zones). For internet-facing traffic the firewall is a hardware 'box' on the extremity of the network, past the 'outward-facing' router and usually connects all of the corporate data at the site to the modem, distribution frame, demarcation point or other highly condensed data stream. It would usually also connect to the VPN concentrator which would be multiplexing a series of VPN streams and de-duplexing them into separate communications streams (or 'tunnels') for communication into the internal network.

An **internal** firewall is so called because it represents a segregation point between two or more security zones within the network. The firewall may separate one department from another, or from the remainder of the network.

An **externally facing** firewall refers to a firewall which separates the internal security zone(s) from the public internet. As described above it is the 'outward-facing' firewall which is the last point through which the data packet must be sent before it reaches the modem, or demarcation point.

3.6

3.6 Explain the purpose of various network access control models
- 802.1x
- Posture assessment
- Guest network
- Persistent vs non-persistent agents
- Quarantine network
- Edge vs access control

802.1x is a certificate-based access model requiring the same certificate to be present on both the client and server before a data encryption channel (a 'tunnel') can be formed. If the certificate is not present on one of the endpoints to the tunnel, encrypted data cannot be read as the certificate is used as part of the decryption and encryption process. However although this is where we see 802.1x be used in the main, we need to look deeper at how this works.

It is an IEEE standard for Port-based access control which involves three machines (or 'parties'): the supplicant, an authenticator and an authentication server. The supplicant would be the client PC wishing to access a resource on the LAN. The authenticator is a network device such as a wireless access point or switch. The authentication server would be a RADIUS or DirectAccess server using EAP.

There are similarities with the firewall and the 'virtual wire'. The authenticator only will allow access for the supplicant once the identity of the supplicant has been validated and the supplicant authorised to access the specific location on the LAN. 802.1x allows the supplicant to provide their credentials (e.g. username and password using Kerberos, or a pre-signed digital certificate). The supplicant sends this authentication data to the authenticator who passes this data first to the authentication server. Once the server confirms that the details are valid, the authenticator then allows access to the network resource requested.

Posture assessment is the evaluation of system security based on the applications and settings that a particular system is using. This may include the operation of, also security strength of a client firewall, ensuring that all updates have been added (within the past 3 months) and that a virus definitions database update has been performed in the last 2 weeks, also that a full virus scan has been completed and that there are no threats on the system. The security software installed on the client may also need to be one of a few 'known good' solutions otherwise the criteria may still not be met. In Microsoft terminology this is referred to as 'Network Access Protection'.

A **guest network** is a means for visitors to access the internet and other non-threatening resources whilst remaining unable to access the more secure corporate network. Physically the same network infrastructure is used, however as the user has not authenticated as a member of the corporate staff the 'implicit' function has not been to deny but instead to provide 'guest' access, or the guest has been granted with a 'guest' Kerberos username and password which will provide access to this area.

The **guest network** is in some situations full physical access to the main corporate environment and restriction takes place through Account Control Lists on resources and shared folders, however some systems give 'guest' user accounts the same level of privilege as a standard user, which may be more access rights than we deem proper. Therefore a guest network is a separate area on the network where the guest cannot gain any understanding of the corporate network data structure, software installed across the network or any other corporate information pertaining to the actual internal network. The 'guest network' is often a webpage or limited 'cloud' enabling access to a limited selection of corporate resources as well as limited and controlled access to the internet. 'Public Wi-Fi' in a restaurant would be an example of a 'guest network' as the guest cannot see any information such as the restaurant EPOS or CRM software and yet the wireless router they are connecting to may well physically exist within the internal network.

Persistent v non-persistent agents – a Network Sentry is an application which validates the configuration of the client as they join the network. If the client is 'unhealthy' (as with NAP) then the client is warned that remedial action is needed before it is able to join the network. The client is given a 'quarantine IP address' by DHCP which allows it to be able to be maintained by the network without giving access to network resources other than those needed to upgrade the client. This is referred to as the **quarantine network**.

The **persistent agent** provides nonstop monitoring and automatic remediation and control, whereas **non-persistent agents** require network administrator intervention, or for the client to disjoin and re-join the domain to perform another system 'health scan'.

Edge vs access control – Edge control refers to a demarcation point between a server and a virtual switch which are the endpoints of the virtual network environment and the physical network. An 'edge' device monitors and manages the flow of traffic leaving the internal network onto the other security zone, or media. This is very much a physical demarcation. However, Access control breaks up the network into logical security zones, or 'domains' which span the physical network (or 'sites'). Access to resources is not necessarily bound by physical limits are services span the sites. Access to resources is dependent on the group to which the user, or device, is a member of and the extent to which (the 'scope') the user can access.

3.7

3.7 Summarize basic forensic concepts
- First responder
- Secure the area
  - Escalate when necessary
- Document the scene
- eDiscovery
- Evidence/data collection
- Chain of custody
- Data transport
- Forensics report
- Legal hold

The Network+ course now encompasses a series of security concepts and techniques. Within this section we will consider Forensic concepts. Forensics in relation to IT security refers to the scientific method of gathering and examining information about the events of the past but extends this further to the safe collection of and examination of data without tampering and ensuring that any evidence gathered may still be admissible in court. This may only be true if specific checks and procedures are following and these are covered in this section.

From a data perspective the **First Responder** is a member of staff who is first on the scene to respond to an incident. Typical incidents may include the following:

Fire, Flood, Earthquake or some other physical disaster where the network will need to be 'saved' or actions taken to protect immediate data.

In the event of a power loss, the **First Responder** is the person with Server authority to close down the servers gracefully, take backups of immediate data without interrupting the backup schedule and as saving as much data as can be saved within the time provided by backup power.

The **First Responder** may also switch over processes and systems to backup failsafe systems.

In all of these scenarios, the **First Responder** has a duty of care to protect life, also to do all that it is possible to protect the network and corporate data from loss, harm or in the case of security, leaking to a third party, or the public network. It is to this end that a First Responder may choose to take drastic action (e.g. to remove a network cable) to quickly stop the loss of data from the system, then deal with any infection whilst the machine is isolated from the network.

Securing the area, or 'lockdown' is a process of alerting the wider site of an emergency situation, next to take action to electro-mechanically lock physical doors, windows (etc.) to prevent egress. This may be done if there is a suspected data breach such as if a theft is in the process of taking place in order to trap the would-be 'villain' from escaping with whatever confidential data they may possess. Whilst melodramatic, it is more commonplace to simply secure an area by locking a cabinet, or closing a lockable door. Security doors are so-called in that they are intended to close behind you and egress is only possible by the use of a security technique such as a key fob or swipeable ID card, knowledge of an access code, or to be permitted to leave by another member of staff who has access to the door control.

Escalation in this respect refers to the 'chain of authority' provided to staff. Any member of staff may hold a suspicion that a person is not who they claim, for example a visitor may have lost their ID badge and not be able to give a proper account of themselves, therefore asking the individual to wait nearby within a secured area whilst the staff member can inform a member of the security team, or their line manager shows correct adherence to procedure as other more senior-level (clearance) staff may be able to take action such as to check visitor logs, or even to issue a replacement ID badge. Whilst this seems to be a very procedural, or draconian measure the act of referring a security matter to a senior colleague may be entirely innocent and part of the normal security process.

Escalation may include the involvement of a trained security guard who is capable of taking evidence, conducting an interview, or to escort the individual off the premises, alternatively to refer the matter to the Police for further action where the individual may be removed, formally charged, or arrested.

The term **escalation** itself refers to an increase in the intensity or seriousness of something. Escalating in terms of data refers to the action of access to a data file, or its change having to be made by a person with more ('higher') security privilege whereas for corporate security we are referring to the actions a staff member may take to stop, question, or intervene with the actions of an individual. Certain processes have to be undertaken by a designated member of staff, or group and so this individual will have to be informed that their presence is required in order to take further action on the incident.

The process of documenting the scene refers to the action of the first responder to give a full account of the incident, at the time that it took place. The **Forensic report** provides a chronological account of the incident from the time the first problem was encountered to the final steps. No subjective information should exist in the report – it must be entirely factual detailing all observed problems in as much technical detail as can be obtained. To support this, system logs from routers, firewalls and even logs within servers and client PCs are used to give precise timestamps where technical events have occurred.

The documentation is from the perspective of the first responder and details their observations as time elapsed as the incident occurred. Supplementary documentation is also from the viewpoint of the person involved with the incident.

eDiscovery refers to the discovery of files and documents in electronic format for their use as potential evidence in a case (e.g. civil litigation, or a government investigation). Electronically Stored information (e.g. files) can provide a series of problems for the legal profession as their authenticity is commonly brought into question. Local rules and processes do change from state or country to country and so may only be admissible if certain regulations are followed in how they were obtained, stored and brought to the attention of the court.

Files are often put into **legal hold** status, meaning that the file is under the protection of the court. During this time, the file may be converted to other formats and may be analysed so that text can be extracted and made searchable.

One of the problems present is in the access to and 'shelf life' of data stored electronically. A server may embargo documents and also restrict access to specific individuals, so the access control list and document management configuration on the server is also very important. Electronic files often will also contain 'metadata', that is additional information about the file which is extra to the viewable content on the document (e.g. a Word processed document also contains META data showing the author, the date it was created, when it was last accessed and the version number). If handled incorrectly, for example a file type conversion or 'extracting' of a file as a different type (e.g. PDF to JPG), metadata is not captured and it said to be 'spoiled'.

Data is collected by a variety of techniques, but one of the most common is to perform a bitwise copy of the entire hard drive, or partition onto another blank external hard drive. This can then be inspected remotely without concern of damage to the data stored on the original drive (referred to as the **data integrity**). Imaging software which can perform an exact bitwise copy is extremely useful but presents an interesting problem – we now have two physical copies of the data we need to protect. Whilst one is designed to be held in a secure manner until it is needed by court, the other can be investigated and analysed. However, there must be an unbroken audit trail, from the time of the incident and the data's 'discovery' at the time of the incident through to its eventual use within court. An audit trail would show when the original was locked away and two looked after it, when safes were opened and so forth, but more importantly that the device was only handled by an authorised and qualified individual and only for a specific purpose. With the 'copy' of the data the problem is more complex as many different forensic analysts, each a specialist within their own field may need to have access to the evidence and at different times of the investigation. It is extremely unlikely that further copies would be made, or that the data under inspection would be placed onto a network, rather the second hard drive, the 'copy' is handed from individual to individual and the security log is updated as work progresses and as the device changes hands. This log must be entirely unbroken otherwise the solicitor fighting against the admission of the evidence could rightly claim that the 'chain of custody' is unbroken and that a third party may have replaced, or tampered with the investigation at this point. Whilst probably implausible in a secure environment, it would render the evidence unusable from a legal perspective.

Data transport – during transport the evidence (e.g. a smartphone) will be sent from site to site in a shut-down state to avoid any changes to the device, intentionally or not, during transit. For example, a mobile phone may contain a GPS receiver which otherwise would update the phone's location. In the case of copied hard drives, the drive is bagged and sent in an unpowered state.

However, the opposite may be true – you may need to keep the device running and also in a state where it cannot be tampered with until it arrives at the destination. To this end, a HotPlug Field kit will supply power to a laptop (a portable UPS) whilst also preventing physical access to the laptop (it is held within a security protected case). A possible scenario where this may occur is if you need to continue to access a laptop after the user has left, or has been injured and is unable to operate the device for you (e.g. may have been mortally wounded) and telemetry or security data still exists on the users' account (e.g. in a murder scene, the attacker leaves and the victim writes a note onto the laptop but was unable to finish the note and to save it before losing consciousness).

A HotPlug Field Kit

Domain 4

Troubleshooting

The term 'troubleshooting' refers to activities which provide information and then are able to remediate a problem encountered on the network. By problem we are usually referring to a misconfigured service, an inactive service, an inaccessible service or other problem affecting services and data offered on the network.

4.1

4.1 Given a scenario, implement the following network troubleshooting methodology
- Identify the problem
    - Gather information
    - Duplicate the problem, if possible
    - Question users
    - Identify symptoms
    - Determine if anything has changed
    - Approach multiple problems individually
- Establish a theory of probable cause
    - Question the obvious
    - Consider multiple approaches
        - Top-to-bottom/bottom-to-top OSI model
        - Divide and conquer
- Test the theory to determine cause
    - Once theory is confirmed, determine next steps to resolve problem
    - If theory is not confirmed, re-establish new theory or escalate
- Establish a plan of action to resolve the problem and identify potential effects
- Implement the solution or escalate as necessary
- Verify full system functionality and if applicable implement preventative measures
- Document findings, actions, and outcomes

The CompTIA Network+ exam takes great pride to, quite correctly, educate network administrative staff to follow the correct troubleshooting procedure, to avoid pitfalls or shortcuts which may result in a lack of correct information, a 'quick fix' or in fact a repeat of previous steps as they have been improperly carried out. The CompTIA troubleshooting methodology is designed to ensure that all persons who are carrying out the remediation, or 'fix' are fully armed with the correct information before work is carried out, so that 'guesses' are avoided and options to 'eliminate the obvious' are built into the methodology.

Identify the problem – this may sound obvious but in network troubleshooting finding the exact cause and location of a problem can be quite time consuming. For example, an Ethernet network wired using a Coaxial cable may suffer from a cable 'break', particularly if T-junction 'spurs' are used to connect new PCs as connectivity will be lost if the cable is 'jolted' or moved accidentally. Finding the 'break' may take some time involving a process of PINGing from a series of different locations on the network, or even the involvement of a Time-Domain Reflectometer to measure the distance from a key point to the actual break in a cable. TDRs are not cheap and simply asking a class of delegates who can connect and who cannot when all as sharing a simple bus network common cable may be much quicker.

As part of the identification stage out aim is to eliminate the obvious, but to use questioning techniques along with technical observation to find out what the problem is perceived to be.

In order to identify the problem, we will attempt to **gather information**, through direct objective observations of the scene, or by physically checking the system. Our purpose is to gather as much relevant information pertaining to the problem. If possible, once we have observed and understood what we perceive to be the problem, we will try to re-create it, or refer to notes, a knowledgebase or internal database of previous faults and fixes in order to narrow our search further. In order to obtain a timeframe, also which activities have been tried already to fix the fault, also an understanding of the user's perspective as to what is precisely wrong (useful if the technician cannot get to site and is reliant on user information of the problem, such as in a First-Line technical support call). Here, **questioning techniques** are used to focus the conversation on the specifics of the problem encountered by the use of open questions to allow the client to elaborate, also closed, technical question to affirm specifics of the problem.

Armed with information as to what the problem is, the technician may decide to try to **duplicate the problem** if it is safe to do so within a test environment. In the case of a virus, or unsafe activity, researching the problem online would also count as relevant at this stage to envisage how the problem was created, the impact of the problem and also how it may be resolved.

Through analysis of the problem we can **identify symptoms** – what does a system look or act like once it has been effected in this way? Symptoms are factors which imply that the system has been affected in a specific way. For example, a boot sector virus may cause the system to not boot and a specific error message is generated. The denial of services on a server will be evident with warning and error messages in the event log. Equally, the administrative tools > services page will list services which are expected to load on startup. These services may, for some reason such as a script switching them back off, may need to be restarted – a temporary fix but showing how rogue code may impact on a system.

We are therefore **determining if anything has changed**. To help with this it is good practice to have a list of used services on each client. Where different users or department may have specific needs, this list of applications and service may change, but if the 'expected' services are listed and from this we can determine what has changed, then we may be able to postulate if there is a common pattern, or connection between the elements which have changed. (e.g. a virus may programmatically stop the Defender service with a view to undertaking other actions which otherwise may have been detected by the Defender service).

There are a number of **key questions** which are vital when investigating a fault:

- When did this start?
- What is the extent of the damage? (this system, or network-wide)
- Is the cause of the damage obvious?
- Who was using the system both at the time of the incident and since the incident? (Who else may also have been affected?)

- Which resources / website were visited at the time that the incident was noticed?

The incident may in fact lead to a cascade of different problems to the system. The investigating technician may determine a common pattern which in itself shows that one or a few problems encountered may lead to the presence of a wider issue. However, each problems need to be **considered separately** until it is possible to perform a holistic 'fix' if this is possible.

Once we have a thorough understanding and have documented what we believe to have happened and of how the system has been impacted, we need to determine how the problem was caused. We would be quite literal and not assume anything. Question the obvious options available (e.g. did the user visit a website which has not been checked for viruses? Did the user ignore any warning messages from the antivirus software and by doing so overridden any safeguards, causing the affected file to be downloaded anyway?).

It is possible that in order to fix the fault several **different courses of action** may be taken to remediate the problem:

- Spend several hours attempting to disinfect the system, repairing OS damage in the hope that the system does not become re-infected or other 'dummy' files or registry entries have not been missed which may re-infect the system. This is the most labour-intensive option and whilst it may seem obvious to fix the fault, if the system affected is standard and images exist then there are other options which are quicker and more reliable.

- Attempt a rollback to a previous state in the hope that this 'previous state' is free of the problem. System files will be re-written and hopefully the system will be returned to a working state. There is no guarantee that the infection, or problem has been solved.

- Re-image the machine from a previous image taken recently. The machine will quickly be returned to a working state however any recent updates, recently installed applications or locally-saved documents will be lost in the process.

- On a corporate network, a WDS server can remediate the rebuild by installing the OS and applications in stages based on which AD security group the system is associated with. This would however need the system to be present on the network, but booting across the network, rather than into the infected system which may then in fact spread the problem across the network.

As an example, there may be ways to shortcut a network problem by using the **OSI model**. Trainers often dispute as to where to start with the OSI model – some assert that we should always start with the **bottom layer** (Physical) and work from this up to the application and eventually to the user actions. Other trainers consider the problem from the user **down through** the model through the various conceptual layers to the eventual physical wiring. In reality, we are presented with a problem which equates with one layer of the OSI model, so we may in fact start with a middle layer and then work to adjacent layers.

As an example, consider a call from a user on a corporate network to a support technician, complaining that they cannot access a shared folder, just created recently on the network.

You verify that the shared folder exists on the network as from your workstation you are able to navigate to the folder. You ask the user for any specific error messages. You ask the user to navigate to the folder again via UNC path (e.g. \\Server\NewShare). They do so, there is a delay and the error message is again given. You ask the user to navigate to the hosting system storing the shared folder by UNC path (e.g. \\Server\SharedFolder). This succeeds and proves that the 'Server' machine is available to the user's computer, negating the need to check wiring, or IP addressing. You ask the user to use the IP address of the server rather than the name 'server'. This would show that there is no DNS problem. Accessing the old shared folder located on the same system proves that DNS is resolving to the correct machine. The problem is therefore higher in the OSI model. The fact that the user can access one folder and not another infers an access issue and so the access control list should be checked to ensure that the user is present on the ACL and has sufficient permissions to access the new shared folder.

Once we have hypotheses of potential causes we can perform a series of tests to eliminate causes until we can be confident that we have the most probable cause. This approach is referred to as 'divide and conquer'.

> *"Once you eliminate the impossible, whatever remains, no matter how improbable, must be the truth."* - Arthur Conan Doyle

The next step is to test the theory to determine the cause of the problem. Naïve technicians at this point, if they are aware of the problem and know how to fix it, may be tempted to simply fix the fault, charge the client for their time and leave. This would not however stop the incident from happening again – the client has not been educated and no further safeguards have been put in place to harden the system. If we are aware how the problem occurred in the first place, then we could take further actions to stop a repeat of the incident, also would have a greater awareness of the problem.

e.g. a virus may be present on the system, however reviewing recent internet activity may reveal the site where the virus was inadvertently obtained. This URL can be added to the corporate 'blacklist' ensuring that other systems will not be able to access the site and therefore will not be affected.

The confirmation of a theory prompts the technical team to be able to take **additional steps to resolve the problem**, also to ensure that other systems across the network will not be affected.

If the theory is not confirmed, we return to the evidence and backtrack to possible gather more evidence. Once more information has been obtained which changes our theory we can establish a new theory. Where the technician is unable to produce a new theory, the complexity of the matter may necessitate a need to escalate the issue to another partner technician, or to Second-Line support. Where the problem is beyond the skills of Second-Line and the problem is of a specialist nature, Third-line support consultants may be involved.

Once a theory is confirmed by evidence, the technician needs to **determine the course of action** they will take to remediate the problem:

- Do we only need to repair one system or is the problem network-wide?

- Is there a need to educate staff?
- Will we need to replace damaged components?
- Which is the best, quickest and most effective method to repair the system and data (the 'image')?
- Would my actions fully repair the system or are further actions required?
- Am I using additional software to repair the system which may have an impact on applications or data? (E.g. a vulnerable XP system may be updated to Windows 8.1 however application compatibility will need to be set and some applications may not work with 8.1 and will need to be virtualised, or moved to another system.)

The next step will be to actually **perform the fix** (remediation). If the fix cannot or is not allowed to be performed by the support technician, the matter will need to be escalated to a colleague, or **escalated** (e.g. in the case of a Network Manager who would have higher security privileges and be able to perform network hardening.)

Once the fix or repair has been completed, we need to verify that we have full system functionality by comparing known services and applications installed before the incident are again available and that there has not been a performance drop caused as a result of the fix. At this point if we are able to perform some 'hardening' to ensure that the same problem does not occur again, it would be applied at this stage.

Finally, we need to **document the findings, our actions and any outcomes** we have noticed so that our change management process is followed. Other technical staff needing to work on the system in the future will need to know about any additional work, changes and configurations which make the system configuration different to 'base' (usual configuration). This can be eliminated by deploying a WDS or imaging strategy.

Exam Tip: Although we cannot give precise specifics of the exam, we can tell you that you will be given a brief scenario which describes actions taken at one phase of the network methodology. Your job will be to determine which stage activity is taking place, or to consider what stage occurs next. Answers will be the stage titles as they appear in the standard methodology, but may not appear in order.

You may also be asked to present the stages in order.

4.2

4.2 Given a scenario, analyze and interpret the output of troubleshooting tools
- Command line tools
  - ipconfig
  - netstat
  - ifconfig
  - ping/ping6/ping -6
  - tracert/tracert -6/traceroute6/traceroute -6
  - nbtstat
  - nslookup
  - arp
  - mac address lookup table
  - pathping
- Line testers
- Certifiers
- Multimeter
- Cable tester
- Light meter
- Toner probe
- Speed test sites
- Looking glass sites
- WiFi analyzer
- Protocol analyzer

In this section we will be discussed the different tools used when troubleshooting a system. We will consider the benefit of the tool and how it is used, also what results we would expect to see by using the tool. Most of these software tools are already installed as part of the system.

IPCONFIG (IFCONFIG on Linux systems) is a command-line tool which provides basic IP configuration data for all NICs and Tunnels on the system. Using the default command with no switches will give the main IP address for the system, however IPCONFIG / ALL is useful in that it also provides additional information such as:

- Whether the host IP address was provided by DHCP
- The media state (e.g. Wi-Fi may be disconnected)
- The host NIC IP address, subnet mask and default gateway
- The MAC (link-local) address of the NIC.

IPCONFIG in normal mode

Additionally, with the /ALL switch we can learn:

- Host name and DNS information
- IP address of the DHCP and DNS servers
- DHCP lease expiry
- Are we using NetBIOS over TCP/IP

This tool makes for a good starting point to determine the IP configuration settings of the host NIC quickly. If there is a misconfigured gateway, this may be the reason why a NIC can communicate with other systems in the subnet only.

An IP address statically assigned to the same IP number as another system will cause a conflict on the network. If the IP address is assigned by DHCP what should happen is that the configurable IP address (DHCP) will default to 0.0.0.0, meaning cannot communicate to any host on any network, prompting you to set an IP, or to check for IP conflicts. This can be a common problem for legacy photocopiers and printers which had to be manually assigned an IP address in the firmware.

The **IPCONFIG** tool also can be used to flush the DNS cache of any rogue entries. If the system has been the victim of DNS poisoning, the /FLUSHDNS switch will clear the local DNS cache and prompt the client system to check with the DNS server for any new requests.

Exam Tip: Expect to be asked about an APIPA scenario, where the DHCP server is uncontactable either due to a BOOTP router blocking traffic between subnets, or a DHCP server is turned off. APIPA is an 'emergency' system (used to be referred to as 'Network zero', or 'auto configuration') whereby all hosts on the subnet obtain an IP address starting 169.254.x.x where x.x is a random set of numbers. The idea is that each IP address should be unique. However APIPA addresses are non-routable, so it is not possible to use a host in an APIPA state for Internet connectivity.

NETSTAT is a command-line tool showing all currently active connections on the system. This is useful to determine if there are any unknown background services attempting to communicate without the knowledge of the user.

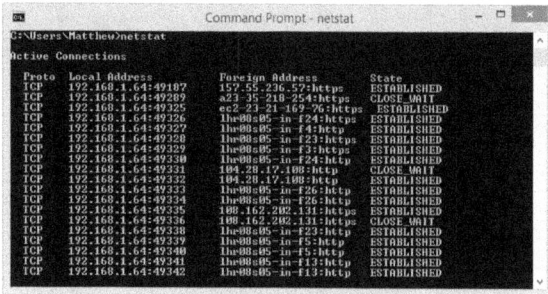

NETSTAT active ports

PING stands for Packet Internet Groper. It is a major tool in the ICMP suite. However, routers and managed switches can block ICMP traffic. PINGs are a major cause of Denial of Service as a PING command can be looped, or can be sent indefinitely (known as the 'Ping of Death'). A 'ping' is a test packet sent to a specific IP address. Domain names can also be 'pinged' and the test packet is resolved and send to the machine we are trying to reach. A 'ping' command sends 4 test packets of a set size, in sequence and records the time taken for a response to be received. This enables us to see if the next node in the network map from this point can be reached and also if there is any congestion on the cable, or if the node we are trying to reach is itself congested.

By 'pinging' a node several hops away in a physical sequence (e.g. through a switch, through a router into another subnet, through a switch and then to the end node) we can determine if this path is viable. This will suggest to us if there is a break in the path (e.g. a disconnected cable, or a misconfigured router).

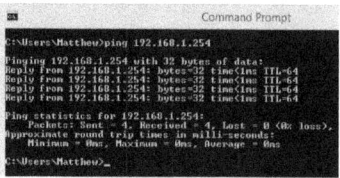

PING test to router

On an IPv6 network, the Ping -6 switch will send an IPv4 test packet. In the case of the example below I am 'Pinging' the loopback address for IPv6 on my local NIC. By doing this we are proving that the NIC is working, that the TCP/IP protocol stack is working, that IPv6 is enabled and that the NIC is able to process this data.

(NB: *Ping6* was a separate command to perform this action on XP systems.)

Testing with Ping -6

In the above, what we are however not testing is the physical condition of the actual port within the NIC. To do this, we need to use a loopback plug which will send any outward bound data back in through the input pins creating a data loop and affirming connectivity.

A loopback plug

Traceroute (*Tracert* on Microsoft Systems) is a command-line tool which will show the path taken to send data packets across the network. For the internal network it will show common pathways or trunk lines used to reach the destination. The use of the -6 switch (or on some systems 6 is appended to the command name) infers that the trace will take place using a test IPv6 packet.

Traceroute is useful as a mapping tool to determine the pathways taken from router to router to ensure that no routing loops are occurring, or to check that the most effective route is being chosen. If the Network manage is aware of a faster route at one point in the pathway, they may choose to amend the router configuration to favour the preferred route.

TRACEROUTE to www.google.com

NBSTAT is a useful tool for displaying NetBIOS statistics on the internal network.

A NETBIOS name check of known groups on the host PC.

NETBIOS is a legacy system used in the days of Windows 95 and NT. It was a simplified version of DNS which was flat is structure, not hierarchical. The WINS (Windows Internet Naming Server) is an earlier, basic version of the modern DNS in that it resolved hostnames to IP addresses. NETBIOS protocols can be run across the TCP/IP network for backwards compatibility. With modern system it is unlikely that network problems will be presented if the corporate network has moved over to DNS. However, workgroups and homegroups may be misconfigured, or may contain hidden groups in use by spyware. These may be revealed through the use of **NBTSTAT**.

Tip: there are several switches connected with NBTSTAT. Usually you will want to run the command to resolve names and to view remote tables from other neighbouring hosts. Switch:

–a will resolve a remote host by its name.
–A will resolve a remote host by its IP address.
–R will reload the NETBIOS cache.
–s lists the session table
–RR releases and refreshes the NETBIOS system, clearing the cache and restarting communication with WINS.

NSLOOKUP (Name Server Lookup) is a command-line tool environment. It is a powerful tool able to print but also to set domain information. It is used to edit the local NS cache. Typically **NSLOOKUP** will list the location of the default local gateway by its DNS name and IP address, however more extensive configuration of the local NS table can be performed. As modern domains rely on the presence of a DNS server **NSLOOKUP** is only used to edit specific configuration cache information, although it is often easier to flush the cache with IPCONFIG. NSLOOKUP is used to manually locate and to resolve other servers and routers across the network.

NSLOOKUP resolves the home router, but cannot see a domain

(R)ARP ((Reversible) Address Resolution Protocol) is a similar resolving table able to resolve IP addresses to MAC addresses. The **ARP** cache can be used to determine the ARP address we are sending to a specific machine. It is the ARP cache which is poisoned in a 'man-in-the-middle' attack.

ARP cache for a local PC

A **RARP** command gives the reverse information – given the MAC address, which IP address is it currently assigned to? The RARP tool is not available on client systems however the ARP tool is.

The MAC address table is a table found on routers and switches, listing the MAC address discovered to be connected to each switchport. Once the MAC is present on the table after a result of receiving a 'handshake' packet from the newly connected node's NIC, the node is said to be 'discovered' (or 'learned').

Access to the MAC table will easily show if there is a connectivity problem between the affected node and the switch / router.

Attached Devices

Wired Devices

#	IP Address	Device Name	MAC Address
1	192.168.1.7	SQA-PERF-PC	D4:BE:D9:8A:B5:90

Wireless Devices (Wireless intruders also show up here)

#	IP Address	Device Name	MAC Address
1	192.168.1.8	optiplex-936c99	02:0F:B5:C4:7C:C8
2	192.168.1.10	sqa-dell_5300	02:0F:B5:28:31:20
3	192.168.1.250	WN2500RP	02:0F:B5:3C:59:E3
4	–	–	E0:24:B2:3C:59:E4
5	192.168.1.10	sqa-dell_5300	02:0F:B5:28:31:20
6	–	–	E2:24:B2:3C:59:E4

[Refresh]

A typical MAC table on a managed switch

Exam tip: *You may be presented with a network diagram, event logs and switch MAC tables in order to determine where there is a 'break' in the network.*

Pathping is a command-line tool found on servers. It is an advancement of the standard PING, (combining the features of PING and Tracert) in that it is able to ping across the network from node-to-node until the end point is reached. This will enable the Network Manager to determine if there are any slow connections, or congestion between nodes, or on a specific node and allow the Network Manager to take remedial action.

A sample PATHPING trace

A **line tester** is a device capable of checking connectivity on a line (e.g. telephone line). Rather than checking electrical connectivity, the presence of the carrier line data is detected. On advanced testers, the tester itself is capable of sending a test signal to a node. For telephones, a 'butt set' is a line tester which is clipped to the telephone cable in order to check for connectivity. The technician will be able to hear a dial tone and even to use the cable to dial a test number to ensure that connectivity is present.

A typical 'butt-set' line tester

A **cable tester** is a device which will check for electrical continuity in a network cable. One end of the cable is connected to one end of the device, the other end is connected to the other side of the device. A test electrical signal is sent on each wire in turn, lighting LEDs on both sides of the device. Any break in continuity either by socket pins not connecting to the cable it is crimped to, or a wire break within the cable itself will cause the LED pair not to light up.

A **cable tester** is often used to ensure connectivity on manually-crimped cable during the cabling of patch and installed cabling (e.g. within Plenum space).

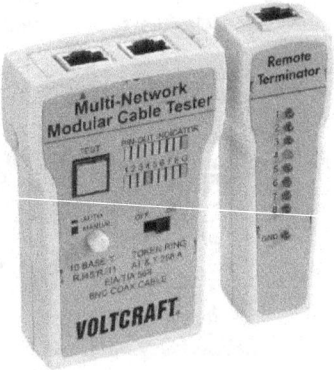

A cable tester

A **cable certifier** fulfils a legal requirement when laying installed cable. As it needs to be cut to length and manually crimped, not only is connectivity important but also the resistivity of the cable a measure of its quality. Building insurance regulations now require that any cable which has been manually installed needs to be checked for compliance by a cable certifier. The device proves that the cable has been properly terminated and that data speeds, noise and attenuation are within tolerances expected within the medium. The certifier produces a report which can be used to guarantee the quality along the length of the fitted cable.

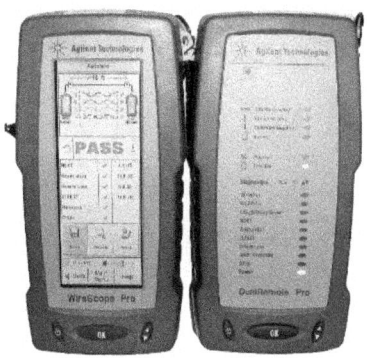

A cable certifier

A **multimeter** is a simple way of testing for electrical connectivity between a component within a system (e.g. across a fuse, or resistor) but can also be used to give an accurate reading for current, voltage and resistance of a circuit. A resistance of infinity would infer a connectivity break at this point in the circuit suggesting that a component would need to be replaced.

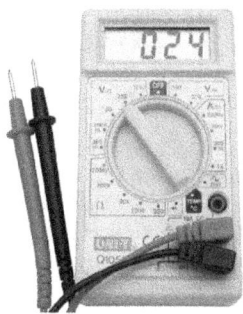

A multimeter

A **light meter** is a device used by photographers to determine the ambient light levels of a room in order to calibrate the camera (referred to as *black balancing* and *white balancing*). The device is also useful to ensure that room lighting meets Health and Safety lighting luminance levels.

Imagine a scenario where you need to label patch cables in a switch room, but the patch panel has been left as a mess and you need to determine which 'end' is for which cable. To find the end of a cable can be difficult. A **Toner probe** can help here. This is a device in two parts – a sounder and power unit to send a signal across the cable and a 'screwdriver'-like sensor which is tapped on the end of the cable until the correct one powered by the probe's power unit is found at which point a 'beep' is sounded. A common make is *Fox and Hound* and this is why the toner probe is still today referred to as that. Electricians also use single-unit toner probes to determine where live wires are housed within walls to ensure that they do not inadvertently drill into a power cable.

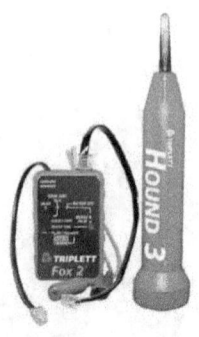

A 'Fox and Hound' toner probe

A **speed test site** is a website which will test your broadband speed, within your local area. Some sites are ISP-specific, some can test direct to your local cabinet, or to your local exchange. The site will give you an overall rating (upload and download speeds) and also usually inform you of other providers in your area. This would be useful if you are planning to evaluate a location for commercial use but need to host web services at the location. One typical site is http://www.broadbandspeedchecker.co.uk

A **looking glass site** is an entry point to obtain information, or even to access a **looking glass server**. A looking glass server is a server which allows people to view routing information for internet routers with a view to ensure that traffic is flowing effectively. http://www.traceroute.org contains a list of looking glass servers across the world.

A **Wi-Fi analyser** exists as either a dedicated hardware device or as an application. It is a wireless network scanner tool useful to identify channels in use, overlapping and conflicting channels. By obtaining this information we can determine the best course of action to take to eliminate overlap or conflict on the wireless network, typically by adjusting device channels. This link is to Wi-fi analyser for Android.
https://play.google.com/store/apps/details?hl=en&id=com.farproc.wifi.analyzer

A **protocol analyser** is a device, or application which will capture and allow the user to analyse signals over the network. Typically the application will allow the user to search or filter by specific port, or by a protocol. *Wireshark* and *Microsoft Network Monitor* are examples of this. Typically data is represented as an IP packet and is visually broken down in relation to the OSI model. The user can inspect parts of the packet and by so doing focus on areas of interest.

4.3

4.3 Given a scenario, troubleshoot and resolve common wireless issues
- Signal loss
- Interference
- Overlapping channels
    - Mismatched channels
- Signal-to-noise ratio
- Device saturation
- Bandwidth saturation
- Untested updates
- Wrong SSID
- Power levels
- Open networks
- Rogue access point
- Wrong antenna type
- Incompatibilities
- Wrong encryption
- Bounce
- MIMO
- AP placement
- AP configurations
    - LWAPP
    - Thin vs thick
- Environmental factors
    - Concrete walls
    - Window film
    - Metal studs
- Wireless standard related issues
    - Throughput
    - Frequency
    - Distance
    - Channels

In this section we will consider practical problems we may face with our wireless network and how they may be overcome.

Signal loss refers to the complete loss of, or weak signal either caused by the main access point being out of range, therefore by attenuation to a point where there are a significant number of dropped packets and the network connectivity is no longer effective. This may be remedied by the fixing of the access point (in the case of an inactive access point), the turning of the aerial to face the direction of transport (if the signal is weak), the replacement of the omnidirectional areal with a directional, a parabolic or a Yagi antenna. The signal may be boosted at source in order to clear the distance and improve the number of accepted packets, or the answer may be to fit a Wi-Fi repeater in order to regenerate the signal and by so doing extend the distance.

Whereas signal loss refers to the inability to receive the pure signal, **interference** refers to the interruption of the pure signal through 'crossover' with other RF signals, or by 'white noise', or even by EMF (electro-motive force). For example a factory may have three-phase machinery and unsuppressed motors which would generate a high amount of EMF. Equally within an office, fluorescent lighting can generate substantial EMF as can mains power cables, so network cables are laid perpendicular to power cables and away from fluorescent lighting. Also with wireless signals, cordless phones and microwave ovens produce EMF on the same frequency as Wi-Fi.

Adjacent channels within the Wi-Fi bandwidth only generally overlap on the rising and falling curves. These curves are quite sharp and therefore there is only a small area which will suffer from crosstalk. However the remedy would be to alter one wireless access point to not broadcast on the adjacent ID number to its neighbour. Where these channels are said to be of neighbouring channel IDs and physically adjacent, there is a strong likelihood of interference in which case these IDs are said to be mismatched. Where the neighbouring devices share the same ID, there will definitely be dropped packets as both Wi-Fi devices may be transmitting at the same time. To counter this, the IDs on one or on both Wi-Fi access points are adjusted accordingly. These channels are said to be not only **overlapping**, but **mismatched**.

The **signal to noise ratio (SNR or S/N)** refers to the amount of usable data which has been received. We are comparing the desired signal strength to the background noise. The ration is of signal power to noise power, referenced in decibels.

This ratio in data terms is now considered with the **Shannon-Hartley theorem** which provides to us the maximum rate at which information can be transmitted over a channel with a given bandwidth in the presence of noise. There is a degree to which the signal is usable, which this theory considers.

$$C = B \log_2 \left(1 + \frac{S}{N}\right)$$

C is the channel capacity in bits per second;
B is the bandwidth of the channel in hertz (passband bandwidth in case of a modulated signal);
S is the average received signal power over the bandwidth (in case of a modulated signal, often denoted C, i.e. modulated carrier), measured in watts (or volts squared);
N is the average noise or interference power over the bandwidth, measured in watts (or volts squared); and
S/N is the signal-to-noise ratio (SNR) or the carrier-to-noise ratio (CNR) of the communication signal to the Gaussian noise interference expressed as a linear power ratio (not as logarithmic decibels).

Referenced from Wikipedia

Device saturation refers to the face that a device can only send and receive a limited number of packets whilst multiplexing. When it reaches its limit it is said to be congested, in terms of data flow. This could apply to CPU usage, RAM, hard disk drive access as well as NIC data transfer.

Bandwidth saturation however specifically refers to the total usages of the complete bandwidth for transmission capable by the wired, or Wi-Fi device. This is separate to the capabilities of the system as a unit, and internal data transfer.

An **untested update** is an update rolled out across the corporate (production) network without prior testing. This could lead to instability, or the complete lack of operation by systems which may not be able to cope with the requirements posed by the software upgrade, leaving the system in an unworkable state. Major impacts could be a system upgrade to all machines which only just meet the current OS specification, rendering every PC unusable.

Best practice is to test an update within a test environment, also to use standardised hardware and images across the whole environment as much as is possible. By so doing this reduces workload for testing teams. Once the tested update can be approved (a manual process by the network administrator) the update can be safely rolled out by **WSUS**, or **Intune**.

If the Wi-Fi NIC connects to the **wrong SSID**, there will still be a connection to part of the network, however security levels, access geography may not meet with expectations. SSIDs are often password protected, however if the user can connect to various SSIDs they will find access to different shares including areas of the network not normally accessible. A good ACL with implicit deny will help in this situation to ensure that the would-be adventurer is unable to access anything they should not be able to.

As mentioned earlier, a weak **power level** will render a packet unreadable, or unusable, therefore will be dropped. By increasing the power level it should be possible to increase the signal to noise ration to ensure that a 'clean' signal is received by the recipient.

An **open network** is a network which is not security protected, or has reduced security restrictions allowing external (public) parties to also communicate. An 'open' network is not considered to be safe.

A **rogue access point** refers to an 'evil twin' or a secondary access point outside of the control of the internal network and corporate security staff but is broadcasting a legitimate SSID. Other users connect to the WAP and by so doing reveal their IP address and login details. Some RAPs can act as 'man in the middle' by forwarding packets on to the legitimate access point, but allowing a hacker to inspect the packets at this point, gaining valuable security information.

The **wrong antenna type** refers to two different problems. As a physical problem, the omnidirectional antenna may not produce enough of a focussed signal to reach the WAP, whereas the direction antenna may do. However, the term *antenna* is misleading as it may also refer to the WAP itself and the protocol used to transmit the signal (e.g. *802.11a* not *g*)

Incompatibilities may exist even though the OSI and *DoD Networking model / Internet Protocol* suite may seem generic and cross-platform. There may be a problem that at the application level data that is usable to a Microsoft platform is not usable for an Android app because the Android app has not built-in import filter for the data being received.

Wrong encryption - if the expected encryption type at the receiver does not match the sender, then the data packets being received me be received in actuality, but may not be possibly decrypted and read by the receiving host. For this reason it is important that the same encryption protocol is used for both transmitting stations and receiving stations. This problem most often arises when a receiving station (host) does not have an 802.1x certificate installed.

Bounce refers to the use of another node to transfer the data packet from in an attempt to confuse and hide the original transmission source.

MIMO (Multiple In, Multiple Out) refers to the 'stereo' nature of 802.1n which makes use of dual-channel transmission and by so doing the timeframe difference between the signals captured by the receiver determine any changes between antennae which may help with timeframe, geographical placement or encoding.

The **placement of an Access Point** is vital – too high and the signal may not be received within the 'doughnut' pattern of an omnidirectional antenna (and so a direction antenna may give a better transmission result). Too low and building components: walls, beams and EMI will interfere with transmission. Specific wireless protocols use more susceptible to physical impediment than others due to the way in which the signal is sent. 802.11a uses orthogonal frequency-division multiplexing which sends a narrow-beam transmission, therefore the data beam can be intercepted by physical blocks. Type b and g however use different multiplexing methods to a which allow more of the signal to reach the destination.

Access points are not intended to overlap except at the range extremities ensuring that the roaming client can traverse from AP to the closer, stronger AP without loss of signal.

An Access Point can be **configured** to work in Infrastructure mode, or ad-hoc mode. This refers to the type and level of security used to authenticate and to send on to the network. For a PAN, we would expect to use 'ad-hoc' and for a domain we would be using 'infrastructure' due to the additional authentication levels required to access the domain.

Lightweight Access Point Protocol (LWAPP) is a management protocol used to control several access points at once. This can be used to roll out configuration changes to many, or to all APs on the network, negating the need to repeat configuration instructions or to manually configure APs to the same settings. LWAPP is synonymous with *Airespace* and *Cisco* hardware systems and is designed to make configuration of a set of APs easier.

Thin v Thick – A 'thin' Access Point only contains enough intelligence to perform basic Wi-Fi packet switching tasks. Network intelligence (e.g. packet routing) is managed by the neighbouring switch. This makes the thin AP cheaper to purchase, but also efficient as there are fewer protocols in use and therefore fewer features, therefore the attack surface of the AP system is reduced. Attacks would therefore have to be direct, however security has been targeted to protect the transmission protocols used. This makes the Total Cost of Ownership less and ensures that the only traffic sent (routed) is heavily managed by other devices (e.g. NIDS, managed switch, or firewall).

The Thick AP however refers to a standard Access Point used for general access. It contains a large array of features some of which may be misused by hackers to obtain alternative routes into the network than conventional traffic. The larger system also means therefore an increased attack surface. Although these APs are more generic and are easier to come by than 'Thin' APs, costs may be higher. Whilst a 'Thick' (or 'smart') AP can be stripped down to act as a 'Thin' AP, this will require configuration.

Environmental factors – as discussed earlier, physical neighbouring component may impede the transmission of a signal to its destination node. Thick, load-bearing **walls** often contain steel girders. Stone walls are also famous for degrading (reducing) the signal to a weak state. **Window film** (often found within triple-glazed windows) can also reduce radio signals, as can **metal studs** within walls. Other equipment which give or radio leakage such as cordless phones and microwave ovens (these transmit 'noise' on the 2.4 GHz 'b' band).

There are a number of metrics we can also use to determine the effectiveness of transport:

Throughput refers to the rate at which successful packets are delivered. It is the measure of successful packet delivery. Throughput is not the same measure as the amount of packets which can be sent within a given time period, as some packets are affected and therefore unable ('dropped') upon receipt by the destination node.

Frequency refers to the carrier frequency used to transmit the signal. The frequency used also defines the wavelength of the signal, therefore the quality, or amount of data which can theoretically be transmitted, although modulation, multiplexing and the width of the beam also account for the signal data transmission speed. Frequency is a measure of the amount of radio waves are sent per second. Typical frequencies used are 2.4 and 5 GHz.

Distance refers to the actual direct 'as the crow flies' distance from point to point (e.g. from AP to receiving node). There will be a point at which the signal is weak (attenuation), or has been rendered unusable as what is received has been impacted by other radio noise on the same bandwidth, or by white noise (random noise). Signal quality is measured in 'bars' (although properly is measured in dB), and a signal strength of approx. 55% or lower indicates a high propensity of dropped packets which will slow transfer speeds as packets will have to be resent. Reducing the distance by moving the node closer to the AP should improve the transmission power by combatting attentuiation and removing the amount of noise which could have impacted on the signal, therefore rendering the power of the transmission higher and reducing the number of dropped packets.

Where the node cannot be moved closer, a wireless 'bridge' can be used to regenerate the signal and to send it out again one further time, increasing the range to the node.

Channels refer to specific bandwidths within the selected frequency. As previously mentioned, if two neighbouring devices share the same bandwidth, both will be causing cross-talk which will render both packets being sent as unusable on the receiving AP. To correct this, one device's channel is altered, thereby ensuring that the AP can receive both packets at the same time, but due to the subtle frequency difference no conflict has occurred and both packets are usable.

4.4

4.4 Given a scenario, troubleshoot and resolve common copper cable issues
- Shorts
- Opens
- Incorrect termination (mismatched standards)
    - Straight-through
    - Crossover
- Cross-talk
    - Near end
    - Far end
- EMI/RFI
- Distance limitations
- Attenuation/Db loss
- Bad connector
- Bad wiring
- Split pairs
- Tx/Rx reverse
- Cable placement
- Bad SFP/GBIC - cable or transceiver

A '**short**' refers to the bridging of an electrical circuit and by so doing electricity will flow through the new pathway, affecting the usual flow of electricity through the circuit. A 'short' is so called because of the detour of the electrical flow. 'Shorts' are often very dangerous as electricity is crossing areas of a circuit where it was not intended and this may lead to significant physical damage to components. A short may be caused by poor maintenance or to a lack of care, e.g. the connecting of a cable to a live system where pins are misaligned may cause electricity to flow into the wrong cable. A USB socket B (square, device-end) cable, whilst in theory 'keyed' (it is chamfered to ensure that it can only be fitted one way into the socket) can if forced by fitted upside down. This will lead to a short-circuit where electricity will spark (arc) to other components of the circuit, rendering the device useless. In my example sadly, through neglect and lack of attention 'shorted' the controller card of an external hard drive. Thankfully, the device was powered separately, so voltage was quite low. Nevertheless the external hard disk controller card was rendered useless and the hard disk had to be refitted to a replacement unit.

An '**open**' (or 'open circuit') refers to a gap, or break within a cable wiring, or solder lanes. As a result electricity cannot flow through the pathway and therefore the circuit is not completed. A voltmeter can be used to demonstrate that electricity is not flowing through a location within a circuit.

Where the '**open**' is on a circuit board, this may be repairable by adding additional solder to close the gap. For cabling, replacement of the damaged cable with a known good, or by repairing the section of cable will repair the fault. When a circuit is said to be 'open' it is considered to be powered down. However, if only part of the circuit is affected by the 'open' other parts of the circuit may still be live, so caution is advised.

For wireless Ethernet cables a TIA standard defines the wiring sequence (TIA-568 for Ethernet) as indicated in the diagram below:

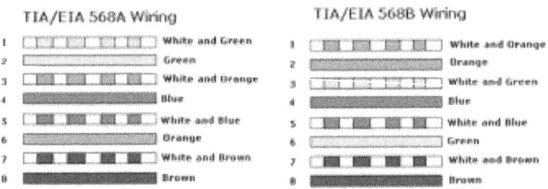

TIA 568 A and B wiring sequence

Where the Ethernet cable is connected with sequence A or sequence B at both ends, the cable is said to be a '**patch cable**' and is used to directly connect a device to a switch. Where the cable is sequence A on one end and B at the other end, the 'swap' will create a data loop. This cable is referred to as a '**crossover cable**'. It is used for router uplink ports to connect to neighbouring routers, also for a basic 2-PC connection, in order to directly connect 2 PCs together without the need of a switch as an intermediary device.

Cross-talk refers to interference in the form of data from another transmitted stream. Where two data cables lie adjacent, or two neighbouring wires are used to transmit the data signal, 'bleed' from the one wire will affect data being sent on the other to a point where the data being transmitted will be unusable. In order to counter this, we send the binary opposite of the data signal on a neighbouring wire and twist both wires together across the cable, so any 'bleed' forms in fact cancellation as we progress along the wire.

Near-End Crosstalk (NEXT) refers to the signal bleed from two neighbouring, untwisted wires. NEXT is a measure of the signal strength between the affecting wire and the affected wire. Recommendation is to avoid air gaps and ensuring that the cable pair in an Ethernet remains completely twisted into the junction box, or socket. Poorly made Ethernet cables with unstranded wires at the socket will definitely lead to NEXT at this point, reducing the performance of the cable.

Far-End Crosstalk (FEXT) refers to the measure of crosstalk (as above), measured at the extremity of the cable, from the transmitter. This measurement will clearly indicate a weakness in the signal caused by both attenuation as well as crosstalk. Where the measurement of NEXT and FEXT values are low, the cable is considered to be effective.

Electromagnetic Interference, or **Radio-Frequency Interference** refers to other factors which could impede the 'hygiene' of the data being transmitted, whether wired or through air. Electrical equipment such as high-voltage three-phase circuitry, unsuppressed (unshielded) electric motors and fluorescent tubes do give out ('bleed' EMI). Network **cabling placement** should be laid avoiding power cables wherever possible and if there is a need to traverse one, this should be done perpendicular to the power cable in order to minimise the exposed surface area. For EMI problems, the most obvious, but still expensive solution may be to use a media which would not be affected by EMI (e.g. light, therefore fibre-optic cable).

Our transmitting equipment will naturally have a range which will be affected by signal strength and physical impediments. Our transmission distance will therefore be limited based on our environment and so the theoretical distance effective by a specific protocol / standard may not be completely reached in the physical world.

Attenuation (dB loss) refers to the weakening of the signal as it travels. A signal will be exposed to interference such as white noise, signal bleed (RFI) from other equipment and this will impact on the usability of the signal. A signal can be regenerated by another Access Point, or 'wireless bridge'. The same is also true for wired networks with the use of a bridging unit, or switch.

A **bad connector** can lead to intermittent (but full) connection. The physical weight, tension, or twisting of a cable however can cause connections to become 'open' and therefore the signal is intermittent, or permanently stopped until maintenance is actioned. Where a cable is transmitting several channels or data streams using different pins, the connection 'break' of one pin would lead to only part of the connection being affected (e.g. one data channel) and this may make it harder to find the cause of the problem.

With **Wi-fi** this problem may also manifest on poorly configured APs which will constantly retry to send the packet using an ad-hoc network. Some data elements are received but as authentication has not taken place only those elements which have been allowed onto the network are visible. This problem manifests itself as a network status message on the client PC indicating a constant switching between 'online' and 'offline'.

Bad wiring refers to a loose wire within a wired circuit. The movement of the cable, or the weakness of a solder join may be a weak point within the circuit which may cause intermittent connectivity, or in the case of higher voltage systems arcing (electric sparks) which may ignite surrounding materials and cause a fire.

Bad wiring may also refer to poor cable management which will increase the amount of time needed to find a specific cable should further maintenance need to take place. Systems which have grown organically are notiorius for poor cable management.

A poorly managed distribution frame

Split pairs refers to incorrect wiring within an Ethernet cable, so that the return wire instead goes to a different pin. This will cause interference in the cable as the twisted pair are not correctly cabled to the node circuitry. The 'twist' of the cable in this situation would exacerbate the interference on the cable, rather than try to reduce it. A cable tester can be used to determine that the wiring has been successful and to the correct pins.

Tx/Rx reverse – a typical professional Ethernet switch or router supports Medium dependent interface crossover (MDIX) – it is said to be 'auto switching' between crossover and patch-style cabling. MDIX allows the correct positioning for transmission and receive by adjusting for the cable type used. If the device is not 'auto-switching' (does not support MDIX), then connecting the wrong type of cable will result in an 'open circuit' – the cable will not be recognised as present by the system.

Bad SFP / GBIC – A small-form-factor pluggable (SFP) module can be inserted into the SFP module slot on a Cisco Router, providing an uplink optical interfaces, laser send (TX) and laser receive (RX). If the module is inserted incorrectly, the wrong module is used for the model of router, or firmware does not support the module, the module may not work and be said to be 'bad'. A Gigabit interface converter can also convert form a Gigabit Ethernet port to other media types. An SFP is considered to be a small form factor GBIP.

4.5

4.5 Given a scenario, troubleshoot and resolve common fiber cable issues
- Attenuation/Db loss
- SFP/GBIC - cable mismatch
- Bad SFP/GBIC - cable or transceiver
- Wavelength mismatch
- Fiber type mismatch
- Dirty connectors
- Connector mismatch
- Bend radius limitations
- Distance limitations

This section covers various technical problems which may be found with Fibre connections.

Attenuation / Db loss – Fibre is less susceptible to attenuation given that a laser light signal is being bounded along the edges of the fibre filament to the endpoint. However, placement of the end cap (the 'ferrule') can cause some signal problems. Some loss will appear wherever there is an air gap within the connection, notably at endpoints, or a cable junction. Attenuation across the fibre is caused by both scattering of the light path and also by absorption. That said, loss across the cable is typically low. An 8km length of SMF-28 cable transmits 75% of light at 1550nm.

Any rough, or irregular walls of the fibre will cause the light beam to be scattered, or for part of the beam to veer off at a tangent. This scattering has the overall effect of weakening the light beam as light travels across the cable. It is for reasons such as this that the end 'ferrule' (cap) attaching the fibre to the fibre interface is seated correctly onto the cable.

SFP/GBIC - cable mismatch – this is referring to the use of an incorrect cable not supported by the device. A multimode cable can normally not be attached to a single-mode socket given the fact that the cable connector is quite specialised, however, form factor connectors can be fitted across platforms (single mode cable onto a Lucient connector), therefore the cable will connect, but light will not pass through as is expected leading to undesirable results, particularly a light stream which cannot be read by the receiving device. Given the interchangeability of some of the connector types, the connector types cannot be fully relied upon to provide an awareness of whether we are using single or multi-mode fibre. The SFP may be set to only work with multimode, therefore cannot interpret the signals being received.

Bad SFP/GBIC: cable or transceiver – this would refer to a problem with the operation of either the cable (e.g. not connected correctly), or the operation of the SFP (perhaps it cannot be initialised by the firmware?)

A **wavelength mismatch** - when splicing or connecting two fibre cables, the cladding and core must exactly match; even a few microns of mismatch can cause an air gap, attenuation loss, or for the laser beam to be misaligned. If the second joining cable is of a different optical density, the wavelength itself may be distorted, affecting transmission.

We have recently discussed the connecting of a multimode fibre to a single fibre port, or vice-versa. Fibre sockets are interchangeable however fibre media is not and neither are the transceivers / receivers. A **fibre type mismatch** will present no clear beam being sent, or even damage to the receiver.

Dirty ferrules or sockets will mean that a direct or 'clean' connection of the ferrule into the socket is not possible or that the ferule may be misaligned by the presence of dirt, or grit. This will cause an air gap, or a misalignment rendering the beam to be misinterpreted. A good and interesting analogy here is the human eye. Light is focussed through a lens onto the back of the eye where an image is formed, upside-down. If the lens is misaligned, to fat or too thin, the image received at the back of the eye is out of focus.

A **connector mismatch** may cause the light from the ferrule to not reach the receiver at the exact angle and distance required, again causing issues with the receipt of the data beam. Where two fibre cables have been connected and the strands are at different length, light 'bleed' from the edges will be apparent leading to attenuation, or even the inoperation of the cable.

Bend radius limitations - there are limitations as to the extent to which a fibre cable may be bent. Physically, excess stress may snap or increase pressure on the glass at that point leading to a break (30°) is the typical maximum. There the glass is put under strain the optical density of the glass may waiver at this point as the glass is twisted and stretched.

Distance limitations – fibre cables suffer from attenuation so even in a straight line after a length of time the cable data will become unusable. Typical distances are as follows:

- **Multimode fibre** can carry multiple light rays (modes) at the same time by having varying optical properties at the core; essentially light travelling the shortest path (down the middle) travels the slowest. The larger core simplifies connections and takes advantage of the lower cost LED & VCSEL technologies which operate in the 850nm window. Due to dispersion the range is limited so it tends to be used as premises cabling when less than a kilometre. It comes in two core sizes, 62.5 and 50 microns.
- **Singlemode fibre** has a much smaller core size of 9 microns and has a single light path and can travel much longer distances of up to 100km. They require more expensive electronics which operate in the 1310 and 1550nm windows and are typically used in longer distance LAN's, Cable TV and telephony applications.

	62.5/125 OM1 200MHz (850nm)	50/125 OM2 500MHz (850nm)	50/125 OM3 1500MHz* (850nm)	50/125 OM4 3500MHz* (850nm)	9/125 OS1 (1310nm)
100Mb	2km	2km	2km	2km	40km
1Gb	275m	550m	800m	1100m	100km
10Gb	33m	82m	300m	550m	40km
40Gb / 100Gb	-	-	100m	125m	40km

(Cited at: http://www.universalnetworks.co.uk/faqs/fibre-optic-faqs/fibre-types-and-distances.html)

4.6

4.6 Given a scenario, troubleshoot and resolve common network issues
- Incorrect IP configuration/default gateway
- Broadcast storms/switching loop
- Duplicate IP
- Speed and duplex mismatch
* End-to-end connectivity
* Incorrect VLAN assignment
* Hardware failure
* Misconfigured DHCP
* Misconfigured DNS
* Incorrect interface/interface misconfiguration
* Cable placement
* Interface errors
* Simultaneous wired/wireless connections
* Discovering neighboring devices/nodes
* Power failure/power anomalies
* MTU/MTU black hole
* Missing IP routes
* NIC teaming misconfiguration
    o Active-active vs active-passive
    o Multicast vs broadcast

Incorrect IP configuration/default gateway - if the node does not have the correct default gateway configured it will be able to communicate only within the local subnet. This information is usually given out by the DHCP server along with other important 'known IP addresses' such as the DNS server and other key network components. This information can be changed for network-wide distributions on the DHCP server however can also be set manually if the IP configuration has been set as such ('a static IP address').

Broadcast storms/switching loop – if a broadcast is sent to a switch which does not know where to send the packet to reach its destination and by a sequence of routers and switches returning the packet back to the initial switch, a loop is formed where the data will again be sent out. As the sending node has no knowledge of a data loop, other test packets may be sent causing more data and congestion on the internal network to a point where the devices cannot cope with the amount of traffic. This is referred to as a 'broadcast storm'. To avoid these, TTL values are set to low (e.g. 16 hops is considered to be 'infinity', but it is possible to set the hop maximum hop count threshold to 3 or 4 to ensure that the packet is disposed of before it returns to the starting point of a loop).

Duplicate IP – a duplicate IP address on the same subnet is a concern as both nodes will contest for use of the IP address. If the address was manually assigned (static) then it cannot be changed, so most often will still transmit. This is a problem because the Network Administrator may miss the offending node, if this was not configured deliberately. If the IP used falls within a scope and there is no exclusion for the given IP, then the DHCP server will unknowingly provide the IP address to another node on the network. By setting the static IP to be an IP address outside of a scope, or by setting an exclusion within the scope the problem can be avoided. A DHCP-configured node has a failsafe and the IP address will revert to 0.0.0.0, meaning that it cannot transmit.

Speed and duplex mismatch – here, we are concerned with **end to end connectivity**, where the speed of one NIC is set lower at one node than the other (e.g. 10Mb/s and 1Gb/s) then the connection will only be sent at the speed of the slower NIC. Where there is a duplex mismatch, speed may be sent using half of the available bandwidth rather than full bandwidth, again reducing the expected speed.

Where the node is set to an **incorrect VLAN**, the node will not be able to transmit to expected nodes by IP address because the VLAN it has been assigned to may well be using a different IP subnet numbering system. As a result, there will be connectivity to the switch, but not beyond it to any of the nodes which are visible.

Hardware failure in the case of an inactive NIC, or broken NIC port will cause a complete loss of connection. In the case of a node the damage is minor and easily replacement by replacing the NIC for a new similar one able to transmit at the same speed and with the same connection media as the old one, although the MAC address and IP address will also have to be configured to match the old NIC. In the case of a node segment such as a switch or router, impact across the network will be more significant. If many, or all nodes within a subnet cannot connect then it is likely that the problem is at the central point – the switch. If it is the case that a subnet is active, but cannot send data to a neighbouring subnet or to the wider network, the 'bridging' router is unable to forward traffic, suggesting either an uplink connectivity problem a configuration problem on the routing table (e.g. the uplink port is set in 'down-mode' state, not 'up-link'), or that the router is turned off / inactive.

A **misconfigured DHCP** on a modern system using the Automatic IP Addressing system will cause APIPA to provide an alternative random IP within the 169.254.x.x range. This infers that the DHCP server is inactive, however if there is a problem with the scope configuration, such as the fact that the IP address and subnet mask are correct but the default gateway information is incorrect, then only those nodes who have been provided IP addresses assigned by this DHCP on the network will be affected. This will localise the problem and ensure that the Network Administrator realises that the problem is server-side.

A **misconfigured DNS entry**, such as the DNS server IP on a node, will mean that a node can only connect to a resource by its node's IP address. If the first DNS IP address in the local list is in fact a remote DNS server, greater traffic than is needed will be present on the network. If the DNS list however is rectified to point to the IP address of the local DNS server then local cached information (which is normally local site-specific traffic) will already be cached on this DNS server, reducing the need for further queries on the wider network.

If the **interface is misconfigured** (e.g. further NIC settings can be set directly in device manager including the multiplexing mode and top speed of the NIC) then overall performance will not be as expected even though we do have connectivity.

Cable placement – if the network cable runs its entire length and has to traverse areas of high EMI, there is a likelihood of dropped packets and a reduction in the overall transmission speed due to both attenuation and interference. The correct selection of media (e.g. Shielded Twisted Pair rather than Unshielded Twisted Pair), or even fibre optic cable would reduce or negate these effects.

Interface errors – once configured, the NIC is a relatively reliable device however it is possible that data errors can occur within the interface itself. These may be due to problems in converting data formats, or in reading a packet. Error logging can be enabled to check for problems along a cable and packet inspection software such as Wireshark can check for a high number of dropped packets, focussing maintenance and remediation tasks to a specific area of the network.

Simultaneous connections can lead to dropped packets due to crosstalk. A basic RJ45 bridging unit is a device which can combine signals from two cables (female socket RJ45) to one male socket. These can be used to successfully extend the run of a cable however the connection of two live nodes to this device in the hope that it would work as a basic hub, or switch is not a good idea as the packets from the first NIC will repeatedly interrupt the second live node, rendering both as disconnected by the respective nodes. A hub can allow simultaneous connections however, packets sent to a NIC which is waiting to send will cause a delay. In the case of the Hub, the node's NIC has no way of knowing if the packet being received is intended for the recipient until it has downloaded the whole packet and inspected the header to check the IP destination address. If it is not intended for the recipient node, the packet is discarded. We use the principle CSMA/CD for a wired connection (Carrier Sense Multiple Access with Collision Detection). If a 'collision' occurs on the line both the sending and receiving packets are destroyed, the node's NIC will wait for a few milliseconds and then will try again. For wireless connections, the technique used is Carrier Sense Multiple Access with Collision Avoidance. We avoid crosstalk through the use of separate channels, separating data streams to the same Wireless AP, or node.

Node discovery tends to happen on a switch – once the PC node's cable is connected to the switch, a link light is activated indicating the presence of a 'data loop' (a complete Tx circuit and a complete Rx circuit). At this point a 'handshake' frame is sent to the new node or a broadcast signal is received by the switch from the node. Either way this frame will contain the MAC address of the originator. This MAC address is placed in the switch port MAC table and at this point it is considered to have been 'learned' (discovered). If this process has not completed then the switch will be unable to handle requests to this note until the process has finished. Node discovery usually only takes approx. 10 seconds.

Power failure, or an intermittent power source will lead to the rediscovery of connected nodes ('re-learning') which will mean that for a short amount of time the switch will not be in a position to forward frames to their recipient nodes. The process may take up to a minute before the network returns to a steady state (*contention*). Absence of power will lead to a gap in the network at this point. Any service offered by this resource will not be available unless backup systems are already in place along with alternative routes to these devices.

An **MTU black hole** refers a section on the network where packets are being silently 'dropped' without forewarning any monitoring systems, or logging the event. One example of this could be the presence of jumbo frames on an internal network not configured to handle packets of this size.

For routers, a **missing IP route**, such as a 'trunk' route to another router would not necessarily mean that the network has a physical 'hole' if it is possible to re-route traffic through other cabling/pathways, or through other devices. The data transfer would be slower than expected and the missing route may not be discovered until the router is thoroughly checked, or network mapping software tests the speed of each and every pathway.

NIC teaming is the process of configuring two or more NICs to accept traffic to one IP address. The NIC group shares one IP address and can manage data packets into each NIC simultaneously, therefore increasing the available bandwidth.

An **Active-Active** configuration refers to multiple NICS connected to one single switch offering one large 'pipe' of data bandwidth.

An **Active-Passive** configuration refers to multiple NICS which are themselves connected to multiple routers. This method provides fault tolerance and ensures several routes into the NIC team. In A/P mode, one NIC can be dedicated to a task to ensure that dropped packets are kept to a minimum while additional duties are performed by the other NIC in the group as and when needed.

Tip: The following video is a screencast demonstrating how to configure NIC teaming in Server 2012.
http://technet.microsoft.com/en-us/video/microsoft-virtual-academy-nic-teaming-in-windows-server-2012.aspx

Multicast vs broadcast – casting has changed between IPv4 and IPv6. In IPv4, a single packet sent to a single node is referred to as a Unicast. A packet sent to many nodes is a Multicast and a packet sent everywhere is a Broadcast. Broadcast packets are non-routable to are only used within the subnet to locate other resources (e.g. Park of the WDS / BOOTP discovery process, or one of the stages in the DORA sequence for obtaining an IP address from a DHCP server). Multicasts can be routable, but Broadcasts are not. In IPv6 we no longer use Broadcasts and have also introduced a new concept with Anycast – any node who wants the data can join (e.g. for video conferencing, one node can add itself to a list of IPs which will receive the Multicast).

4.7

4.7 Given a scenario, troubleshoot and resolve common security issues
- Misconfigured firewall
- Misconfigured ACLs/applications
- Malware
- Denial of service
- Open/closed ports
- ICMP related issues
    - Ping of death
    - Unreachable default gateway
- Unpatched firmware/OSs
- Malicious users
    - Trusted
    - Untrusted users
    - Packet sniffing
- Authentication issues
    - TACACS/RADIUS misconfigurations
    - Default passwords/settings
- Improper access/backdoor access
- ARP issues
- Banner grabbing/OUI
- Domain/local group configurations
- Jamming

A **misconfigured firewall** will not necessarily block all traffic to a node, but would block specific data types based on the service this data is providing (e.g. port 53 is used to send DNS data). By analysing missing data be checking error logs on the client machine we can see that specific ports are being blocked. This will lead the administrator to next check the firewall settings. This problem should be local – if this is a part-network or full-network-wide problem, then the problem is with a hardware firewall, or software-based server firewall.

Misconfigured Access Control Lists would provide error messages in the error log specifying which resource was denied. By checking access on different folders by different members of the same team (AD group) we can determine the scope of the problem. (Is it a problem which exists for one person, or for the group the person is associated with?)

Malware refers to any type of software which is performing an unwanted activity on the network which may impede production, or slow down operations. Malware is a very broad description but usually implies software which is not harmful (e.g. not strictly a virus), but will still need to be disposed of by a network administrator, or service technician. Malware often seems legitimate, purporting to be a virus scanner for similar application which then finds a series of bogus problems and encourages you to buy the full product which will eradicate these nasties for good. It is of course a trick – your PC has not been infected, however the software will regularly interrupt you, reminding you of the 'poor state of the PC' until you take action. Malware can be tricky to uninstall as it buries itself deep into the system. On a corporate network, a re-image would completely eradicate such software.

Denial of Service is a general term to refer to the inactivity of a service expected on the network (e.g. print server down, therefore we cannot print). When referring to routers we use the term to refer to a DoS attack – a deliberate, premeditated attack of the node in an attempt to stop it from being able to function normally either by causing it to shut down, or by flooding it with erroneous data which would impede its ability to perform.

Open ports – a port is only left open when the Network Manager is happy that it will be used for conventional traffic. As ports are specific to the services that port uses it is customary to leave ports open where vital services are in use (e.g. TCP port 80 for HTTP web traffic, TCP port 67 and UDP port 68 for DHCP). There is however a problem – any service can be configured to use any port. Ports are defined for external use – within the network it is up to the Network Manager as to which ports should be used, although normal conventions are often kept.

Closed ports – where a port is closed on the firewall, traffic cannot pass. This is useful where traffic should only pass on this particular port when it is a rare occasion. Here, the Network Administrator will manually open and close the port, or the port control can be association with an application which will make use of the port (e.g OpenSSL and PuTTY, or WinSCP).

ICMP related issues – the problem with the ICMP suite is that in itself it has little to no security. Tools which form the suite can be used programmatically and maliciously by would-be hackers to perform actions on the network which although were intended for Network Monitoring and Management, or basic communications, could in practice cause a DoS. PING is a perfect example of this as it is possible to send a test packet indefinitely to a router, also to forward the request to send the test PING to other PCs in the subnet. This is referred to as a 'smurf attack'. The eventual result will be congestion on the router until it shuts down. A PING attack from one machine (e.g. using the PING –t switch) is referred to as the '**Ping of Death**'.

An **unreachable gateway** is caused by the fact that the router's IP cannot be reached. It may be misconfigured on the router (in which case all connected nodes will be affected), or the default gateway information on the IP configuration page for the affected node has been wrongly typed. Pinging the gateway (if the router has been set to accept ICMP packets) should revela if the IP configuration is correct.

One problem with **legacy firmware** is that it is likely to have been attacked, or hacked and is therefore vulnerable if discovered. One major benefit of upgrading the firmware for a router is the ability for the firmware to provide new security protocols (hardware permitting). The same is true of a **legacy OS** (refer to previous chapter where a buffer overflow attack allowed an external user to obtain access to an unpatched Windows XP system)

A **malicious user** is any person who means to cause, or does in actual fact cause harm on the network. Where this user is a member of staff, the user is referred to as a 'trusted user' because they are in a position of trust, have an active security account and therefore their user account is also trusted by the system. An **untrusted malicious user** refers to any other external entity who obtains access into the network with a view to causing harm.

Packet sniffing is the process of inspecting traffic flowing across one connection with an attempt to obtain information about the type of data, or even to extract valuable data sent 'in the clear', or in a form which can then be unencrypted later. *Wireshark* or *Microsoft Network Monitor* are typical network analysis packet software which can give a bitwise account of the data packet. Taking the analogy further, *Kane and Abel* can augment a data packet before sending it on across the network in its altered state. This software is often used in man-in-the-middle attacks.

An **authentication issue** refers to a denial to a service or node at the *Active Directory* (access and authentication) / *Access Control List* level (permissions). The user has incorrectly supplied the necessary password or identification information and as a result data being sent cannot be unencrypted, or the attempt to send has been denied at source. Where there is a file certificate issue, the absence of a valid and 'live' certificate will cause encrypted traffic to be sent but will be unreadable.

A **TACACS** or **RADIUS misconfiguration** will mean that any user data supplied from an external source will not be correctly (if at all) forwarded for authentication to an Active Directory Domain Controller. Where the RADIUS server does not reside in the same domain as the ADDS server, there is a requirement to create a domain trust first to that any traffic being forwarded from the RADIUS server can be processed (without a domain trust in place, the data is implicitly dropped by default.)

A **default setting** is the **password** which appears in the user manual and was set in the factory. Pressing the 'factory reset' button will return the configuration to factory settings, including the password. If this password is known to a malicious user, they may also be able to obtain access to the router first, blocking the legitimate Network Administrator whilst obtaining further configuration information about this portion of the network particularly as 'network discovery' takes place.

A **backdoor** is a secret password entered into the system programming. It was customary for the author of a program to enter a means to bypass whatever security tiers had been placed on top of the original application. Backdoors are considered to be extremely dangerous, in fact the more module approach taken with Java and C# programming allows programming teams to identify any such extraneous code which may be hidden within the program structure.

In networking, one possible backdoor technique was the 'hard wiring' of IP addresses and URLs into the local machine, thereby bypassing the existing domain. This is still used with test 'sandbox' networks where one PC may need to access resources not publicly published and therefore not known to the local DNS server.

We have mentioned in a previous section **APR poisoning** – the misconfiguration an ARP entry will cause an IP packet to be misdirected to the wrong location.

Banner grabbing is a process of enumerating the network by analysing traffic and determining the structure of the network. *Telnet* and *Netcat* can both be used to investigate services and variables available on the network in order to build up a picture.

We have in this chapter already discussed configuration scope and its effect. If the effect is across a subnet, or **domain**, it is said to be a domain-wide misconfiguration. For one affected PC it is said to be **local** to the PC. Where access is managed by Active Directory, scope and authentication level is controlled by AD. Where the local SAM database and local ACL refers to a locally shared resource, the configuration is said to be **local**.

Jamming is the process of sending blocking data in a controlled attempt to stop a device from receiving legitimate data. A DDoS attack is an example of **Jamming**.

4.8

4.8 Given a scenario, troubleshoot and resolve common WAN issues
- Loss of internet connectivity
- Interface errors
- Split horizon
- DNS issues
- Interference
- Router configurations
- Customer premise equipment
  - Smart jack/NIU
  - Demarc
  - Loopback
  - CSU/DSU
  - Copper line drivers/repeaters
- Company security policy
  - Throttling
  - Blocking
  - Fair access policy/utilization limits
- Satellite issues
  - Latency

This section will consider common WAN issues:

The loss of **internet connectivity** for a WAN may infer that communication is only authenticated for the local intranet, or that the wireless router is unreachable or out of range, or that the wireless router itself is having problems further up the line connecting to the ISP-managed router. Home routers in particular are susceptible to DDoS attacks and flooding, but more usually the client node wireless NIC has been powered off (laptops have a power switch for the Wi-Fi NIC to conserve power). If the Wi-Fi NIC has been absent on the network for some time and the Home router is also acting as the DHCP server, the IP address used by the Wi-Fi NIC may need to be reset. This requires the command IPCONFIG /RENEW to force a renewal.

An **interface error** can refer to the NIC being unable to communicate, the IP protocol stack not correctly installed on the device, or that there are a large number of packets being dropped. This may be due to range, interference, or an incorrect access mode in use (e.g. Ad-Hoc rather than Infrastructure).

Split Horizon route advertisement is a process whereby a router is prevented from advertising its pathways which lead back to an interface which it has already learned, thereby preventing routing loops from being formed. In the sequence node A, B, C, router C never advertises its route back to A.

Split Horizon DNS refers to the presence of more than one DNS server on the same domain, or subnet, each with a different DNS database with separate data. It can be used to provide a different list of DNS records for internal and external users. However as a system it is not recommended. Split Horizon DNS refers to the fact that different users accessing the system at the same entry point, but because they originate from different locations (e.g. internal and external network users) therefore obtain access to whichever list they should see based on where they are connecting from. Split Horizon DNS can be complex to set up and to maintain and is not always recommended.

Interference refers to wireless interference (e.g. RFI) present in the locale between the router and client. This has been covered in previous sections.

Router configuration – the role of the router is to route traffic to other networks, or subnets. For this the routing table needs to be correctly set to uplink to other routers. For this the correct port, speed, direction and IP address of the receiving router need to be placed in the routing table. If this information is incorrect, then traffic cannot be passed to its destination.

Customer premise equipment refers to other devices which support the network:

Smart jack/NIU – this is typically the demarcation point (**demarc**) for the Telecoms Provider at which point they can test the health of the connection up to the house. In the UK, we refer to this as the 'master socket'. Any traffic within the house from the Smart Jack cannot be tested by the Telecoms provider and falls into the control of the local network team. It is also referred to as a **Network Interface Device / Unit**. ISDN T1 lines are fitted with 'intelligent' Smart Jacks which can check connectivity up to this point and report the line status back to base.

Loopback is both a command-line tool accessible through IPCONFIG, but also a low-level hardware plug capable of proving connectivity for a NIC port.

A **CSU/DSU (Channel Service Unit/Data Service Unit)** is a device able to connect a digital router to a digital circuit such as an ISDN T1 line. The CSU is responsible for connecting the line to the telecoms network whilst the DSU manages the interface with the terminating equipment (e.g. the router). It is the equivalent of a modem in that the data is transposed into a signal which can be sent across ISDN.

A **line driver (repeater)** is a device capable of taking a signal and regenerating it so that the signal can be sent a further distance. An Ethernet repeater is a powered signal box capable of reading data signals being sent and can resend the signal across a second cable for a further 'run'. This is useful where there are two adjacent sites, but they are out of the maximum range of the selected cable and the move to another medium (e.g. fibre optic) is not financially viable.

A company security policy does not just state who can access but also how much data they can use. In order to comply to this policy it is possible to set **'throttling'** protocols to ensure that bandwidth is not overused by an employee, or that activities which are unsavoury to corporate procedure (e.g. the illegal downloading of videos whilst at work) can be curtailed. **Blocking** refers to the actual complete 'inaccess' to a specific resource, or site. This is usually done by the use of a web proxy server with content filtering.

A 'fair access utilisation' policy refers to the fact that there is an expectation on the part of the user to use the resources available fairly to that other users of the same security level are not impeded and may also access the network to the same extent.

A satellite is capable of transmitting a significant amount of data, however the physical location of the satellite and its distance away from the host node means that there is a delay in receiving the transmission. This is referred to as **latency**, or **lag**. Where the latency may be a few seconds in length, there need to be safeguards within the local system to ensure that the system does not time out, or resend the request whilst it is still being processed.

Domain 5

Industry standards, practices, and network theory

This section will consider some of the standard practices, network concepts and an be used to better understand you network and to make it consistent.

5.1

5.1 Analyze a scenario and determine the corresponding OSI layer
- Layer 1 – Physical
- Layer 2 – Data link
- Layer 3 – Network
- Layer 4 – Transport
- Layer 5 – Session
- Layer 6 – Presentation
- Layer 7 – Application

The Open Source Interconnect model is a conceptual layering model used both for planning and for troubleshooting a network. Each device operates on at least one layer from the Physical layer upwards – the complexity of the device (its 'scope') can be measured by the amount of layers used by the device to perform its functions. It was produced by the International organisation for Standardisation and is a standard reference model for networking.

Microsoft have a similar 4-tier model, referred to as the TCP/IP internet model. This closely resembles Department of Defence Four-Layer Model, developed in the 1970s by DARPA.

Tip: Whilst all three models are 'active' within the IT world, we use the OSI model as it can allow us to understand the scope of a device, also to assist with troubleshooting.

In previous chapters we have considered how to use or to troubleshoot the OSI model, but what is it and how does it work? :-

Physical – here, we are referring to all hardware and the transfer of communication in the form of a signal, through a medium. Whilst this may sound vague, we are referring to electricity, radio waves through air, or light through a glass cable as conventional media. At this layer we are concentrating on the physical media (e.g. cables), junctions (e.g. a hub) or any device which will regenerate the signal (e.g. a repeater, a bridge, a hub).

Data Link – this refers to two separate operations. The 'Data' portion refers to the sending of a data frame and the transmission of data, rather than a signal. The data frame is headed with information specifying which NIC is sending the data, also which NIC we are sending the data to. The data stream has been broken into a data section of a specific size, referred to as a 'frame'. The second portion is the Logical Link layer which is responsible for setting up a 'pathway' between devices in order to send the frame to its destination. At this level we are considering devices such as an unmanaged switch – the connection is established and

LLC is a basic protocol responsible for sending and alerting the receiving switch to be ready to receive the frame. The Data portion is responsible for checking the integrity of the switch.

Network – at this layer we move from focussing on the physical network to the logical design of the network. We provide nodes with a numbering system we have defined to identify nodes on the network based on their location within the logical network (e.g. PCs for the sales department may all share the same subnet (adjacent IP address numbers) but may physically be located at different sites across the country.) Devices at this layer sue the IP address to define how the data is sent on through the network. Managed switches and Routers both use IP addresses to identify the subnet, or to forward traffic onto the correct node.

Transport – At this layer we are concerned with the route taken to reach the destination, where multiple paths are available. The TCP / UDP protocols are responsible for ensuring the transport through the available network. They differ in two ways: TCP is connection-orientated, UDP is not. TCP performs error-checking and requests that the packet be resent if there is a problem. UDP does not.

Session – At this level we are concerned about the system which will manage the data session. We focus here on the file we are to download – at this level the operating system requesting the data is communicating (conceptually) with the operating system hosting the file. The management of the file (download bar, status updates, also the downloading of multiple files from different file hosts at the same time) is dealt with by the OS at this level.

Presentation – This layer considers encryption and file type within the OS. More importantly we also consider and negotiate the transfer type (e.g. ASCII or Binary) between all devices responsible for sending the data to the recipient. If the data is sent in the incorrect format, the data stream will be unusable (e.g. sending a JPEG photo as an ASCII file will lead to scrambled and unusable data. However, sending a pure text file as ASCII will greatly reduce the amount of data needed to be sent.)

Application – This layer refers to the eventual application which will use the data. The application tied to this specific type of data can also be used as a firewall rule to only allow data to be sent (the firewall to be opened) only when the application requests for it.

Whilst the IP model is used across industry knowing the OSI model is more useful as you will be able to troubleshoot with greater accuracy as well as having a more detailed perception of the network. The OSI model considers abstraction layers with the User at the top (Application layer) as this is where the user interacts with the system, and the hardware at the bottom (Physical layer). As referred to previously in this book, the OSI model can be used for troubleshooting and it does not matter where we start as long as we find the fault at the end of our analysis.

Common problems that may be encountered are:

- Cable breaks, broken equipment – Physical
- Switching issues, switch still 'learning' routes, or unprogrammed – Data Link
- Data unable to be sent out of the subnet – Network
- Data blocked by a firewall – Transport
- File download is ended or paused mid-transfer by the user – Session

- Eventual downloaded file contains strange symbols instead of punctuation – Presentation
- The file is downloaded and opened in the browser – Application.
- The file is requested and the firewall opened, allowing a Remote connection to be established (firewall rule is in place) – Application.

5.2

5.2 Explain the basics of network theory and concepts
- Encapsulation/de-encapsulation
- Modulation techniques
    - Multiplexing
    - De-multiplexing
    - Analog and digital techniques
    - TDM
- Numbering systems
    - Binary
    - Hexadecimal
    - Octal
- Broadband/base band
- Bit rates vs baud rate
- Sampling size
- CDMA/CD and CSMA/CA
- Carrier detect/sense
- Wavelength
- TCP/IP suite
    - ICMP
    - UDP
    - TCP
- Collision

Encapsulation is the concept of adding additional information to the data being sent. At the most basic level, a data frame is a portion of the file. It contains a 'header' which identified where the data is being sent to and where it has come from. Additional information is added to the data frame as it traverses the various layers of the OSI model as each service adds its own data to the original frame, so when the frame is sent to the receiving host, it realises the type of data that is being sent, how it should be managed and handled, which protocols are being used, where in the logical network the data is coming from and then where physically (which route) the data is coming from.

De-encapsulation refers to the opposite process – as the packet is sent from the sending host to the receiving host various network devices will strip off the additional data as it is used. The receiving host receives only the final information available. This will still be an encapsulated IP packet, but during transport the intermediary routers may well have placed extra header data which helps the packet be sent from network to network. Eventually the file is re-pieced and saved, ready for use.

Modulation refers to the change in the signal, which is used to represent the data by a change in the medium. For analogue modulation, a change in the signal will be used to convey a specific data value, whereas in digital modulation, the change in the signal is not necessarily exact – we measure either a signal or absence of signal at a point in time, which is translated into binary data (this is the difference between **analogue and digital modulation**). A modem is a modulator-demodulator device capable of converting sound signals into data and also the reverse.

Multiplexing ('muxing') is the process of combining different signals together for transmission across one medium. Two signals are sent at two different frequencies and by doing this do not interfere with each other.

Demultiplexing ('demux') is the reverse process – as the specific frequencies used are known, we can extract from a combined signal specific data from one medium, at the receiver station.

Time-Division Multiplexing is a circuit multiplexor method where synchronised switches at one end of the line can be used to send signals along a common path. The switches each take turns to send their own respective data streams. These are commonly used with ISDN lines.

In terms of networking, three numbering systems are used:

Binary is a two-state system used not only to represent digital data, but is heavily used within subnetting and IP addressing.

Hexadecimal is now very commonly used with IPv6 given the fact that it is an 128-bit addressing system. Hexadecimal is a system using 16 numbers within its base, rather than 2 (or 10 with denary). It is commonly used for RGB values within computing (e.g. *FF* would represent 255, *100* would represent 256). This allows us to reference large numbers by the use of only a few characters.

Octal is an 8-base system (values 0-7, so *10* represents 8). It was used in early programming language systems and there is an easy correlation between Hexadecimal and octal (given that an octal number can be directly easily transferred to Hexadecimal).

Tip: Not to be confused with Octal, the Octet refers to 8-bits of an IP address. In an IPv4 address 32 bits are grouped into 4 octets named w,x,y and z.

Broadband references the sending of data as an analogue signal. The transmission is first split into several different transmission segments which could be sent at the same time, making best use of the available bandwidth. A **broadband** communication is one-way, so in order to send and to receive at the same time two 'channels' are needed (one as an uplink, and one as a downlink). This can either be achieved through the use of two separate cables, or by using two different frequencies and transmitting across the same cable.

Baseband refers to the transmission of a digital signal through the media as a single channel using the entire bandwidth. **Baseband** is bi-directional, so it is possible to transmit and to receive signals across the same medium.

Sampling refers to the conversion of data such as a sound wave into small, discrete sections, referred to as 'samples'. A sample is therefore a set of values within a specific timeframe. These samples, once put in sequence allow the original data to be reconstituted.

The problem is that the amount of values stored within a time sequence, if small, will cause the eventual reconstitution of the original waveform with some degree of error. If only a few values are stored, the reconstitution will be crude and quality will be lost. Sampling is particularly important when encoding video and audio for transmission. If the number of values in the sample is small important video or sound data will be missed. A **sampling size** refers to the size (in bits) of the data captured per segment. The higher the size, the better quality the sample, however this will increase load on network transfer.

Carrier Sense Multiple Access with Collision Detection (CSMA/CD) is a system used on wired networks to determine if the line is in use. A good example here would be several PCs connected to a common cable on a Bus network. Here, many PCs wish to send packets at the same time. If two PCs send their packets at the same time this will cause an overload (a **collision**), both sending devices wait for an indefinite period and then attempt to resend the packet in the hope of no further collision. As there is a degree of randomness in the wait it is likely that both packets will not collide.

Carrier Sense Multiple Access with Collision Avoidance is a similar system used for wireless networks. Here, different channels are selected to completely avoid a collision.

In reality we use a carrier sense system which is able to determine if there is a connection in place which can be used to transfer the data. This is different to **Carrier Detect (CD)** which is a control signal found on RS-232 serial cables when connecting a PC to a modem. The CD signal is used to affirm that the device is connected to the PC. **Carrier Sense** however is a similar means of determining if there is a live link form NIC to switch port.

Wavelength – if we consider a sine wave, the wavelength is the distance the wave travels before the waveform repeats. This can be measured from any point on the wave. The wavelength is measured in metres and is commonly associated with radio waves and Wi-Fi. There is a direct connection between the amount of waves which are sent within a given time (the frequency) and the wavelength as follows (where speed of light = 299,792 km per second):

Wavelength = Speed of light ÷ Frequency

The **Internet Protocol (TCP/IP) suite** is a series of protocols and instruction sets which manage the communications of end devices in order to send data by communications handshaking (TCP), check for errors in sent packets (TCP), transmit to whoever is listening (UDP), identify the route to be taken to reach the end node (IP). It is a management framework which works on top of the physical transmission of data frames from switch to switch. TCP/IP provides 'end to end' connectivity from the requesting to the sending nodes. It allows routers and switches to auto-negotiate routes and instead focuses on how the endpoints send and receive data. It states how data should be split into packets, the packet sizes, where the packets should be addressed and routed.

By having a common standard on all machines, packets can be understood, also will form a common structure.

Internet Control Message Protocol (ICMP) is a key protocol within the TCP/IP suite. It is used by routers to send error messages to other routers, or to end nodes, but also can be used to forward query messages. ICMP also features a variety of command-line tools to check the health and status of nodes (e.g. PING). ICMP traffic can be blocked, or ignored by routers, if this has been selected.

User Datagram Protocol is used to send data in a 'send it and forget it' fashion. Data is sent to selected endpoints, but is considered to be a connectionless protocol in that no 'handshaking' takes place to set up a logical link between the endpoints. People can connect to an existing UDP stream without affecting the stream and will not need previous data – this makes it an ideal protocol for video or audio conferencing, but a poor choice for file transfer. UDP does not perform any form of error-checking on the packet therefore mistakes are often found. This would be fine for a video stream which may have an erroneous pixel, or 'dropout' for a few frames, but would not be acceptable for the transmission of a file, which needs to be completely perfect (bitwise).

Transmission Control Protocol is the opposite of this. It is considered to be a reliable protocol – a logical 'handshake' takes place between endpoints, packets are checked to ensure that they are valid at the receiving node, but also if a packet was erroneous, missed or incomplete it is resent. It is therefore ideal for file transfer and makes up the majority of network traffic.

5.3

5.3 Given a scenario, deploy the appropriate wireless standard
- 802.11a
- 802.11b
- 802.11g
- 802.11n
- 802.11ac

There are several wireless standards currently in use. This section will consider situations where these may be used:

802.11a – this standard is capable of transmitting at 54Mb/s which is an advantage over 802.11b. It is however prone to physical obstructions and may require expensive professional equipment. Its use of the higher 5Ghz frequency reduces the range somewhat and so more access points are needed than with other Wi-Fi standards.

802.11b – this standard is capable of transmitting at 11Mb/s but over considerably longer distances. It is also more reliable than 'a' in that it is not as easily affected by physical obstructions. It was available for home networking from 1999. Transmission is at 2.4GHz which does make it prone to radio interference such as from cordless phones, baby monitors or microwave ovens.

802.11g – this standard has replaced the earlier models. It is highly secure and backwards compatible with 'b' and has become the main standard for computing networking both at home and for the corporate environment. It continues to use 2.4GHz but allows 54Mb/s over this frequency.

802.11n – this standard uses a 'stereo' MIMO signal through a pair (or several pairs) of antennae, allowing for triangulation of signal and higher speeds. It was first introduced in 2009 and is now the standard communications type for Wi-Fi routers. It can operate on either the 5 or 2.4 GHz frequencies. 'n' can achieve a typical 70Mb/s and a maximum of

150Mb/s given no radio interference. 'n' is susceptible to Bluetooth interference, if there are Bluetooth devices within range. 'n' is backwards compatible with 'a', 'b' and 'g'.

802.11ac is a new standard expected to be embedded into our lives within 2015. It introduces data transmission rates of 1Gb/s on a wireless LAN and 500Mb/s on a single link. This may negate the need for wired connections for corporate or home networks, moving forward. It is based on the same MIMO technology used in 'n' with a wide RF bandwidth, 8 MIMO streams, downlink multi-user MINO for up to 4 clients and high density modulation. By combining these tremendously fast data streams with USB v3, it will be possible to have completely wireless cloud solutions or video servers streaming HD-TV signals to 4th generation phones.

5.4

5.4 Given a scenario, deploy the appropriate wired connectivity standard
- Ethernet standards
  - 10BaseT
  - 100BaseT
  - 1000BaseT
  - 1000BaseTX
  - 10GBaseT
  - 100BaseFX
  - 10Base2
  - 10GBaseSR
  - 10GBaseER
  - 10GBaseSW
  - IEEE 1901-2013
    - Ethernet over HDMI
    - Ethernet over power line
- Wiring standards
  - EIA/TIA 568A/568B
- Broadband standards
  - DOCSIS

For wired solutions, the following Ethernet standards are in use:

10BaseT – originally developed in 1984, this system provides a basic connectivity using category 3 twisted pair cable providing 10Mb/s over 100 metres. This is used for small soho networks and for internal connections where data transfer requirements would be small.

100BaseT – an extension of the 10BaseT model using higher grade category 5 cable and NICs which can support the higher bandwidth (due to higher bit rates). It is referred to commonly as **Fast Ethernet**. This is now (and has been since the demise in popularity of Token Ring since 1996 onwards) the de-facto standard for basic Ethernet connectivity as 10BaseT has been phased out.

1000BaseT – **Gigabit Ethernet** is capable of transmitting 1Gb/s over 100 metres. This is now the common NIC type found in most home and corporate environments. It uses all 4 pairs within the cable to transmit the signal.

1000BaseTX is an adaptation of Gigabit Ethernet using Category 6 cable (more expensive that Category 5e, and less common in the UK). It uses two unidirectional pairs in each direction.

10GBaseT released in 2006, this provides 10Gb/s over an Ethernet connection. Category 6a grade cable is required in order to transmit this over 100 metres. On its own, category 6 cable will only run over 55 metres. One drawback is a slightly increased latency in comparison to other forms of 10G cabling available.

100BaseFX – Fast Ethernet over Optical Fibre. It uses two single strands of fibre (one to transmit and one to receive). It can run 100Mb/s over 442 metres, or to 2KM making it an ideal means to connect two adjacent sites on a campus network.

10Base2 is best known as 'Thinnet'. It uses a thin coaxial RG-58A cable and was popular in the 1980s as a simple means to connect small networks. 10Base2 is by todays' standards obsolete. It allows a run of 10Mb/s over up to (theoretically) 200 Metres.

NB: Not listed in the objectives however is still referred to is 'Thinnet' – 10Base 5, which used a thicker RG-8 coaxial cable and allows 10Mb/s over a theoretical maximum of 500 Metres.

10GBaseSR is a **short-range** implementation of Gigabit Ethernet using multimode fibre to send 10.3Gb/s over a maximum range of 26 Metres. For 62.5 micrometres, OM1 has a range of 33 metres. For 50 Micrometers OM2 can transmit up to 82 metres. OM3 can transmit up to 300 metres. OM4 can transmit up to 400 Metres. OM3 and OM4 are the chosen cable type for internal connectivity within buildings (e.g. trunk connections between floors).

10GBaseER – **extended reach** is used for city-to-city connections. It can transmit 10Gb/s over 40 kilometres (25 mi) over engineered links and 30 km over standard links.

10GBaseSW is a short wavelength solution for multimode fibre. SW is designed to send 10Gb/s from 2 metres up to 300 metres, but usually would be used to connect SONET networks.

The **IEEE 1901-2010** is a standard for high-speed communication across power lines (e.g. domestic mains sockets providing network connectivity through the shared earth line). This standard has now been revised to **1901-2013**. Transmission of up to 500Mb/s with frequencies below 100MHz. This standard standardises several other previous powerline specifications and introduces the mandatory coexistence Inter-System Protocol. This protocol presents interference caused by the operation of two neighbouring **Broadband (Ethernet) over power line (BPL)** systems. BPL is a system capable of transmitting duplex data across medium voltage AC wiring between transformers. It can also be used on low voltage wiring for domestic and customer sites (240V in the UK, 110V in Europe). This negates the need of separate wiring for data transfer and the cost attached to having dedicated access points or wireless routers. **BPL** uses frequency-hopping spread spectrum to ensure that frequencies in use by other systems, even by the native power supply in this cabling system do not interfere with the network data signal being sent.

Ethernet over HDMI - version 1.4 of the HDMI standard allows for 100Mb Ethernet to be transmitted along the cable between to HDMI 1.4 capable devices. This can be used by your satellite / cable TV provider to provide interactive 'on demand' services by connecting your TV directly to your router (if compatible), or other HDMI data-active devices (e.g. other hardware which support 'interactive services').

Traditionally, although HDMI is a digital transmission system as opposed to DVI or VGA (DVI is a mixture dependent on the DVI type and VGA is analogue), HDMI can carry sound and vision. Early implementations have been to use HDMI for video and audio connectivity to recording devices and satellite receivers, whilst interactive features were offered through a wired connection (Ethernet cable via RJ45), or by a proprietary Bluetooth / wireless connection.

TIA standards 568A / B – please refer to objective 4.4 where this subject is covered in detail.

Data Over Cable Service Interface Specification (DOCSIS) – is a global standard describing high-speed data transfer to a cable TV system. It is used to provide internet access for cable subscribers by using their existing fibre-coaxial infrastructure, negating the need to rewire every home in the country. Standards also define the speed at which data can be sent as '**Dx**'.

5.5

5.5 Given a scenario. implement the appropriate policies or procedures
- Security policies
    - Consent to monitoring
- Network policies
- Acceptable use policy
- Standard business documents
    - SLA
    - MOU
    - MLA
    - SOW

Security policies – this is a document signed and agreed to by corporate staff as part of their employment contract. By signing it their security status in the company and access levels (physically and also to the network infrastructure) are defined here. It is a paper / e-document (though the staff member is usually provided with a hard copy) which has to be read and signed (agreed) to ensure that they will comply to the restrictions imposed upon them.

The document in itself is not legally binding. It is a policy, not legislature. However it dictates best practice, expectations, and responsibilities of the company and of the staff member and is taken to be the absolute standard for employees. Its main aim is to detail what 'secure' means and looks like and to ensure that there is no room for interpretation if any breach of security were to occur.

One derivation of the SP (usually a separate document) is the **Network Security Policy** (NSP). This is a document which details network access and individual user scope. It details the layout of the network and will detail specific security information, so is not intended to be read by the general staff, rather by specific Network Management, Design and Security specialists within the company.

Consent to monitoring – the security policy will contain a section whereby the individual waives part of their legal protection to privacy for the good of the corporation. The company will have, as part of this waiver powers to investigate any undesired act which may contravene good practice within the company (e.g. checking personal emails or Facebook at work may be explicitly mentioned and for some corporations is enforced stringently).

Although phone tapping is strictly regulated in many countries the laws surrounding internet usage are vague. The individual as the right to privacy to an extent, although freedom of information has now been curtailed with the extensive monitoring of internet traffic which may be aimed at activities which are against the public good (e.g. terrorism). It is for this purpose that organisations such as MI5 and GCHQ work to investigate and to draw a picture of the current threat to the country. Police investigations focus on individuals who may be attempting an illegal activity.

With regard to the corporate environment the key takeaway is that Consent to monitoring is a reduction of civil liberty at the cost of protecting the corporation. IT security staff are able to check how their system is being used given that the individual staff member is representing the company in their dialogue with external agencies. E-mail is one of the most important communication types here – corporate emails are representative of the company and not the individuals' view. They are also kept – an email sent outside of the company may well be forwarded, or kept, even made public such as in a situation where it may be used as evidence against the company in a news article. Emails are archived usually for 7 or 10 years depending on the security situation. All public-sector organisations monitor and archive emails by default. These may be made available under a public information request (or at least non-corporate sensitive content may be), so are never completely private.

Acceptable Use Policy – As part of a corporate security policy, the AUP may exist as part of one large policy document, or may be a separate document. It is usual to find that it is updated and managed separately and updated as new threats are discovered. This document lists what activities are considered acceptable and tries to list examples of activities or content which may be considered unacceptable. This document defines acceptable working practice. The AUP must be concise, particularly where there are known threats to the corporate network, or where a decision has been taken at 'top level' to restrict access to public sites. Some companies make the decision to curtail the use of any personal public site (e.g. *Youtube, Facebook, Twitter*), taking the view that these are not conducive to work and also that workers may post sensitive corporate information to these public sites whilst at work. Colleges and schools often face this dilemma – does private, individual access to these sites affect productivity? Does it pose a security leak? Conversely the action of banning such sites needs to be within line of corporate security policy – the staff member must have agreed to the policy before they are allowed access to the network.

The AUP should also define sanctions which will be taken in the event of a breach. These may range from informing the staff member's line manager with a view to taking disciplinary action. A fine may be imposed, or even in severe cases, dismissal. In the case of a 'tracked leak', the corporation may take legal action against the perpetrator.

The AUP may also consider 'fair usage'. There may be specific times of the day highlighted where staff can work with large files, or for the health of the internal network large file downloads may not be permitted if the health of the network (e.g. congestion) is affected.

For home users, a fair usage policy within the subscription will detail that an individual household operating a shared line to the cabinet would have an adverse effect on their neighbours' bandwidth if they were to download or stream large amounts of data, or if usage is not 'typical' to what would be expected by a certain access package. Where the individual household has 'broken' the policy a warning letter may be sent, the service capped, or suspended altogether.

An interesting concept to raise here is *Microsoft Azure*. Azure is an example cloud solution for individual or corporate use. You can store SQL databases, which are 'always on'. You can host websites and worker processes, program in C# and run the application in the cloud without the need for a host OS. You can store BLOB files (binary, large object) and also run virtual machines, in fact your own virtual network. Data is managed through ISO standards, so confidentiality is assured on a legal basis. Uptime is guaranteed through 'high availability' – copies of the data are kept on different machines across the globe and the reserve machines can be used as a 'failover'. Azure has a credit system and the user is billed for the storage and processing time used. Azure imposes a negative cap so that if credit runs out, the cloud will shut down, making services and VMs inactive until the account is topped up. This imposes usage monitoring onto the client. Systems can also be scaled up and scaled down to other pricing plans based on demand, should this be required.

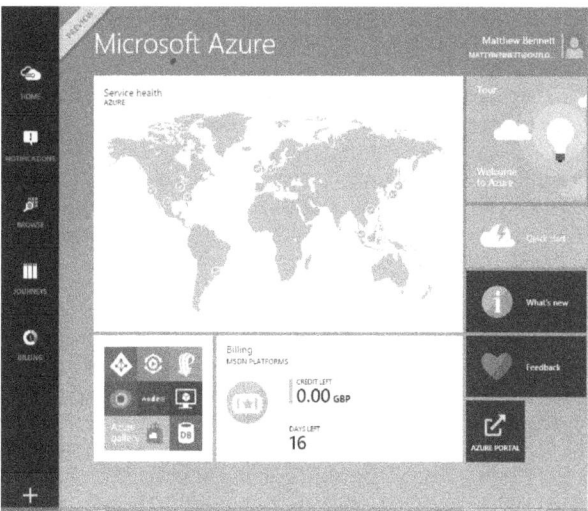

The Azure 'Ibiza' management portal dashboard

You will also find a number of standard business documents which pertain to your role within a corporate IT team, whether in Technical support or a call centre:

Service Level Agreement (SLA) – an SLA is a contract between you and an external agency. It defines a series of targets and measures, detailing what is expected from the service you are offering. In the corporate environment your customers are actually other departments (other staff), not just external customers.

A measure in the SLA may be that the call centre team answer every call (call answer is measured as a percentage and the target is 100%), within 3 rings (monitoring software will check the time the customer has been in a queue). IT remedial work will be graded on the severity and risk to other users. For example, a printer used by one individual may be graded as low priority, meaning that the fix may not occur until after 24 hours have elapsed as there may be more pertinent jobs to remedy first. A PC problem affecting one user may be fixed within the working day, whilst a server failiure with no remediation, or a broken switch will affect many users, possibly the entire network and so this will receive a high priority.

If targets defined in the SLA are not met, the department will be fined. It is therefore in the whole team's best interests to ensure that all activities are in line with the SLA.

Two key company start-up documents are an 'Articles of Association' and a **'Memorandum of Understanding'**. A 'mem and arts' collectively define the nature of business he company will undertake. When a company is incorporated these documents are drafted to define to the open market the nature of the business.

In the case of a limited company with several directors, a Memorandum of Understanding defines the relationship they have with each other in respect to activities and ownership of the business. The areas of influence each director has will be clearly stated and how the directors will work together is also listed. However, a Memorandum of Understanding can extend not just to the directors but may detail how each department communicates with each other, detailing standard communication routers, procedures and courses of action to take in order to log a task. In larger enterprises departments have defined work roles and to undertake work not listed within the usual function may be in effect a breach of the understanding between the departments. This view is referred to and is negatively referenced in the UK as 'compartmentalisation'. In the UK, a MOU between departments is referred to as a **Concordat**.

For the external public customer, other acts and laws take precedence. A call centre representative for example may get a request for something out of scope which will need to be dealt with by a different department. However, the CCR may not be able to log the request, or transfer the call, instead asking the customer to dial a different number. This is legally dangerous as the CCR is representing the company as a whole. The external customer has no knowledge of internal procedures and do not need to know this either as it does not affect them. Where a good has been sold to a customer the Sales of Goods and Services Act allows the customer to contact any person within the sales chain to be able to remedy the problem (e.g. retail shop where it was bought, or manufacturer). Equally from this perspective the customer is contacting the 'corporate body'. This is a common problem with Internet Service Providers – organisations which have split roles (e.g. a customer service team, billing team, technical team and then external fault-testing engineers).

The **Modern Language Association** produce an expected style for business communication. Standard business letters conform to standard formatting and layout and this sets the expectations of letters. With regard to formatting and style, MLA defines the margin width to 1 inch on all sides of the documents. The first line of paragraphs should be indented (tabbed once). One space should be left after a punctuation mark. Font size should be 12 and legible (e.g. Arial, Verdana or Times New Roman are considered acceptable). Whilst this does not seem directly connected with Networking the MLA standard defines professional documents and expectations from the reader, defining professionalism.

A **Statement Of Work SOW** defines work activities, expectations (deliverables) and the expected timeline to be used in order to complete the work. The SOW is used commonly within Project Management methodology to state how the work will be carried out. The SOW is often used alongside with, or as a replacement to a contract of work.

5.6

5.6 Summarize safety practices
- Electrical safety
  - Grounding
- ESD
  - Static
- Installation safety
  - Lifting equipment
  - Rack installation
  - Placement
  - Tool safety
- MSDS
- Emergency procedures
  - Building layout
  - Fire escape plan
  - Safety/emergency exits
  - Fail open/fail close
  - Emergency alert system
- Fire suppression systems
- HVAC

In this section of the course we will consider practicalities of working with equipment, and provide an overview of safety practices:

Electrical safety considers not only the safety of the individual but also that of the components which may be affected by a 'short', or by ESD. The key element here is that the component and operator are properly grounded, also that power to the device is off at the mains. The reason for this is that any accidental slips of tools may cause a short, damaging components. There are also issues with airflow and ionised air as well as moving parts which could harm the individual (e.g. printer rollers).

Users are reminded to remove ties or jewellery as these may get caught in the device, or cause a short.

Grounding refers to the connection of the earth circuit of a device to the earth provided by the mains wiring system. This is typically connected to the physical earth through a conductor rod, thereby all devices share a 'common earth', negating any possible potential difference. By connecting the operator to this same Earth, they are also sharing the same PD as the device, therefore cannot cause an ESD discharge. This can be done by using an ESD wrist strap attached to a grounding mat which in turn is attached to a mains plug through a grounding plug.

PC devices are not 'double insulated' in that they have metal cases and are wired with an earth wire to the mains 'ground' through the mains plug. Laptops and printers however (as with other plastic-shielded devices) are 'double-insulated' – the casing cannot conduct electricity, forming a barrier.

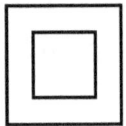

Double insulation symbol

 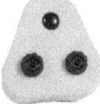

A grounding plug (front and back)

A grounding mat and cable

Electrostratic Discharge (ESD) is the transmission of current, where the electricity is of a different potential difference. For example, your skin will carry a static charge and by simply moving you may gather static electricity. This in itself is not harmful, but the transfer of electricity through an air gap or by making contact with an electrical circuit, casing or solder will cause a transfer of energy. If the transfer is over 20V (which is relatively small) then circuitry, especially delicate RAM chips will be affected. This damage may not be immediately obvious and it may not be until weeks or months later when addresses in RAM cannot store data.

A major consideration of working with heavy machinery, also network racking is that such cabinets are tall and heavy, even if empty. They need to be loaded from the base upwards, therefore ensuring that the centre of gravity is low, reducing the likelihood that the case will topple. Cabinets are bolted to floor plates which will reduce the likelihood of toppling. Cabinets are also attached (hooked) to the wall.

The movement of heavy machinery (plant) requires the use of lifting equipment and cannot be done manually. This may include a 'sack truck', or on some sites a mini forklift truck.

Tip: *For an overview of a data centre where plant can be seen, please view this video describing the Google data centre in the US.*
http://www.youtube.com/watch?v=PBx7rgqeGG8

Components in a cabinet are stored in racks. These devices are quite heavy and need to be secured into place (bolted) with screws to metal cabinet runners, so each component (usually this would be a blade server) can be pulled forward. Other cabinet equipment such as switches or a hardware firewall are bolted at the front and side and cannot be pulled forwards. Some 1U devices are half the depth of standard devices and these can be used with 'double cabinets' (ones where both the front and rear are accessible, so that double the amount of devices can be added). Devices are share a standardised height, measured in 'U'. 1U is the equivalent of 1.75 inches (4.445 cm).

Consideration must also be made to airflow within the cabinet. With 'sealed' cabinets, cold air is pushed through the devices themselves and hot air is directed through the cabinet away from devices and into an air conditioning unit.

Cabinets are placed in a room where there are plenty of network data connections available, or one data pipe can take the cabinet to the distribution frame. Adequate power sources would also need to be available (at the base of the cabinet is a power distribution grid which earths and supplies power from the mains supply, conditioned, into UPS boxes, or directly into the components. Most cabinets have a proprietary cable from the power box to the rear mains AC intake port (the 3-pin D-shaped plug is referred to as a 'kettle plug' because this is where they were originally used.)

Cabinets are placed with sufficient gap surrounding the cabinet to allow a technician to get to all sides of the cabinet. Floor-plated cabinets are 'in-situ', meaning that they cannot be moved, although some cabinets can be turned around. The cabinet is placed in a location where airflow can be managed through dedicated A/C units, or where ambient airflow is being used, the room itself can be temperature controlled.

Tool safety – the standard toolkit contains chip removal tools, screwdrivers, pliers, tweezers and a screw pot. The main concern is that the incorrect tool may damage components but also shear the driving head (e.g. on a screwdriver, if a 'posidrive' (Phillips) screwdriver is used, but the head is smaller than the plus notch in the screw head, inadequate torque can be generated. If the operator overturns the screw the screwdriver may slip and shear off parts of the metal in the notch, 'blinding' the screw.

The correct size screwdriver will ensure adequate torque can be generated to release the thread. If a screw has been 'blind-headed' it is possible to hammer a flat-head screwdriver into the screw head notches and if there is sufficient purchase, the screw can be undone. Alternatively, drilling into the head and then spinning the drill in reverse will unscrew a stubborn screw. All of this may damage components, so has to be done carefully.

The following advisory form from www.toolboxtopics.com details some of the problems you might encounter when using a tool, along with advice about how to correctly use a tool:

Hand tools can cause many types of injuries:

1.	Cuts, abrasions, amputations, and punctures. If hand tools are designed to cut or move metal and wood, remember what a single slip can do to fragile human flesh.
2.	Repetitive motion injuries. Using the same tool in the same way all day long, day after day, can stress human muscles and ligaments. Carpal tunnel syndrome (inflammation of the nerve sheath in the wrist) and injuries to muscles, joints and ligaments are increasingly common if the wrong tool is used, or the right tool is used improperly. Injury from continuous vibration can also cause numbness or poor circulation in hands and arms.
3.	Eye injuries. Flying chips of wood or metal are a common hazard, often causing needless and permanent blindness.
4.	Broken bones and bruises. Tools can slip, fall from heights, or even be thrown by careless employees, causing severe injuries. A hammer that falls from a ladder is a lethal weapon.

To avoid such injuries, remember the following safety procedures:

1.	Use the right tool for the job. Don't use your wrench as a hammer. Don't use a screwdriver as a chisel, etc. Go back to the tool house and get the right tool in the right size for the job.
2.	Don't use broken or damaged tools, dull cutting tools, or screwdrivers with worn tips.
3.	Cut in a direction away from your body.
4.	Make sure your grip and footing are secure when using large tools.
5.	Carry tools securely in a tool belt or box. Don't carry tools up ladders. Use a hoist or rope.
6.	Keep close track of tools when working at heights. A falling tool can kill a co-worker.
7.	Pass a tool to another person by the handle; never toss it to them.
8.	Use the right personal protective equipment (PPE) for the job. Follow company instructions for selecting and using safety eyewear, steel toed shoes, gloves, hard hats, etc.
9.	Never carry sharp or pointed tools such as a screwdriver in your pocket.
10.	Select ergonomic tools for your work task when movements are repetitive and forceful.
11.	Be on the lookout for signs of repetitive stress. Early detection might prevent a serious injury.
12.	Always keep your tools in top condition. A dull blade or blunt point can lead to injury.
13.	Store tools properly when you stop work.

A key document shipped with any consumable is a Materials Safety Data Sheet (MSDS). It contains information about the manufacturer, percentages of ingredients used, information on the toxicity of the substance and safety precautions you may need to take whilst working with the material. The MSDS will have the contact address for the manufacturer and also information on how best to dispose of the item and packaging once the cartridge is exhausted (e.g. ink cartridge).

This link is for a toner cartridge for an HP printer:

http://www.hp.com/hpinfo/globalcitizenship/environment/productdata/Countries/gb/lj_92274a_gb_eng_v08.pdf

Emergency procedures documentation are mandatory documents which detail what to do in the event of an incident, e.g. fire. They detail who is the responsible person who can take further action than a typical employee would be expected to. They detail a route map of nearest emergency exits. They may instruct which fire extinguishers are in use and which type of fire to use a certain extinguisher on. They may also detail how to escape from a room fitted with fire suppression equipment (e.g. Halon gas). The **building layout** design needs to ensure that there are no areas where an individual may be trapped, especially in the event of a fire. Fire escape routes would be listed on a **fire escape plan** – a map visually presented, a different one for each room, showing egress (**emergency exits**) in the event of a fire.

Staff are bound by law (Health and Safety at Work Act 1974 (HASAW)) to read all relevant health and safety documentation, to keep up to date on H/S legislature provided by the company and also to comply with operating procedures in the event of an emergency. Fire testing is also covered under these regulations – fire drill may happen frequently in large organisations to ensure that staff are following procedure. Corporately the company is obligated to comply with these regulations, also to provide all necessary equipment and to check that it is in working order (e.g. filled and tested fire extinguishers, EVAC chairs for stairwells).

It's a fact of life – systems will fail. However we design means into the equipment to respond to such failure. A **fail-safe** is a system within a device to ensure that in the event of failure the 'fail-safe' mechanism will come into effect, causing the minimum of harm to the device, other devices or to people in the vicinity. An example could be in the event of a fire, all electronically locked doors would unlock allowing personnel to exit.

A **fail-secure** system is, but with one key difference – emergency systems would ensure that data is kept secure, rather than try to protect human life. A Fail-secure system would cause doors to lock, preventing unauthorised access to parts of the building thereby keeping the data physically secure.

A **fail open** valve is a control valve which in the event that the part fails, will leave the valve open. A **fail close** valve will leave the valve closed in the event of failure.

Finally, not present in the course but still very relevant is the concept of a 'dead man's handle'. This is a mechanical, or electric device which needs to remain closed whilst the device is in use. For example a DM switch on a lawnmower is closed during operation of the lawnmower. The release of the DM switch would instantly cut the power to the engine. This ensures that a lawnmower cannot continue out of control if it leaves the hand of the operator. For example, if the operator were to suffer a heart attack, or were to fall and let their grip on the lawnmower fall, the mower would stop instantly and therefore not pose a danger to others.

Flymo laynmower.
(The DM handle is the orange handle at the top of the unit.)

An **emergency alert system** is an independent system which will monitor for fire, power outage or other incidents and notify operators to take action. Automated systems such as those in use within SCALA systems (e.g. in a power plant) can close down affected systems and redistribute load to other systems extremely quickly.

Aside: One key EA system is the 'four minute warning' public broadcast system. (The system was also favoured by the US as they were able to also receive the warning alert as it would be passed from UK monitoring stations to US stations, giving the US over 30 minutes of warning time). In the event of a 'nuclear attack' (the detection of inbound missiles targeted at the UK). The population was to be notified by means of air raid sirens, television and radio, and urged to seek cover immediately. Radio stations even today are fitted with a government override and can broadcast the emergency message, overriding normal TV and radio transmission. This system was managed by the *United Kingdom Warning and Monitoring Organisation (UKWMO)* at Strike Command in High Wycombe. The transmission however would originate from BBC Broadcasting House, London. This system was in use between 1953 and 1992 but has now been retired.

> *Did you know?:* The air attack warning is immortalised in *Frankie Goes to Hollywood: Two Tribes*.

The UK used a national siren system – siren poles located one in each district to alert firemen to be area. These were designed to alert flooding in an area. The propensity of the telecoms phone network has now negated the need for this system, also the removal of Police Telephone *Doctor Who* boxes which were originally used (one in each district) by policemen as a mini-office, also as a temporary cell to house any arrested person until further help from the police station arrives.

Duplication of process – Although no longer explicitly covered in the Network course this security process also is considered a mechanical process although in reality this process involves human interaction. In military operations we would need a decision to be ratified, so in the event of a command which would have a major impact (such as, using the military analogy, firing a missile), one individual should not have complete authority to be able to do this alone. An arming procedure would typically be confirmed and operated by two persons of rank to be able to perform the action. Both would have their own ID codes and keys which are unique to them. Both must perform the same actions at exactly the same time. Both are physically distant from each other so that one person cannot reach over and press sequence buttons at the same time.

In IT terms, DP is used when synchronising two systems manually (e.g. a timed domain trust), but would not be common for Network Security. High availability is met through clustering or by moving to a cloud system where duplicate instances of server services provide this requirement.

A **Fire Suppression system** is a mechanical pipe under pressure with heat sensor valves fitted onto the pipe. Some systems also have explosive compression units on the pipe 'rose'. The pipes are filled with an inert gas (e.g. Halon, although Halon is now not often used and more environmentally friendly gasses are used.) which is capable of chemically reacting with and removing the oxygen in the air. Modern FS systems spread an oxygen depleting powder, rather than a gas, but much to the same result. The problem however is that the powder sticks to IT equipment and it is difficult to remove after the incident has occurred. However this is more preferable to a melted server room.

If you are present in a server room and a fire has just started, the FS system will react, the charges will explode and the room will be filled with oxygen depleting powder, or Halon gas. The room must contain an Oxygen mask and cylinder, a 'panic button' to allow egress, overriding automated fail-secure systems.

HVAC refers to the heating, ventilation, and air conditioning systems present within the corporate building. These regulate airflow, humidity and temperature for each room and can be controlled within each room, at air conditioning units, or from a central control system. Some managed offices do not allow staff to make changes to the temperature. For data storage systems, reducing the ambient temperature can help with the control of server temperatures, reducing the risk of server reboots, or automatic shutdowns to protect the server.

5.7

5.7 Given a scenario, install and configure equipment in the appropriate location using best practices
- Intermediate distribution frame
- Main distribution frame
- Cable management
    - Patch panels
- Power management
    - Power converters
    - Circuits
    - UPS
    - Inverters
    - Power redundancy
- Device placement
- Air flow
- Cable trays
- Rack systems
    - Server rail racks
    - Two-post racks
    - Four-post racks
    - Free-standing racks
- Labeling
    - Port labeling
    - System labeling
    - Circuit labeling
    - Naming conventions
    - Patch panel labeling
- Rack monitoring
- Rack security

The **Intermediate Distribution Frame**, opposed to the Main Distribution Frame is a connecting area where the transmissions from several floor switches come together and are concentrated, then sent through higher-density cabling to other buildings (the Combined Distribution Frame), or to the MDF.

Data sent through the IDF may be from different discrete systems, although it is more common to simply use an 'Ethernet' network for all business systems. Older IDFs would have a section of cabling specifically for VoIP / Video Conferencing, a separate section for telephony and another section for data network management ('Ethernet', fibre and coaxial links) however with the onset of Unified Communication all of these are not combined into 'Ethernet' (Cat 6 and Fibre) connections, reducing the physical size of the IDF considerably.

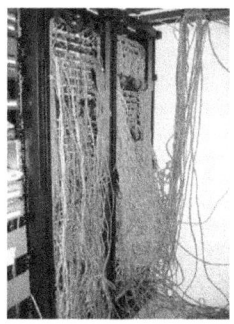

An Intermediate Distribution Frame

The **Main Distribution Frame** is a point at which all IDFs connect as do connections from the outside world. We use the distinction of the internal network as the **inside plant** and the external network as the **outside plant**. Often much larger and forbidding than the IDF, the MDF is a large cabinet, often accessible from front and back, with 110 (or for older systems 66)-block panels, connecting main cabling to the network. The purpose of the MDF is for termination and patching. You will often find the MDF in the basement of the main building on a campus and is where the telecommunications demarcation point/Smart Jack is placed. Older ISDN exchange systems and phone switch units are also housed at this point. You may also encounter VPN concentrators – a device capable of multiplexing and de-multiplexing signals sent across one cable.

A Main Distribution Frame

Cable management refers to how we cable, tie and label each cable. This is a process of labelling and identifying each cable in both a physical and logical form. On the Physical plan of the building we will consider which cables are located where, and the respective cable runs. Cables are identified by their socket number and cable type. Regarding the logical, we use IP addressing to determine which socket relates to which IP address. As many cables travel across the same plenum floor space, they are tied together and laid on cable trays. The tying of cables (with cable ties) enables us to stay tidy whilst also keeping like-purpose cables travelling the same 'run' together.

A **patch panel** is an endpoint for a connecting cable taking data from a room socket. It is labelled with the same ID number as is on the socket and from the panel, further patch cables can take the data to a specific port in a local switch. By doing so we can then provide data management and transfer to the correct port and then to its destination. For our purposes the patch panel is and interface device allowing us to extend from the switch to the NIC. A patch panel contains to intelligent circuitry, rather extends the run of the line from the switch to the NIC.

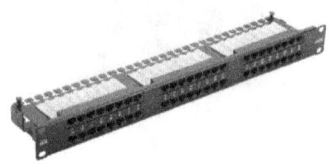

A patch panel

Power management refers to not only the software profiling of a PC based on use, but also the physical remediation strategies and hardware which can be used to negate problems on power lines. These problems include sags (brownouts), cuts (blackouts) and spikes (surges). Where we use capacitors within the power line we are able to reduce spiking through line levelling. This is often included into more expensive mains adaptors and is referred to as 'line conditioning'. Additional conditioning is possible through the inclusion of a Line Conditioner – a dedicated device providing additional power during a sag and cutting additional power during a spike. One simple way for performing line conditioning is through the use of a **UPS** box. This is a battery backup box also sensing if main line power is present. If not present power switches to DC backup power. The **UPS** contains not only a battery but also an **inverter**, capable of converting battery DC power to AC for use by the system. It also informs through serial or USB cable to the server how much time is remaining in the battery. When the mains power is cut, an audible signal alerts the operator that we are running in 'backup' mode.

A power converter is a device designed to rescale the power type from alternative current, to direct current, or vice versa. This enables the use of stored DC power to usable AC. Power supply boxes within the PC also then re-invert and downscale power from AC to usable low-power DC (3.3, 5 and 12v, DC+ and DC-)

A **circuit** is a completed electrical wiring between several electrical components which when arranged in the order prescribed work to perform a purpose. The most basic form would be a switch, cell (battery) and a lamp. Pressing the switch would complete the circuit (making it 'closed'), and so power can flow (current, from the negative terminal to the positive terminal). Electrons flow from $-^{ve}$ to $+^{ve}$ through the circuit and by so doing electricity (energy) is conveyed. A **circuit** describes a working system, but also can refer to a physical circuit board.

Tip: The term breadboard refers to a motherboard not installed into a case, but directly powered within its insulation packaging, in its transport box. This enables the electrical installer to check that power flow meets requirements and that all circuits are closed before then screwing the mainboard (motherboard) into the casing.

Power redundancy refers to alternative power lines which can be used to provide additional 'top-up' power to the main line.

Device placement refers to not only the physical placement of equipment from a health and safety but also from a power and data perspective. We place systems next to other units based on need and as close as we possibly can. We also ensure that power can be reached and that data cabling is with acceptable distances, reducing attenuation as much as possible.

Air flow asks us to consider 'hot' and 'cold' zones – areas where air can be used to cool and to extract heat from devices and into a/c units capable of cooling air for recycling through the system. Closed cabinets contain directed airflow in the form of 'hot' and 'cold' pipes, pushing cold air through devices and removing hot air to 'grey' areas, or into an a/c unit.

A **cable tray** is a metal support which will hold cabling (data and power) within the plenum. It is designed to keep cables in place and also to catch any cables which are loosened. Cable trays can be found behind the back of office desks to keep cables tidy, as well as within the plenum area.

A **rack** refers to an area within a cabinet which supports a device, such as a server, or switch. Rack space is measured in the number of ports contained within the device (its 'capacity'), and its height (measured in U). Rack mounting refers to the bolting of devices into rack guides at the side and front of the cabinet. Some 'racks' are, as kitchen drawers are, placed on runners, or have supporting back plates to allow devices to be pulled forward for easier access.

A **server rail rack** is used with blade servers to allow the blade to be pulled forwards and the inspection top cover removed so that internal components can be inspected and changed (these are modular). Cabinets typically contain a server rail rack in the middle for a monitor and keyboard (KVM) used to control the resident server(s).

A **2-post rack** is exactly that – an iron or aluminium frame with a vertical post at either side in which horizontal trays are connected to it. Devices are bolted to the trays and side posts. It is used as a floor focal point, or Intermediate Distribution Frame. They are not designed to be moved, rather are bolted to a floor plate.

A **4-post rack** offers more stability and is used with heavier equipment such as blade servers. They are common within the media industry for amplifiers and sound equipment as well as with IT network kit. The standard height of a 4-post rack is 19 inches. 4-post racks are not portable and usually are not on castors, so are immovable once bolted into place.

A **free-standing rack** is a cabinet / rack which is not connected to a floor plate which provides stability. FS racks are usually no higher than 19 inches and are mounted on castors. They can be wheeled out and turned around enabling easy access to front and rear.

Labelling (e.g. Patch Panel labelling) – the line from a wall socket, the cable used to make the connection and the patch panel are all labelled with the same 2-stage system. (e.g. 01-039 would indicate floor 1, port 39). This is physically identified on the wall socket label and patch panel label.

System labelling refers to the logical labelling in place across the network. This may refer to IP address, or DNS address.

Circuit labelling refers to the voltage on each wire, purpose of the wire, system the wire is part of and also the direction of current (for DC), eg -12V.

A naming convention is used to typify the type of cable in use. Cables are labelled in side of the cable (e.g. Cat 5e UTPX) for a factory made UTP Cat 5e crossover cable.

The health of a **rack** can be **monitored** through remote sensing equipment. High-end racks contain an environment computer which monitors the power distribution and temperature to each device within the rack. This is reported back to a central collection store where power loads and airflow or a/c can be adjusted automatically.

Rack security – racks are usually placed in secure rooms ('switch rooms'). The room itself is locked and only allowed access to designated IT staff. Within the room the rack is locked (there are locks on both front and back), obstructing access to unauthorised staff.

5.8

5.8 Explain the basics of change management procedures
- Document reason for a change
- Change request
    - Configuration procedures
    - Rollback process
    - Potential impact
    - Notification
- Approval process
- Maintenance window
    - Authorized downtime
- Notification of change
- Documentation
    - Network configurations
    - Additions to network
    - Physical location changes

Change management – the process of managing a project, project management has an agreed endpoint at which time responsibility is handed from the PM team to the owners. Any further adaptations from the original (and paid for) plan has to be undertaken upon committee approval and will be budgeted separately as additional work, over and above the original planned work. Change management is a process of documenting, approving, budgeting / financing and accepting changes to equipment, procedure or data since the original plan.

An example may be the rollout of a Service Pack. The company originally purchased 'out of box' copies of an operating system, but there has been a subsequent rollout (service pack). One rollout justification would be to 'harden' the system due to hacks into vulnerabilities inherent in the original OS. Management approve the further work, however work is documented with a version control number, the work is costed and time allocated to staff to perform the upgrade.

Documenting the Reason for change – the first step is to explain why a change is needed. This may refer to reports and case studies of other similar systems having been compromised. This is documented for use by the change management committee. This panel meet to discuss if the change poses a risk (both if we were to leave things as they are, but also the risk or upgrading and its effect to the existing network). The panel also agree upon a timescale and costs for the upgrade. The reason is then written into a change management form and supporting report. The change receives a CM number and is tracked during work to the system with a separate Gantt chart.

Change Request – the form detailing the change to take place which needs to be considered by the CM committee is referred to as a Change Request form. This form details the reason for the change, responsibilities, scope, effects if the change fails, effects if the change does not take place, impact of the change, impact of issue (e.g. disaster zone) if the change were not to take place, or to fail. The document also documents expected timescales, staffing and costs.

Tip: An example Change Request form is available for download at:
http://www2.cdc.gov/cdcup/library/templates/
CDC_UP_Change_Request_Form_Example.doc

Configuration procedures – any change to the existing system will need to be documented. This will be a technical document listing the changes which will need to be followed, plus signoff from an IT manager to state that this configuration has been tested prior to rollout across the production network. The document is a list of step-by-step instructions detailing how to perform the adaptation to the existing system.

Rollback process – it is possible that for some PCs the 'fix' does not work, or conflicts with existing software. This is certainly the case with compatibility issues, or hardware drivers. A Rollback Process is a list of instructions which will undo the 'fix' already performed, returning the computer to an earlier state before the fix was applied. The absence of a rollback process may in fact cause the PC to be rendered unusable (in some cases) and necessitate a need to rebuild the image. One simple solution on a homogenous enterprise system is to re-deploy the image from a central WDS server. This may 'push' a standard image, or rebuild the image based on PC use and location.

Potential impact – here, we are considering the scope of the change to a system, whether the change is positive or negative. From an operational perspective we are interested in whether the PC can engage with other PCs and to what extent it can/cannot do so. The concern with viruses is that they may significant impact changes very quickly to a system, also to the network. Equally, power loss can affect part of the system or key components thereby stopping specific services across the global network even in parts which have full power (e.g. loss of a DNS server).

When changes are to made to the system, affected users need to be **notified** in advance. The main consideration here is that a low-level system change would need the hardware to be rebooted, or powered off before hardware maintenance can be taken place. Network devices may have to be disconnected from the main network (brought offline) before work can take place to remedy a fix. Notification may be in the form of a network message, email or intranet post, depending on the severity and immediacy that the staff are informed in good time to close any applications which may rely on the service in question, also to save data to ensure that it is not lost by a technician performing a network change.

Approval process – changes to the system have to be approved before the work can be carried out. This requires signoff by a manager with authority to allow the change to take place. Measures will need to be taken to ensure that the work can be undertaken without loss of productivity, or data such as:

- Carry out work out of hours
- Switch to secondary systems (failsafe)
- Store data in a temporary storage area and upload to the main storage area when work is completed.

A **maintenance window** is the agreed amount of time a maintenance operation will take to complete. This is planned in advance and approved by management before work starts.

Authorised downtime refers to the agreed amount of time machinery, or services on the network are allowed to be turned off. Any changes are made whilst the system is offline, but must be finished by the agreed uptime start.

Notification of change – any changes to the operation of a system (e.g. changes to the user interface, to functionality or to operating procedures) need to be provided to staff who can make the necessary changes to how they would normally conduct the affected task. This may come in the form of an advisory leaflet, an intranet document, an email or simply a network message. As it lists changes to existing procedure from the original build, the notification forms part of change documentation.

A change to a **network configuration** may result in the redrawing of a logical or physical diagram. This may include the adaptation of a CIDR subnet grouping by Subnetting or Supernetting the existing subnet.

Additions to a network may be pencilled in, but it is customary to print the final version, replacing the existing network map and indicating the change within a revision in version control. Duplication of equipment such as a secondary DNS will include a configuration of how other DNS systems will interact with it. The benefits of additions may include new services, or a wider data reach. Disadvantages may include a larger PC footprint, thereby a slower system using more data in RAM, therefore slowing down operational capacity.

Physical location changes may impact on physical access to equipment, but also the number of hops to get data from its source to the wider network. We need to consider access to data and power points as well as the suitability of the new physical location from a security and safety perspective. (e.g. Will the new floor support the weight of the cabinet?)

5.9

5.9 Compare and contrast the following ports and protocols
- 80 HTTP
- 443 HTTPS
- 137-139 Netbios
- 110 POP
- 143 IMAP
- 25 SMTP
- 5060/5061 SIP
- 2427/2727 MGCP
- 5004/5005 RTP
- 1720 H.323

- TCP
  - Connection-oriented
- UDP
  - Connectionless

The following section considers the fact that across the wider global network specific ports are used for specific purposes, despite the fact that any port number could theoretically be used on any firewall within the internal network. Common ports are as follows:

80 HTTP – this is used to transfer standard, public, unencrypted webpage traffic. Port 80 is a general port so can also be used for other purposes tied with general access.

443 HTTPS – this is used specifically for encrypted traffic to websites, such as for payment pages on e-commerce sites. It relies on an Internet Certificate present to guarantee connection. This certificate is used to create a virtual tunnel between endpoints (server and client PC).

137,138,139 NETBIOS – this is a legacy system used to translate the computer name of a specific workstation on the network to its respective IP address.

110 – POP3. The Post Office Protocol is used to receive and to store email messages, accessible by the client with email client from the email POP server.

143 IMAP – The **Internet Message Access protocol** is used for web access to email, such as via Yahoo, or Hotmail.

25 SMTP – The **Simple Mail Transfer Protocol** serves two purposes – mail can be sent from one email server to another, email server health can also be assessed with this management protocol. However its main client-side use is to actually outwardly send emails to the recipient's email system.

5060/5061 SIP - Session Initiation Protocol is used by VoIP systems to establish a voice connection between systems. A session containing a media stream is set on the client, managed through the network, routed and eventually received by the receiving endpoint.

2427/2727 MGCP – an advancement of the **Simple Gateway Control Protocol**, **Media Gateway Control Protocol** is a text-based signalling and control protocol used in VoIP systems. It uses Session Description Protocol to determine and negotiate media streams used in a call session. Real-time Transport Protocol is used to frame the media streams. Data streams are sent in a 'master-slave' format to forward data from node to node.

5004/5005 RTP – This refers to **Real Time Streaming Protocol** (RTSP) for Microsoft Windows Media streaming services. 5004 is used to deliver data packets and media data. 5005 is more often used to send packet loss information. 5004 and 5005 are also common ports for Yahoo Messenger's voice chat system.

1720 H.323 is a system used by Microsoft NetMeeting, also for voice-over IP call set-up (for call control signalling). H.323 refers to the standard for audio/visual communication on a packet-switched network.

TCP – The **Transmission (Transport) Communication Protocol** is a **connection** (**stateful**) system where endpoints first establish that both are ready to receive the data stream. Next, each packet contains error correction (hashing) is added to the packet to that the actual data can be checked against the hash which will verify that it is exact. If the packet fails, the packet is resent. There are 65535 TCP ports on a firewall.

UDP – The **User Datagram Protocol** is a **stateless** (**connectionless**) system. Data is sent irrespective of any endpoints available to listen to it. There is no error correction for this system, so data is received 'as is'. This means that the packet is 'lighter' due to the absence of any error checking data. UDP is popular for video streaming as glitches will not adversely affect presentation.

5.10

5.10 Given a scenario, configure and apply the appropriate ports and protocols
- 20,21   FTP
- 161   SNMP
- 22   SSH
- 23   Telnet
- 53   DNS
- 67,68   DHCP
- 69   TFTP
- 445   SMB
- 3389   RDP

20, 21 FTP is used in the connection to a public FTP site in order to download files, a website, or a GIT repository. In itself FTP is not secure, but additional security connections are available to secure connection (authentication) or to encrypt the data stream.

161 SNMP (Simple Network Management Protocol) is used to send management instructions to other IP devices on the network, such as to check for connectivity, system health or to forward configuration information. SNMP is an accepted protocol amongst NICs, Switches and Routers. SNMP spans the whole OSI suite, including commands at the application level. Servers can use SNMP to report their status to a waiting collection point (e.g. a client PC).

22 SSH (Secure Shell) is used to create a secure connection between endpoints. It is commonly used with OpenSSL / PuTTY or Remote Desktop to establish and to maintain the connection between the connecting and target machines.

23 Telnet – an older but popular management system is Telnet. This is used to send remote commands from a client PC to a target PC. However, you need to authenticate to the target PC, so need to present the username and password of an account which will be accepted by the target PC. However, all information is sent between the two PCs 'in the clear'. Telnet is not an encrypted channel.

53 DNS (Domain Name System) – this is used to send DNS requests and resolves between the client and DNS server. DNS resolves name requests to IP addresses to inform the client the specific IP address to use to then forward communication directly to the computer by its IP address. DNS servers can also forward requests onto either other internal DNS servers, or to the internet root servers (referred to as 'root hints').

NB: For further information refer to Iterative v Recursive queries.

67,68 DHCP (Dynamic Host Configuration Protocol) – DHCP in this context refers to the DORA process where broadcasts and unicasts are used to request a new client IP address, also to locate a DHCP sever on the network. Not only is a client IP lease provided but also a series of other significant IP addresses that may be useful to the client. These 'signpost' IP addresses may identify other key network components such as the location of DNS servers, Default Gateways (Routers), IIS (Web Servers) and other services. Upon second presentation of the client onto the network, the final 2 stages are used ('RA') as the DHCP IP address is already known to the client.

69 TFTP (Trivial File Transfer Protocol) – a lighter protocol to FTP is the Trivial File Transfer Protocol. A file request is sent, but no checking takes place. If the file is only part received, or a packet is damaged this affected area is not resent. TFTP is not a reliable protocol and so should not be used for files where file validity needs to be assured.

445 SMB – Server Message Block is an important protocol provides network shared access to files, printers. It is considered to be an inter-process communication system, in that is it controlled by the OS and defines how and which parts of files to send from one PC to another. We often consider the fact that file data is stored on a hard drive as 'blocks', and that data is transferred as a 'low level' system however in reality the OS takes the responsibility of managing the transfer. SAMBA is one implementation of SMB used on typical systems specifically for file transfer through the internal network.

3389 RDP – Remote Desktop Protocol uses two channels. Port 22 establishes the connection and encryption, also manages the health of the connection, whereas 3389 is used to send the actual input/output data from the target PC to the client.

www.ingramcontent.com/pod-product-compliance
Lightning Source LLC
Chambersburg PA
CBHW060834170526
45158CB00001B/160